DISTANCE EDUCATION

STATEWIDE, INSTITUTIONAL, AND INTERNATIONAL APPLICATIONS: READINGS FROM THE PAGES OF *DISTANCE LEARNING* JOURNAL

SECOND EDITION

A Volume in
Perspectives in Instructional Technology and Distance Education

DISTANCE EDUCATION

STATEWIDE, INSTITUTIONAL, AND INTERNATIONAL APPLICATIONS: READINGS FROM THE PAGES OF *DISTANCE LEARNING* JOURNAL

SECOND EDITION

COMPILED BY
MICHAEL SIMONSON

EDITOR OF *DISTANCE LEARNING* JOURNAL
DEPARTMENT CHAIR
INSTRUCTIONAL DESIGN AND TECHNOLOGY
FISCHLER SCHOOL OF EDUCATION
NOVA SOUTHEASTERN UNIVERSITY

ISBNs:
  Paperback: 978-1-68123-641-4
  Hardcover: 978-1-68123-642-1
  E-Book: 978-1-68123-643-8

Printed in the United States of America.

CONTENTS

PART III:
INTERNATIONAL APPLICATIONS OF DISTANCE EDUCATION

Introduction

Michael Simonson

istance Education: Statewide, Institutional, and International Applications, 2nd Edition, is a collection of the best and most important articles from the pages of *Distance Learning* journal, a professional publication written by practitioners for practitioners. *Distance Learning* journal is a premiere outlet for articles featuring practical applications of distance education in states, institutions, and countries.

During the 15 years of publication of *Distance Learning* journal there have been hundreds of articles published that explain the efforts of practitioners who are involved with implementing, operating, or evaluating distance education programs. This book of readings is a compilation of some of the most important articles pub-

Michael Simonson, Editor, *Distance Learning,* and Program Professor, Programs in Instructional Technology and Distance Education, Fischler School of Education, Nova Southeastern University, 1750 NE 167 St., North Miami Beach, FL 33162. Telephone: (954) 262-8563. E-mail: simsmich@nsu.nova.edu

lished in *Distance Learning* journal. This book is designed for emerging and experienced practitioners who wish to learn from the efforts of others—efforts based on science and research with an emphasis on what is practical.

This book of readings is organized into three sections:

- *Section I: State-Based and Statewide Approaches to Distance Education:* The 10 articles in this section explain distance learning efforts on a statewide or local educational level.
- *Section II: Institution-Based Applications of Distance Education:* The 12 articles in this section explain distance teaching and learning in colleges, schools, governmental institutions, and the military.
- *Section III: International Applications of Distance Education:* There are 10 articles in this section that present distance education initiatives in Nigeria, the Caribbean, Belize, the Congo, and other countries.

Distance education is defined as institutionally based formal education where the learning group is separated and where interactive communications technologies are used to connect students, teachers, and resources for learning. *Distance Learning* journal supports this definition by publishing manuscripts that concentrate on distance education practices where this definition is applied.

The field of distance education—inclusive of distance teaching and distance learning—has matured to the point where research-based best practices are now available in the literature of the field. While

ix

research provides a foundation for any field seeking the status of a profession, it is also important to understand the successes of those who are implementing research. This book of readings is a compilation of success stories that demonstrate the impact of science on the practice of a field. Articles were selected because they have direct impact on not only the present status of distance education, but also on its future.

Finally, this section of this book of readings ends with an "And Finally" column, the last of which is titled "Educational Colonialism." Distance education has been proposed by some as THE solution to many worldwide education problems—even to the point of imposing distant solutions to local concerns—read and enjoy—agree or disagree.

Part I
State-Based and Statewide Approaches to Distance Education

Florida Virtual School
Blended Learning

Dana Baugh

INTRODUCTION

Florida Virtual School (FLVS) is synonymous with distance learning in the state of Florida. It is the first completely online public high school in the state and is widely recognized as the most efficacious online school in the United States. In 1996 in Orange County, Florida a "web school" was set up as a pilot. Later in 1996 the Florida Department of Education awarded a $200,000 grant to Alachua County in Gainesville, Florida and Orange County in Orlando, Florida. After the two counties partnered, the program officially began as Florida High School with 77 students, in 1997. The online high school

Dana Baugh,
School Counselor,
Miami-Dade County Public Schools.
E-mail: dehb101@hotmail.com

began with six courses and seven staff members. All courses abide by current state standards and the school is accredited by the Southern Association of Colleges and Schools/AdvancEd.

FLORIDA VIRTUAL SCHOOL TODAY

FLVS is comprised of five schools. Their part-time schools consist of Florida Virtual School Part Time K–5, Florida Virtual School Part Time 6–8 and Florida Virtual School Part Time 9–12. All students in charter, public, and private schools in all 67 Florida districts in Grades K–12 can participate. The part-time schools enroll students who take courses as a supplement to their courses in a traditional school. The enrollment is a on a rolling basis and the school runs year round (FLVS, 2013b).

The other two schools reside under the Florida Virtual School Full Time umbrella. These schools are Florida Virtual School Full Time K–8 and Florida Virtual School Full Time 9–12. Students who enroll in FLVS full time make FLVS their school of record. These schools have the calendar of a traditional school and award diplomas. In addition, FLVS offers clubs, activities, and scholarships (FLVS, 2013b). FLVS Global was created in 2000 to serve international students (FLVS Global, 2014). In the 2002–2003 school year the online high school began an in-state franchise program. As of the 2012–2013 school year, 57 districts in Florida were part of the FLVS franchise program. Through this program districts are trained in FLVS policies and procedures and operate as a component of FLVS (FLVS, 2013b).

In the 2012–2013 school year FLVS offered more than 120 courses across all grade levels and varying academic levels inclusive of regular, honors, and Advanced Placement level courses. In the same school year, part-time FLVS students finished 410,962 half-credit courses and FLVS full-time students finished 51,409 half credits. By the end of the 2012–2013 school year FLVS had 1,702,811 part-time completions and 76,281 full-time completions in its entire history. As of August 2013 FLVS employed 1,140 full time faculty, 485 support staff, and 45 adjunct teachers (FLVS, 2013b).

FUNDING

As of the 2003–2004 school year the FLVS program became funded as a statewide virtual school in the Florida Education Finance Program. According to this model, the school receives funding only if students complete courses successfully. In 2013, the state legislature made changes to virtual school funding. Prior to July 1, 2013 brick and mortar schools were given a specific amount of funding for offering six classes per student, although FLVS was given one sixth of that for every supplemental course the students took online. However, since July 1, 2013, FLVS now earns the same amount that has historically been given to brick and mortar schools. So now if students enroll in additional online courses the brick and mortar school loses funds and FLVS experiences lower funding. The funding change is equal to one seventh instead of the original one sixth. Therefore, as a result of funding issues in addition to lower enrollments FLVS experienced its first reduction in staff. A total of 177 full-time and 625 part-time employees lost their jobs in the summer of 2013 (Associated Press, 2013).

LEADERSHIP

Julie Young, who was the founder and chief operating officer of FLVS, announced her retirement on February 5, 2014, after 17 years as its leader (Clow, 2014). On March 1, 2014, Ronald Blocker became the interim president. Blocker previously served as superintendent of the Orange County Public Schools district before retiring in 2012 (Postal, 2014). The FLVS Board of Trustees is currently conducting an international search for a new chief operating officer.

INNOVATION LED BY LEGISLATION

Innovation in this case was led by transformative legislation otherwise referred to as the Digital Learning Act. This was signed into law by and was effective as of July 1, 2012. The legislation was incorporated into House Bill 7197. Beginning with the 2011–2012 cohort (that is, the class of 2015) Florida students are required to take one high school credit course online in order to graduate. Students can take the online course in either middle school (6–8) or senior high school (9–12). Students who have an Individualized Education Program (IEP) can be exempt from this requirement if their IEP states that online courses are inappropriate for them. Also students who have an IEP and have less than one year left prior to graduation can also be exempt (FLVS, 2014b). However districts cannot require students to take the online course in addition to the courses they are enrolled in during the traditional school day (FLDOE, 2012).

All FLVS courses count toward the online graduation requirement credit. Students can earn the online credit if they take a one-credit course and they have completed both segments. However, if students complete only one segment of a one-credit course they will not earn the online credit. However, students who take a .5 credit hour course and complete that one segment will be awarded the online credit

(Florida Virtual School, 2014b). In essence, the Digital Learning Act made online learning mandatory yet accessible for all students.

BLENDED LEARNING

Schools are battling budget constraints and small numbers of teachers. This has led many schools to consider the implementation of blended learning. According to the United States Secretary of Education Arne Duncan, with the "new normal," schools are going to have to provide more educational opportunities for students with fewer resources (Horn & Staker, 2011, p. 2). Essentially blended learning may fill that void. Blended learning is defined as: "any time a student learns at least in part at a supervised brick-and-mortar location away from home and at least in part through online delivery with some element of student control over time, place, path, and/or pace" (Horn & Staker, 2011, p. 3).

The concept of blended learning is broken down into six different models. The first model is called face-to-face driver. This model consists of a traditional teacher providing all of the instructional content with face-to-face contact with students. Web-based learning is used on an as-needed basis in addition to the regular instruction. This usually takes place either in the classroom or the computer lab. The model is being successfully implemented in Leadership Public Schools, a group of public charter high schools in California. This district uses this model with their Hispanic, English for speakers of other languages students. These students use computers in the traditional classroom to learn the curriculum in a self-paced environment. The textbook is online and has also allows students to read content with a translation capabilities (Horn & Staker, 2011).

The second model is Rotation. In this model students alternate using a set schedule between being in a traditional classroom and experiencing online learning on an individualized basis. In this case the traditional teacher reviews the work students complete online. Carpe Diem Collegiate High School in Yuma, Arizona allows students to use one period for online learning and another in a face-to-face classroom environment. This is done for each course at the school. Each day the students have two to three rotations (Horn & Staker, 2011).

The third model is the Flex Model. With the flex model students are able to get the majority of their curriculum using a web-based system. However, there are teachers in the lab to provide the students with assistance if needed. AdvancePath Academics in Williamsburg, Virginia has a very impressive flex model. They facilitate their dropout prevention programs through the flex model. Students are in the computer lab working on a course; however certified teachers are available to provide one on one or small group assistance if necessary (Horn & Staker, 2011).

The fourth model is the Online Lab model. With this model students are in a traditional school computer lab yet the curriculum is provided using a web-based platform. The teachers are all web-based; however, noncertified individuals monitor the students. Students who participate in this model usually also have traditional courses. Miami-Dade County (Florida) Public Schools has widely implemented this model as a result of their lower number of teachers. They developed Virtual Learning Labs (VLL), which are facilitated by FLVS. With the VLL's the students' courses are completed online through FLVS. Although the students are supervised by an adult, no traditional instruction is provided (Horn & Staker, 2011).

The fifth model is the Self-Blend Model. The self-blend model involves students taking web-based courses in addition to their traditional school day. This is similar to the online lab model; however, with this model students are not completing their assignments in a school computer lab during the school day. These students are completing their assignments at a separate location after the school day has ended. Many students take online courses after school. Many online schools such as FLVS and Michigan Virtual School offer students single online courses (Horn & Staker, 2011).

The sixth and final model is the Online Driver. With this model students take courses completely online. The teacher communicates with the students via the web. These programs may require a face-to-face experience at some point however; this may not be needed. Often these programs offer activities and some other traditional components. Albuquerque (New Mexico) Public Schools' eCADEMY uses this blended learning model. These students initially meet with a teacher in a traditional environment. However, they transition to an online environment. Although students who are able to sustain at least a C average can continue to work online independently, some students choose to use the technology labs at the traditional school site (Horn & Staker, 2011). FLVS primarily uses the online lab model, the self-blend model, and the online driver.

How FLVS Conducts Blended Learning

The Online Lab model is noted as the FLVS version of the blended learning model with its Virtual Learning Labs. FLVS partners with many school districts on an individual basis. However, FLVS references Miami Dade County in relation to defining its program. FLVS reveals that in Miami-Dade County the courses are taken in a completely online format in a computer lab within the school building. The individuals monitoring the labs are referred to as Lab Facilitators (FLVS, 2013a).

Florida Virtual School Virtual Learning Lab Pilot

Florida Virtual School piloted its Virtual Learning Lab in Miami Dade County during the 2010–2011 school year. The pilot consisted of a total of 56 middle and senior high schools in the area. SRI International conducted a study in November 2011 evaluating the success of this program. However, the study focused on 38 high schools. In order to gain information for the study seven high schools were visited. Students, facilitators, administrators, and FLVS personnel were interviewed. Enrollment and demographic information was also used in the study. The study found that in order for a Virtual Learning Lab to be successful there needs to be strong leadership, consistent communication, and parents need to be informed. The study also revealed the many benefits of the Virtual Learning Lab for students. These benefits include but are not limited to greater access to courses, flexible scheduling, pace control, independent learning, and an excellent method for students to gain their online graduation requirement (SRI International, 2011)

The study also identified the skills students should have to prosper in an online lab environment. These skills include: reading skills, time management, self-direction, self-motivation, learner independence, oral and written communication skills, sound academics, and comfort with technology. There is no lab without a facilitator; the study also pointed out the top skills that would be needed to become a successful facilitator. These include, being a student motivator, communication with the web-based teacher and knowledge of best practices. In addition, facilitators should communicate with parents and staff. Being knowledgeable about the course was not ranked at the highest level for making a successful facilitator. Student support is also need in terms of monitoring student progress, working with the guidance counselors, and giving content support if necessary (SRI International, 2011).

VLL Versus Blended Learning Community

A VLL and a blended learning community (BLC) are very similar yet different. Both offer online courses in a lab setting. However, VLLs offer instructional support, meaning that an online teacher physically visits the class. With blended learning, students receive instruction in a completely online model in VLLs, while students are able to have face-to-face contact with the instructor visits for BLCs. For BLCs and VLLs, FLVS gives the instructional materials online, and qualified teachers as well as training for the facilitators. The facilitators do not need to be certified. Labs need computers, telephone, and a listing of the course offerings FLVS (FLVS, 2014b)

The Future

After the pilot, one Miami-Dade administrator said that they would like to enhance the curriculum with FLVS courses in the future. Another future concern is funding for facilitator positions. Before her retirement, Julie Young described the future of online blended learning for FLVS and discussed how she would improve course offerings. She mentioned the implementation of gaming such as the Sims and Minecraft. In addition, Florida Virtual School has added a social media course. FLVS currently partners with most districts for blended learning. Furthermore, FLVS has implemented BLCs in all of the high schools in Miami-Dade County (Riedel, 2014).

References

Associated Press. (2013, August 8). Florida virtual school lays off hundreds of teachers. *Tampa Tribune*. Retrieved from http://tbo.com/news/education/florida-virtual-school-lays-off-hundreds-of-teachers-20130808/

Clow, T. (2014, February 6). President and CEO announces retirement from Florida Virtual School. [Press Release] Florida Virtual School.

FLDOE. (2012, December 07). Online course graduation requirement. Retrieved from http://www.fldoe.org/eias/dataweb/tech/onlinegrad.pdf

Florida Virtual School. (2013a, January). Blended learning: How it works in Florida Virtual School. Retrieved from http://www.flvs.net/areas/aboutus/Documents/Research/Blended_Learning_White_Paper.pdf

Florida Virtual School. (2013b). Florida virtual school2013–14. Retrieved from http://www.flvs.net/areas/contactus/Documents/Florida_Virtual_School_Summary.pdf

Florida Virtual School. (2014a). Digital learning act - FAQs. Retrieved from http://cwww.flvs.net/areas/faqs/Pages/digital-learning-act.aspx

Florida Virtual School. (2014b). Online learning solutions for my school or district. Retrieved from http://www.flvs.net/educators/Pages/learning-solutions.aspx

FLVS Global. (2014). What is FLVS global. Retrieved from http://www.flvsglobal.net/about-us/

Horn, M. B., & Staker, H. (2011, January). The rise of k-12 blended learning. Retrieved from http://www.christenseninstitute.org/wp-content/uploads/2013/04/The-rise-of-K-12-blended-learning.pdf

Postal, L. (2014, February 27). Ron Blocker to lead Florida Virtual School while it searches for next president. *Orlando Sentinel*. Retrieved from http://www.orlandosentinel.com/features/blogs/school-zone/os-ron-blocker-florida-virtual-school,0,5480109.post

Riedel, C. (2014, February 2). Using online and blended learning to help students design their educational experience. *The Journal*. Retrieved from http://thejournal.com/Articles/2014/02/11/Using-Online-and-Blended-Learning-To-Help-Students-Design-Their-Educational-Experience.aspx?Page=1

SRI International. (2011, November). *Implementing online learning labs in schools and districts: November 2011 lessons from Miami-Dade's first year.* Retrieved from http://www.sri.com/sites/default/files/brochures/implementing_online_learning_labs.pdf

Simonson, M., Smaldino, S., Albright, M., & Zvacek. S. (2012). *Teaching and learning at a distance: Foundations of distance education* (5th ed.). Boston, MA: Pearson.

ACCESS Distance Learning
A Teacher's Perspective

M. Danyelle Hillman

INTRODUCTION

Alabama Connecting Classrooms, Educators, and Students Statewide, better known as ACCESS, is an education initiative developed through the Alabama Department of Education. ACCESS Distance Learning was launched in state of Alabama in 2006, funded through the line item budget through the state department of education. By the end of 2010, ACCESS had grown to the "third-largest virtual education program in the country" (Flanigan, 2012) and received $18.5 million from the state in 2013. During the inception of ACCESS the number of low-income students taking Advanced Placement courses has increased five times more than prior to implementing the program (Flanigan, 2012).

Due to an increase of teachers implementing blended learning, ACCESS is moving its focus toward blended learning in addition to distance learning. As a result of this new focus, in 2010, the official name changed to the Alabama ACCESS Distance and Blended Learning initiative. The enrollment of ACCESS had grown to approximately 44,000 students by the end of 2011.

BACKGROUND

There is no charge to attend courses through ACCESS Distance Learning as long as the students are enrolled in an Alabama public high school and in Grades 9–12. All courses are offered during normal school hours. The school must provide students with computers, textbooks, Internet connections and software. The typical ACCESS Distance Learning classroom contains "computer cameras, monitors and/or projectors for viewing content and teachers, interactive whiteboards, wireless routers and a minimum of 25 tablet computer" (Alabama Policy Institute, 2012).

Classes follow the local school calendar and closely match the school calendars. If the class is an interactive videoconferencing class, counselors will match the student's classes as close to the time as the onsite class in order for the students to interact with the teacher. Students are also eligible to take online or web-based courses.

M. Danyelle Hillman,
Commerce and Information Technology
Teacher, Muscle Shoals High School,
Muscle Shoals, AL.
Telephone: (256) 810-4265.
E-mail: danyelle.hillman@gmail.com

Any student interested in taking a course through ACCESS Distance Learning must make a request through their counselors.

Classes are taught in either synchronous or asynchronous format—or both. The class content containing synchronous format generally uses interactive videoconferencing in the course, whereas the course using asynchronous format is typically more of a web-based course. According to the Alabama Policy Institute (2012), synchronous learning is great way for students to gain knowledge and provide feedback in a timely fashion to assist with misunderstandings. Teachers are contracted to create courses or the state department will purchase a ready-made course with exclusive rights to make changes as necessary (Alabama Policy Institute, 2012).

BENEFITS OF ACCESS

There are many benefits to students, teachers, and counselors who use ACCESS Distance Learning. One major benefit is students, who live in rural Alabama, which is a large majority of students, have an opportunity to take courses not offered at their local high school. For whatever reason these courses are not offered, it does not hold the student back from taking Advanced Placement courses or any other course not available on-site. In the 2010–2011 school year, one of every five students took one course through ACCESS Distance Learning in rural Alabama. In that same year, in micropolitan areas one of every seven students took one course, while one of every 14 students took a course in the metropolitan districts.

Teachers have the ability to learn new methods of teaching, whether through synchronous, asynchronous or blended format. ACCESS Distance Learning provides different methods for teachers to be successful. Teachers are engaged and interactive with their students. Another benefit for teachers is teaching for ACCESS Distance Learning provides a supplement to the teaching income they are already receiving.

Counselors also benefit through ACCESS Distance Learning because now they have more classes to offer students in areas such as Advanced Placement, foreign languages, electives, and higher mathematics. The curriculum is state approved; therefore, there is no need to worry if it meets state standards. The teachers are highly qualified; therefore, the school system does not have to stress over personnel backgrounds.

THREE ROLES OF THE PROFESSIONAL AND ACCESS DISTANCE LEARNING

For the professional, ACCESS Distance Learning provides multiple opportunities. The roles to be discussed in more details include the counselor, the facilitator, and the teacher.

COUNSELOR'S ROLE

It is the counselor's responsibility to ensure students are enrolled in the correct ACCESS Distance Learning courses. Course requests are made through the ACCESS Distance Learning online registration link. Counselors determine if a student is ready for a distance learning course through ACCESS. They look for certain characteristics such as good writing skills, communication skills, interest in online learning, computer literacy, and a capacity for independent learning (Alabama Policy Institute, 2012). The student must work closely with the counselor to ensure the best possible course is selected for the success of the student. It is imperative the counselor does not give a student a class he/she is not ready for. The counselor works closely with the facilitator to monitor the student's success in the course throughout the semester and make any notes deemed vital to future decisions.

Facilitator's Role

ACCESS Distance Learning facilitators do not have to be certified teachers. A facilitator is an adult supervisor who serves as the liaison between the student and the teacher. A facilitator must over 18 years of age and must be familiar with web-based instruction. Facilitators in a Title I school must be supervised by a certified teacher. Facilitators must also meet personnel qualifications set forth by the local school system.

A facilitator's responsibilities include monitoring student progress and ensuring students submit their coursework in a timely fashion. If there is a problem with a student, it is the facilitator who acts as the on-site person in charge of the student while the student is in the lab. If the student begins to fall behind, the facility will work closely with the student and counselor to ensure coursework is turned in as it should be. If there are any technical issues, it is the facilitator's job to see to the troubleshooting of the lab equipment. If it is a more complex technical issue, the technology department is contacted.

Teacher's Role

To become a teacher with ACCESS Distance Learning, an interested teacher must first fill out an application and submit the required paperwork, including a recommendation letter from the teacher's principal. Teachers then participate in an interview and attend a 3-day training session. These training sessions are conducted in Madison, Tuscaloosa, and Troy, Alabama. Once selected, ACCESS teachers participate and "attend scheduled, ongoing, professional development" (ACCESS Distance Learning, 2013, p. 2).

By teaching ACCESS Distance Learning classes, teachers learn different approaches to integrating technology in their own traditional classrooms. Teachers believe they always need to learn (Sugar & Slagter van Tryon, 2014); therefore, teachers can use ACCESS Distance Learning as a learning resource. One example is the use of Moodle in the classroom or similar course management software. One teacher noted that using the software program has helped her decide which classroom management program would be useful and user-friendly to her students in the classroom. She also mentioned how using the web-based software is beneficial in monitoring student progress (teacher first initial and last name, personal communication, date).

Teachers must rely a great deal on using technology in the classroom when teaching through ACCESS Distance Learning classes. They must be familiar with the equipment in their classroom in order to troubleshoot problems that. For example, when a teacher is utilizing the interactive videoconferencing class format, they must be able to use the video equipment and the software that comes with it in order to teach their classes to students. If technical problems arise in the classrooms, the teacher must have the ability or knowledge to be able to troubleshoot minor problems. Problems which may arise can include printer issues, saving issues, file retrieval issues and computer freeze and crash issues, just to name a few. A facilitator on-site at the remote school is also beneficial.

While in a classroom setting, if teachers have any problems with an online student, they will first contact the student. Problems that may arise include students not turning in their work, not logging into the classroom, or plagiarism (K. Vaughan, personal communication, 2014). The teacher will contact the facilitator at the student's school to try and resolve the issue if talking with the student is not successful. Depending on the issue at hand, disciplinary issues could go as far getting the student's principal involved, but there has been no need for that type of action.

INSTRUCTIONAL STRATEGY

Teachers using instructional strategies with virtual learning have the ability to utilize the same instructional strategies as used in the traditional classroom. Teachers must continue to plan for reading assignments, textbook use, and media deemed necessary (Marsap & Narin, 2009). No matter the media used to reach students in a virtual learning environment, communication is the key to success (Marsap & Narin, 2009).

When developing discussions for online courses, Berge's (1995) model is useful. It can be used to assist teachers and facilitators when performing multiple duties in both the online and traditional settings. Teachers and facilitators fulfill pedagogical, social, managerial, and technical roles (Safar & Alkhezzi, 2013). When used correctly, this model will transform teachers and facilitators so they can:

- help students become self-learners;
- increase student awareness of the course offered;
- help students become persistent and successful learners; and
- help students becoming lifelong learners (Safar & Alkhezzi, 2013).

One important note to remember when designing a class for e-learning through a virtual school is to create goals, objectives, class outline and major units and topics before doing anything else for the class (Ko & Rossen, 2010). This helps the teacher to have in mind what is being taught when designing the class and can implement the appropriate learning strategies for student success.

CLASSROOM STRATEGIES THAT WORK

When designing a virtual classroom, it is important to remember the standards for this type of classroom just as with the traditional classroom. With the implementation of the Common Core Standards in Alabama, it is imperative the ACCESS Distance Learning courses follow the same rigor and standards as traditional classrooms. According to Buehl (2014), when implementing Common Core Standards, students will be expected to:

- read and comprehend texts of much greater complexity;
- read a higher volume of informational texts;
- perceive, analyze and develop argumentation as readers, writers, speakers, listeners, and viewers;
- expand their academic vocabularies; and
- regularly communicate their understanding as readers and learning through writing.

IMPLEMENTING DISCUSSION QUESTIONS IN ACCESS DISTANCE LEARNING

Discussion questions can either be asynchronous or synchronous. When developing discussions for ACCESS Distance Learning, the teacher must first determine the discussion question format. Does the teacher want the students to have time to reflect on the question and give thought-provoking responses (asynchronous), or does the teacher prefer the students respond to the questions in a timely fashion (synchronous), as in a bell ringer. Whichever response the teacher prefers, the goal and objectives of the class should help foster the decision making.

Ko and Rossen (2010) provided some helpful tips when implementing asynchronous discussions. These tips include:

- The teacher should start the major thread;
- Topics should be narrowed down;
- The class discussions should be organized in a chronological order or sequenced pattern;
- Make the threads personal by addressing the students by name;

- A pattern should be established when responding to posts;
- Facilitate the discussions and help students build on others' responses to aid in class participation;
- Higher order thinking should be stimulated in the students;
- Strategize for controversial topics as they may arise; and
- Cultural patterns should be reviewed.

Whatever type of discussion chosen for the ACCESS Distance Learning classroom, keeping students actively engaged is important.

WEB-ENHANCED AND BLENDED COURSES

Web-enhanced and blended courses are offered by ACCESS Distance Learning. Both provide the necessary tools needed for success in the classroom. A web-enhanced classroom consists of a broad category of content put on a website or classroom management system which may contain material such as a syllabus, class calendar, resources, and discussion boards. In the web-enhanced classroom, actual online participation may be optional (Ko & Rosson, 2010). In a blended classroom, a good percentage of the classroom material is delivered online and student participation and activity is online as well. A blended learning classroom is delivered in both a face-to-face classroom and online as well.

With ACCESS Distance Learning moving its focus to a blended classroom format, here are some tips in implementing a blended course:

- Avoid overloading students with more work than they would have received in a traditional classroom.
- Give clear directions on the goal the students are to accomplish. This helps to alleviate any misunderstandings.

- Give students an orientation of the blended classroom format so they understand how the course works (Ko & Rossen, 2010).

TIME COMMITMENT

Time is one of the greatest commitments a teacher with ACCESS Distance Learning or any virtual school can give. Although time is not spent in a physical classroom with virtual schools, this time can be well spent preparing lessons, recording lectures, developing websites, posting to discussions, answering questions, and interacting with students (Simonson, Smaldino, Albright, & Zvacek, 2012).

COMMUNICATION

Communication is just as important when teaching at ACCESS Distance Learning as it is when teaching at a brick-and-mortar school. Effective communication is necessary with the exchange of ideas, messages and signals (Stancil, 2011). Students are successful when they can see or hear feedback. When a teacher communicates to the students the proper instructions and expectations of a class, students tend to learn better and have a better understanding of how the class will work (Ko & Rossen, 2010). Teachers will also notice behavioral problems are kept to a minimum because the student is well aware of any consequences for his/her actions.

CONCLUSION

Teachers have the ability to set the standards in a classroom, whether it is an e-learning classroom or a face-to-face classroom. Their approach to learning and their ability to identify with their students will determine the success of their students. The teachers' perspective of technology will influence their students' learning in ways they have never imagined. With so much information available, there is room for every student to be successful in an e-learning classroom if only the teacher takes to the time to research and implement the strategies to help his or her students reach their goals.

Classrooms have moved from a teacher-centered approach to a student-centered learning environment. Although student centered learning is not a new approach, the movement toward distance education brought student-centered learning back to the forefront of active learning (Simonson et al., 2012). In today's classrooms, with the implementation of Common Core Standards, teachers must implement more critical thinking skills. Open lines of communication with the students is a key to success as well. With the implementation of Plan 2020, schools have the task of getting students "college and career ready." Because of ACCESS Distance Learning, the third largest distance learning school in the country, the students of Alabama are well on their way to becoming "college and career ready" and ready to compete with other students domestically and globally in both the academic and the global markets.

REFERENCES

ACCESS Distance Learning. (2013, August 9). *A guide for educators.* Retrieved from http://accessdl.state.al.us/documents/EDUCATORS2014-NB.pdf

Alabama Policy Institute. (2012). *Classes without walls: Access Distance Learning works for Alabama.* Birmingham, AL: Author.

Berge, Z. (1995). Facilitating computer conferencing: Recommendations from the field. *Educational Technology, 35*(1), 22–30.

Buehl, D. (2014). *Classroom strategies for interactive learning.* Newark, DE: International Reading Association.

Flanigan, R. (2012). Ala. opens wide access to blended learning. *Education Week, 32*(9), 19–20.

Ko, S., & Rosson, S. (2010). *Teaching online: A practical guide* (3rd ed.). New York, NY: Routledge.

Marsap, A., & Narin, M. (2009). The integration of distance learning via Internet and face to face learning: Why face to face learning is required in distance learning via Internet? *Procedia Social and Behavioral Sciences, 1*(1), 2871–2878.

Safar, A. H., & Alkhezzi, F. A. (2013). Beyond computer literacy: Technology integration and curriculum transformation. *College Student Journal, 47*(4), 614–626.

Simonson, M., Smaldino, S., Albright, M., & Zvacek, S. (2012). *Teaching and learning at a distance* (5th ed.). Boston, MA: Pearson.

Stancil, S. (2011). Wired for success: Alabama's access to distance learning. *Distance Learning, 8*(4), 51–58.

Sugar, W., & Slagter van Tryon, P. J. (2014). Development of a virtual technology coach to support technology integration for K–12 educators. *TechTrends, 58*(3), 54–62.

NorthStar Academy
An Online International School

Kevin Arndt

INTRODUCTION

The world today is more interconnected than ever before. Corporations have expanded and acquired other corporations to become multinational corporations. With the rise of multinational corporations comes the need for education. This education is not limited to internal education of the corporation but also education of the children of the

Kevin Arndt,
Mathematics Teacher, The International
School of Azerbaijan. TISA, Yeni Yasamal,
Stonepay, Royal Park, Baku, Azerbaijan.
Telephone: (623) 523-7740.

employees of the corporation. With this need has come the rise in international schools. International schools are schools that offer an educational program that is different from the national curriculum. Generally this education is done is a language that is different from the language of the country where the school is located. Many of these international schools started as boarding schools for the children of protestant missionaries. They were located in capital cities or centralized locations and missionaries would send their kids to these schools for their education. Schools like Seoul Foreign School in South Korea and Rift Valley Academy in Kenya started this way. Because some of these schools were located in capital cities, this allowed for diplomats to bring families and have their children educated. As the world has evolved to becoming an interconnected planet, many of these schools have expanded their focus to offer educational opportunities for all who qualify to attend their schools. Now most countries and most large cities have international schools. These schools offer diverse international curriculums like the International General Certificate of Secondary Education, or the Advanced Placement, or the International Baccalaureate. The goal of most of these schools is to help educate and train the future leaders of the world.

This article will spotlight a different international school, an online international school.

NorthStar Academy

NorthStar Academy is an international school that differs from other international schools in that it is an online school. NorthStar Academy is a member of the Network of International Christian Schools (NICS). NICS currently has 19 brick and mortar schools located in 15 different countries. The size of the NICS school vary from school-to-school, with population ranging from under 100 students to over 800 students. "The mission of NICS is to establish a worldwide network of international Christian schools staffed by qualified Christian educators, instilling in each student a Biblical worldview in an environment of academic excellence and respect for people of all cultures and religions" (Network of International Christian Schools, 2012, Mission and Purpose section, para. 1). With NICS having 18 different schools in 15 different countries one may wonder why would NICS need an online school? The beginning of NorthStar may explain the desire to have an online school. NorthStar academy was the brainchild of two Wycliffe mission executives. In the 1990s the executives saw the potential power of the Internet for use in education. Through most of the nineteenth and twentieth centuries missionaries had two choices for educating their children. They could send their children off to international boarding schools or they could home school their children. There were advantages and disadvantages in both options. In sending their kids off to boarding school, the children generally received a high quality education that allowed the students access to further education, but families were separated for long periods of time and there were extra costs that families had to cover, such as tuition, boarding costs and travel expenses. In homeschool-

ing, families were able to remain together, but quality of education depended of a number of factors, such as the family's access to curriculum and the quality of instruction coming from the parents, many of whom may not have been trained as teachers. In starting NorthStar Academy it would allow families who live in more remote areas without access to a local international school to have access to a high quality school education for their children and to remain together as a family. In 1998 NorthStar Academy started with 32 students in Grades 7 through 11. In 2008 NICS took over the management of the school and has helped to continue to grow the school to over 1,400 students in Grades 4 through 12. NorthStar Academy students reside in over 70 different countries.

NorthStar Academy has some similarities and some differences in what it offers to their students compared to other international schools. One similarity is in the choice of curriculum. NorthStar offers over 200 different classes. In their course offerings they have chosen to offer typical American curriculum classes, including 18 Advanced Placement courses. Also in their course offerings they have partnered with LeTourneau University and Moody Bible Institute to offer dual enrollment courses. A dual enrollment course is a course where the student pays the university tuition along with the NorthStar tuition and the student receives both high school and university credit for the courses. A way that NorthStar differs is their offering of curriculum to homeschooling parents. In the 2011–2012 school year approximately three percent of school age students were homeschooled (U.S. Department of Education, n.d.). Ninety-one percent of the parents who homeschooled said that they had concerns about the environment of other schools as an important factor of why they chose to homeschool (U.S. Department of Education, n.d.). NorthStar believes it can help these families by offering high quality curriculum to the parents. Parents are given access to the teaching notes, teacher-designed tests, and answer keys. This access can relieve the stress that parents can face in developing lessons and tests for their children. NorthStar sees homeschooling as an area for future growth and will work to further refine course offerings to make sure the curriculum continues to be of high quality.

NorthStar is committed to offering high quality education from a Christian worldview, with educators who understand what it is like to live internationally. NorthStar commitment to high quality education is seen in the school's accreditation. NorthStar was one of the first online Christian schools to receive accreditation when the Southern Association of Colleges and Schools accredited it in 2005. NorthStar realizes the importance of accreditation to the future of its students and so has maintained its accreditation. NorthStar also feels teaching through a Christian worldview is important. Thus all of the educators at NorthStar are required to sign a statement of faith to show that they align with the faith values chosen by the leadership of the school. Also, teachers are given guidance in integrating their faith into their lessons to further emphasize the Christian worldview. Lastly, NorthStar realizes it is an international school and so it strives to hire current or former international school teachers. These teachers have insight into the struggles that the students may be facing living in a foreign country. NorthStar's association with NICS allows for NorthStar to recruit teachers from other NICS schools.

NORTHSTAR'S FLEXIBILITY

Delivery of content can be an issue for online schools. Online schools must decide if they will do synchronous, asynchronous, or a blending of the two for their course offerings. Synchronous class sessions mean that everyone in the class logs into a class session and class is held in this session. An asynchronous class does not have set meeting sessions; instead, videos and/or text-driven lessons are given to students to complete in a designated time frame. Some schools have chosen to blend these two styles of distance learning. NorthStar has chosen an asynchronous approach. With students spread throughout 70 different countries it would be difficult for teachers to find a good time for all their students to attend a synchronous class. The other issue keeping NorthStar from offering synchronous sessions is their students' access to reliable Internet service. Some NorthStar students do not regularly have access to the Internet. These students may be living in extreme rural areas of Africa or Asia. This is where NorthStar is unique. Northstar offers their students two options for their course work; high bandwidth and low bandwidth. In the low bandwidth option when students have access to Internet, they log into their courses and download a certain number of weeks worth of curriculum and upload assignments or activities for their teachers to grade. This pattern is repeated throughout the duration of the course. Because NorthStar is asynchronous, students set the time frame for their classes with the limitation that a full year course must be finished in 52 weeks and a half-year course must be finished in 26 weeks. Giving the students the ability to set their time frame and the ability to download course work in advance to work when they do not have access to the Internet allows NorthStar to be a viable option for students and families who live in remote areas of the world.

NorthStar also offers flexibility to both students and to other NICS schools. NorthStar does not require its students to be full-time students. For instance, parents may want their kids to attend a public school but want their children to also take a bible course. NorthStar is an option for these parents. Students may choose NorthStar because their school is unable to offer a class. By taking the class through North-

Star the student is able to pursue an area of interest. Families use NorthStar to varying amounts. It is not uncommon in a family for one child to be a full-time NorthStar student, while a sibling takes one or two courses. In some families the parents may choose the homeschooling option for one child but for another child they choose for the student to be a full-time student. NorthStar wants to bring this flexibility to its families. NorthStar also partners with other NICS schools. Recently one of the NICS schools lost it statistics teacher. The school was unable to replace the statistics teacher but had 11 students signed up to take the course. The school approached NorthStar to see what NorthStar could do to help fill this need. NorthStar designed an online statistics course and provided a teacher for the course. This allowed the NICS school to continue to offer the course and meet the student needs for the school. This partnership is very beneficial to the smaller NICS schools where course offerings can be limited because of low enrollment. Students are able to take electives that the school is unable to offer because of lack of interest or because it is unable to staff the position.

STUDENT EXPERIENCE

The student experience at NorthStar is important and a point of focus. NorthStar wants its students to interact with each other. In individual classes this is done through discussion topics posted on discussion boards. But outside of classes, students have the opportunity to take part in a number of enrichment activities. This is done mostly through their school communication system, but use of social media and communication technologies such as Skype are also an option for students to connect. Students have the option to be members of over 30 clubs and activities. NorthStar has a functioning student council to help plan activities for students and look out for the interests of the students.

Students can also access areas where they can interact with each other through a bible study or through a prayer group. NorthStar also offers a spiritual emphasis week for their students to attend. In this week students watch live sessions from speakers. They also interact with each other through activities with the goal of helping the students know what they believe and how to best live out those beliefs in the world. The school does not mandate the spiritual emphasis week but would like all students to participate. NorthStar believes that the student experience is important that they offer access to activities and the spiritual emphasis week to all of their students whether full-time or part-time. It also offers access to clubs, activities, and the spiritual emphasis week for the homeschooling families. Even though these students are not official NorthStar students, the school feels that their students can benefit from interaction with other NorthStar students and vice-versa.

TECHNOLOGY AND COURSE DESIGN

NorthStar uses three technology systems with students and parents. The first system is called Genius. Genius is a commercial student information system. Genius works with other online schools and is a good fit for NorthStar. In Genius students apply for admission, register for courses, find their final grades, and ask for transcripts. For courses NorthStar uses BrainHoney learning management system. BrainHoney is another commercial product, and is similar to other learning management systems. Courses are delivered to students through this program. The courses are built in week-by-week format to help students know a pace that will allow them to finish the course within the 52-week or 26-week deadlines. The final system is the communication system. NorthStar has chosen to use FirstClass as their communication system. This choice was made because they are able to host this on their servers and therefore control who has access to the communication held in this system. This system also provides the areas needed for the clubs and activities.

NorthStar courses are designed by the teachers of the course. When a new teacher comes to the school and takes over an existing course, the new teacher is responsible for maintaining the course and updating the course to make sure the course is still relevant and still challenging to the students. New courses are designed by the teachers, who use their knowledge of the subject to design lessons and assignments. NorthStar continues to evaluate their course offering and the rigor in the courses to make sure that they are challenging yet achievable by the student.

FUTURE

NorthStar is also looking to the future. The leadership at NorthStar are starting to look at how they could potentially bring a blended instructional aspect to some of their classes. In this idea, students would potentially travel to a location and have some face-to-face interaction with both their teacher and their classmates. An example of this could be in a chemistry class where students travel to a location to do laboratory work with their classmates and the teachers. The goal of this is to further enhance student learning. The logistics of how NorthStar is going to offer this has yet to be determined and it may be limited to students who reside near a partner school.

NorthStar's leadership is visionary, but maintains its mission of offering high qual-

ity Christian education. NorthStar does acknowledge that there are other options for international students but they do feel their wide ranges of options, such as the bandwidth options and the homeschooling option, gives them a uniqueness compared to other international school. Feedback about NorthStar form parents and students has been mostly positive. They have found that parents and students like the flexibility of the program to where a kid can take one or two or all of their classes through NorthStar. NorthStar has been success in transitioning student to further education. They have found that 75% of their students go on to a 4-year university and another 10% go to a 2-year university. Also, NorthStar graduates have been accepted by great universities. As NorthStar continues to grow, the list of where NorthStar graduates are admitted to college will also grow. NorthStar is truly meeting the NICS mission of having students achieve academic excellence but they are doing this in a unique way. NorthStar is a unique international school meeting the needs of many international families through its programs and is striving to be a great online school.

REFERENCES

Network of International Christian Schools, (2012). Mission and purpose [Webpage]. Retrieved from http://www.nics.org/about/mission-and-purpose

Department of Education, (n.d.). Fast facts: Homeschooling [Webpage]. Retrieved from http://nces.ed.gov/fastfacts/display.asp?id=9

North Carolina Virtual Public School

Preparing Students Today for Lives Tomorrow

Holly Marshburn

INTRODUCTION

Virtual schools are continuing to rise in numbers and the population of students served. Three hundred eleven full-time virtual schools

Holly Marshburn,
P.O. Box 1791,
Carolina Beach, NC 28428.
Telephone: (910) 7074580.

were operating in the United States during the 2011–2012 school year and 338 schools serving 243,000 students in 2012–2013 (Cavanagh, 2014; Miron, Horvitz, & Gulosino, 2013). Parents are considering online learning as an alternative to traditional school because they feel their children do not learn as well in a traditional setting, they need more flexibility with scheduling, and they want their children home where they feel they are safer than in face-to-face schools (Connections Academy, 2014).

BACKGROUND

The North Carolina General Assembly, in 2005, passed the session law, 2006-66, that included the 2007 launch of the North Carolina Virtual Public School (NCVPS) (2014e). NCVPS has grown to become the second largest virtual school in the country (North Carolina Virtual Public School, 2014e). As shown in Figure 1, the NCVPS organization consists of administration, operations, and instruction (Fetzer, 2013). In the 2012–2013 school year, 115 local education agencies (LEAs) and 44 charter

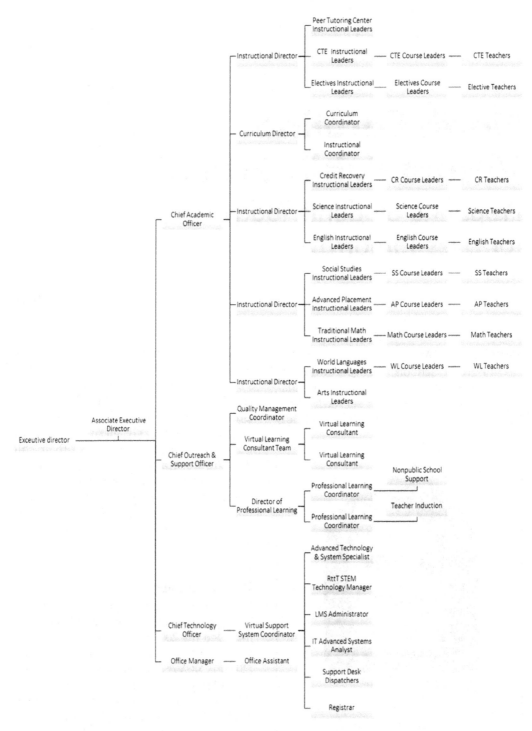

Figure 1. NCVPS organization chart.

schools offered their students NCVPS courses. In addition, 11 private students took NCVPS courses (North Carolina Virtual Public School, 2014a).

NCVPS online courses are supplementary to the classes students take in their district school. Students register for NCVPS courses through their district school and attend a computer lab during their assigned time to complete their online course work. This hybrid model allows for better student accountability and addresses any technology deficiencies students may have at home (Ingerham, 2012). Certain students are allowed to complete their course work from home.

MISSION AND VISION STATEMENTS

The NCVPS mission statements are, (a) "NCVPS provides blended learning and leadership opportunities to empower globally competitive students" (North Carolina Virtual Public School, 2014a, p. 2) and (b) "NCVPS serves learners with high quality online courses and expanded options in education" (North Carolina Virtual Public School, 2014k).

The vision of NCVPS is, "To be a world-class model of blended learning for a new generation of global learners" (North Carolina Virtual Public School, 2014a, p. 2) and to expand minds, expand opportunities, and expand connections through blended and online learning. The faculty and staff of NCVPS strive to always put the students and their learning first (North Carolina Virtual Public School, 2014k).

THREE INSTRUCTIONAL PILLARS

The teaching philosophy of NCVPS has three instructional pillars (see Figure 2): (a) effective instructional announcements and learning blocks, (b) effective instructional feedback on all assignments, and (c) effective synchronous conversations to build relationships. First, the daily announcements have three components: due dates of assignments, sections covering new and old material, and student celebrations. Next, teachers provide quick

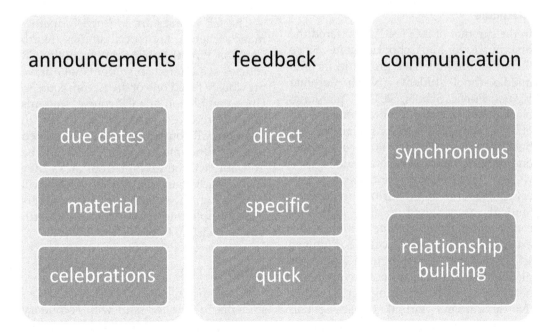

Figure 2.   NCVPS Three instructional pillars.

(within 24 hours) and specific feedback on students' assignments. As a final point, teachers use different interactive opportunities to build relationships with their students and parents (North Carolina Virtual Public School, 2014k). These instructional pillars are instrumental in encouraging students' online learning success.

FUNDING

The North Carolina General Assembly creates and modifies the funding formula legislation for schools' costs for their students' enrollment. Currently, per student, schools are responsible for $235 for summer courses, $349 for block courses, and $438 for year-long courses (North Carolina Virtual Public School, 2014e). These funds cover the instructional, operational, and administrative costs of NCVPS. The budget for the 2012–2013 school year was $15,737,378 for instruction, $1,342,418 for operations, and $1,868,537 for administration (North Carolina Virtual Public School, 2014a).

COURSES

In the summer of 2007, NCVPS offered the first courses for high school students. Since then, the offerings have grown to include middle-school students (North Carolina Virtual Public School, 2014f). Year-long, block, and summer school courses are offered annually. Year-long courses are held over two semesters, block courses last one semester, and summer school lasts 8 weeks. Only traditional and credit recovery courses are offered during the summer. Students are advised to take only one course during the summer due to the extremely fast pace of the courses. Summer school students are not excused from completing their work due to not having Internet access, such as going on vacation (North Carolina Virtual Public School, 2014g). There are four areas of courses offered through NCVPS: traditional; sci-

ence, technology, engineering, and mathematics; occupational course of study (OCS), and credit recovery (CR) (North Carolina Virtual Public School, 2014b).

The traditional courses include honors, arts, career and technical, English, health, mathematics, science, social studies, and several world languages (Arabic, Russian, Japanese, Latin, Mandarin Chinese, Spanish, French, and German). The science, technology, engineering, and mathematics courses are blended and cover the subjects of Earth and environmental science, forensic science, mathematics, and biotechnical and agriculture science (North Carolina Virtual Public School, 2014b).

The OCS courses are in English, mathematics, science, and social studies (North Carolina Virtual Public School, 2014b). These courses follow a blended model with face-to-face time with the OCS teacher and online time with the NCVPS content teacher. The OCS face-to-face teachers are required to complete a one-time, 2-hour, online training session in order to participate in teaching the blended model (North Carolina Virtual Public School, 2014j).

The CR courses are in English, mathematics, science, and social studies (North Carolina Virtual Public School, 2014b). CR courses are offered to students who have previously failed one of the 12 core courses. Upon completion of a CR course, students can only receive a grade of Pass or Fail. In addition, CR courses are mastery-modeled courses. Students are preassessed on the unit and will be exempt from areas they have already mastered and the teacher will identify which assignments the students must complete to master the unit (North Carolina Virtual Public School, 2014d).

SUCCESS 101

As another means to assist high school students to be successful with secondary learning, the course, Success 101, is a one credit, semester-long elective requiring no prerequisites. The middle school equivalent is Middle School Success 101. The focus of the course is study skills, time management, using the Internet, and personal learning styles (North Carolina Virtual Public School, 2014c).

COURSE DESIGN

NCVPS teachers use Moodle or Blackboard learning management systems. There are asynchronous and synchronous aspects required in all courses (North Carolina Virtual Public School, 2014h). All the NCVPS courses meet the North Carolina Department of Public Instruction standards, the Southern Regional Education Board's e-learning standards, and the standards are benchmarked by the iNACOL National Standards (North Carolina Virtual Public School, 2014h).

NCVPS faculty and staff design content for the courses tailored to North Carolina students. The designers for NCVPS follow four main instructional design principles: (a) the universal design for learning principle—content is accessible to all learners through different modalities, (b) supporting students towards higher level thinking, as illustrated in the Revised Bloom's Taxonomy, (c) differentiating content for students' diverse learning styles, and (d) highly qualified expert teachers developing the content (North Carolina Virtual Public School, 2014k).

In 2007, NCVPS courses began with purchased courses from vendors. However, due to the high cost of buying courses or hiring instructional designers, plus the time needed to customize outside courses for North Carolina students, the administration decided to use their own teachers to revise and create courses for NCVPS students (Oliver, Kellogg, Townsend, & Brady, 2010). NCVPS staff offers qualified teachers paid opportunities to revise courses and develop new courses as needed and on an ongoing basis. Teachers with experience with universal design for learning principles, revised Bloom's taxonomy, integrating 21st century skills, creating multimedia, and using Web 2.0 tools collaborate with an NCVPS design team to revise and develop courses (North Carolina Virtual Public School, 2014i).

TEACHERS

More than 500 teachers subcontract with NCVPS part time each semester. Teachers can teach two course sections if they are employed by an LEA and three sections if they are not (A. Pacyna, personal communication, August, 2014). All NCVPS teachers are North Carolina certified highly qualified teachers. Sixty-four percent of the teachers have a master's degree and 4% are National Board Certified teachers (North Carolina Virtual Public School, 2014k). NCVPS teachers are required to attend department meetings, complete necessary reports, keep office hours, and interact often with students, schools, and parents (North Carolina Virtual Public School, 2014i).

The hiring process for NCVPS begins with submitting an online application, a résumé, or curriculum vitae, proof of a Standard Professional II NC teaching license in the subject area to be taught, and three letters of reference. Next, there are two telephone interviews: one with the Instructional Lead teacher and the second with the Instructional Director of the subject area for which one is applying (D. Richardson, personal communication, July 2014). Once applicants are recommended for hire, they must travel to the NCVPS office on the North Carolina State University campus in Raleigh, NC, to complete the hire paperwork, show proof of residency, a social security card, and submit fingerprints for a background check (A. Pacyna, personal communication, August, 2014; North Carolina Virtual Public School, 2014g). Finally, the applicant is ready to participate in the Teacher-in-Training program.

TEACHER-IN-TRAINING PROGRAM

All teachers who are added to the NCVPS work pool are required to participate in the nonpaid Teacher-in-Training program. The program lasts 18 weeks; that is, one semester. The first nine weeks involves an online training that addresses the expectations of NCVPS teachers. In addition, new teachers learn about the NCVPS policies, procedures, best practices, and learning management system (North Carolina Virtual Public School, 2014g). The final nine weeks is a teacher practicum that is much like an internship. The teachers-in-training participate in a mentor teacher's course in their subject area. The mentor teacher gradually adds responsibilities on the teacher-in-training (North Carolina Virtual Public School, 2014k; North Carolina Virtual Public School, 2014a). With the successful completion of all requirements, NCVPS administration can offer the newly trained teachers a section to teach during the next semester or in the future, depending on the number of students enrolled.

STUDENTS

NCVPS administration projected 58,000 students would attend the 2014 fall semester. During the 2012–2013 school year, a total of 47,715 students enrolled in NCVPS courses. Nearly 97% of the students completed their courses, with about 82% passing. However, the results from the end-of-course state standardized testing indicates that NCVPS students consistently perform below the traditional state averages in general/honors, OCS, and credit recovery courses, with the exception of the general Math 1 course (North Carolina Virtual Public School, 2014a).

The most successful online learners are also successful in their face-to-face courses. They are independent, self-motivated, familiar with technology, and have a proficient command of the language. When considering students with disadvantages and comparing the populations of virtual schools to traditional schools, virtual schools serve less: (a) economically disadvantaged—33% less, (b) special education—55% less, and English language learners—96% less (Cavanagh, 2014; Miron et al., 2013). At-risk students who do not yet have the typical success factors will need additional support and attention from faculty in order to be successful. Three strategies in particular are helpful with at-risk students. One strategy is designated faculty follow students throughout their course work. These faculty members can include teachers, counselors, and special education teachers. Another strategy is using technology tools to personalize learning. An example could be using software programs that specifically address the academic needs of the individual student. A third strategy is tailoring instruction to promote success. For example, NCVPS utilizes mastery learning in its credit recovery courses (Archambault et al., 2010).

Students have varying expectations of online learning. Often students do not completely understand the rigor involved with NCVPS courses. Although there are students who try to make themselves unavailable by cutting off communication with the teacher (R. Edwards, personal communication, August 14, 2014), teachers who are able to maintain effective communication with students build relationships that lead to motivating students to complete courses (Oliver, Osborne, & Brady, 2009).

PEER TUTORING PROGRAM

NCVPS faculty choose veteran students to volunteer with the peer tutoring program. These volunteers help other students who are in need of assistance in their courses (North Carolina Virtual Public School, 2014f). The purpose of the program is another means to help raise students' academic achievement and to make the transition to online learning a positive experience. Over 8,000 volunteer hours were reported during the 2012–2013 school year (North Carolina Virtual Public School, 2014a). The peer tutoring program is a unique idea that other virtual schools are considering adding to their programs.

PARENTAL INVOLVEMENT

Parents have several ways to stay abreast of their children's progress. A virtual open house, parent–student handbook, and the NCVPS Virtual Support Center are available online for assisting with making online learning and course procedures clear. Parents have access to their children's online courses. The online learning contact and advisor are available at the students' home school to answer questions and provide assistance. Teachers make weekly or biweekly contact with parents and are also available to answer their questions during office hours, through e-mail, text messaging, Blackboard instant messaging, and telephone calls (North Carolina Virtual Public School, 2014k; W. Kraft, personal communication, August 6, 2014). Parents are encouraged to reach out to the NCVPS teacher with any questions or concerns.

NEW HANOVER COUNTY SCHOOLS

With over 100 districts and dozens of charter schools involved with NCVPS, one of the largest consumers in North Carolina is New Hanover County Schools. The LEA, New Hanover County Schools (NHCS), began its involvement with NCVPS in 2007. Approximately 30 students began course work during that first semester on two separate campuses (W. Kraft, personal communication, August 6, 2014). NHCS is the third largest LEA enrolling students in NCVPS courses with 2,300 students in the 2012–2013 school year (North Carolina Virtual Public School, 2014a) and almost 2,500 students in the 2013–2014 school year (W.

Kraft, personal communication, August 6, 2014).

During the summer of 2011, NCVPS exclusively offered all summer school credit recovery courses for NHCS students. NHCS's growing involvement with NCVPS led to the LEA adding additional positions in order to help guarantee a high level of student success. The supervisor of online learning was added, and each high school campus gained a virtual academy coordinator. The Virtual Academy Coordinator is in charge of the computer lab where students complete their NCVPS online course work (W. Kraft, personal communication, August 6, 2014).

Seven of the eight middle schools also offer online courses. As of the 2014–2015 school year, the seven middle schools share three Virtual Academy Coordinators, about one person per every two schools. Approximately 300 NHCS middle school students were involved with NCVPS in 2013–2014. These students were closely screened as high achieving eighth graders who were ready to take high school classes (W. Kraft, personal communication, August 6, 2014).

BENEFITS

The administration of New Hanover County Schools found definite benefits to offering NCVPS courses. One of those benefits is the ability to expand course offerings. Typically, NHCS is not able to offer courses such as Mandarin Chinese and Japanese language courses. Not enough students request these courses to make them cost effective for face-to-face classes. A second benefit is opening up students' schedules so that they are able to take certain courses. For example, if students have only a certain block of time available during their day at their district school, they can take an NCVPS course during that time (W. Kraft, personal communication, August 6, 2014).

VIRTUAL ACADEMY COORDINATORS

Virtual Academy coordinators help students with skills such as understanding the learning management system, how to contact their online teacher and ask for help, and troubleshooting issues that come up with assignments. Not all students need the additional help; however, the support is there for those who do (W. Kraft, personal communication, August 6, 2014).

The Virtual Academy support structure was implemented in 2012. It is a model of support that begins with the Virtual Academy coordinators. They are trained on the two learning management systems: Blackboard and Moodle. In addition, they help students advocate for themselves and instigate parental involvement. They also coordinate communication with all stakeholders in the NCVPS process: parents, counselors, principals, NCVPS teachers, and others. At the traditional high school, teachers hold weekly after-school tutoring sessions. The Virtual Academy coordinators set up this face-to-face tutoring for students who are struggling or need a little extra help with their online course. In general, Virtual Academy coordinators synchronize the support that students need and make a significant impact on their online academic success. Of the nearly 2,500 NHCS students who took NCVPS courses in 2013–2014, there was nearly a 90% pass rate and approximately 68% of the students earned a B or higher. Not only are the students passing, they are doing well (W. Kraft, personal communication, August 6, 2014).

A second area of focus is mindful scheduling of online courses. The individual students' abilities are taken into consideration when scheduling online courses. For example, students who struggle with biology are not placed in online chemistry. The Virtual Academy support structure is most successful with students who have been placed appropriately in courses (W. Kraft, personal communication, August 6, 2014).

New Hanover County Schools is unique in that it has dedicated positions to support the implementation of NCVPS. The current superintendent of NHCS is a positive influence on the implementation. NCVPS is a focus for NHCS administration and it is an expectation that the program will continue to grow in the county. The utilization of the resources for the NCVPS program sets the students up for success (W. Kraft, personal communication, August 6, 2014).

CONCLUSION

North Carolina Virtual Public Schools is a growing program throughout the state. The NCVPS administration, faculty, and staff maintain focus on the students and their learning. Policies and procedures have been put in place to assure student success, such as parent and student involvement, teacher training in best practices for online learning, courses catered to the needs of North Carolina students, and local support at the district level. The NCVPS organization is a part of the change of 21st century schools that is preparing today's students for jobs that do not yet exist (EF Explore America, 2012).

REFERENCES

Archambault, L., Diamond, D., Brown, R., Cavanaugh, C., Coffey, M., Foures-Aalbu, D., & Zygouris-Coe, V. (2010). Research committee issues brief: An exploration of at-risk learners and online education. *International Association for K–12 Online Learning.* Retrieved from http://files.eric.ed.gov/fulltext/ED509620.pdf

Cavanagh, S. (2014, March 11). Online schooling. *Education Week.* Retrieved from http://www.edweek.org/ew/articles/2014/03/12/24report-2.h33.html

Connections Academy. (2014). 2014 parent survey. *Entertainment Close-up.*

EF Explore America. (2012). *What is 21st century education?* [Video.] Retrieved from https://www.youtube.com/watch?v=Ax5cNlutAys

Fetzer, L. (2013). NCVPS organization. [Presentation.] Retrieved from http://prezi.com/hkcqt5pymodp/ncvps-organization/#

Ingerham, L. (2012). Interactivity in the online learning environment: A study of users of the North Carolina virtual public school. *Quarterly Review of Distance Education, 13*(2), 65–75.

Miron, G., Horvitz, B., Gulosino, C. (2013). *Virtual schools in the U.S. 2013: Politics, performance, policy, and research evidence.* Retrieved from http://nepc.colorado.edu/files/nepc-virtual-2013-section-1-2.pdf

North Carolina Virtual Public School. (2014a). 2012-2013 annual report. Retrieved from http://www.ncvps.org/wp-content/uploads/2013/12/NCVPS-2012-13-annual-report.pdf

North Carolina Virtual Public School. (2014b). Catalogue. Retrieved from http://www.ncvps.org/index.php/courses/catalogue/

North Carolina Virtual Public School. (2014c). Course descriptions with prerequisites, textbook, and tech requirements: Success 101. Retrieved from https://docs.google.com/document/d/11ycvAQANAAywtWtxcpSJjw_OM_9PP31mldcTra6kc_A/edit#heading=h.a67bee95fbf6

North Carolina Virtual Public School. (2014d). Credit recovery. Retrieved from http://www.ncvps.org/index.php/courses/credit-recovery/

North Carolina Virtual Public School. (2014e). Funding formula and financial information. Retrieved from http://www.ncvps.org/index.php/funding-formula-and-financial-information/

North Carolina Virtual Public School. (2014f). History. Retrieved from http://www.ncvps.org/index.php/about-us/history/

North Carolina Virtual Public School. (2014g). OCS blended learning. Retrieved from http://www.ncvps.org/index.php/courses/ocs-blended/

North Carolina Virtual Public School. (2014h). Quality assurance. Retrieved from http://www.ncvps.org/index.php/parents/quality-assurance/

North Carolina Virtual Public School. (2014i). Summer school guide for 2014. Retrieved from http://www.ncvps.org/index.php/summer-school-guide-for-2014/

North Carolina Virtual Public School. (2014j). Teach and coach for NCVPS. Retrieved from http://www.ncvps.org/index.php/teach-for-ncvps/

North Carolina Virtual Public School. (2014k, July 30). Virtual open house [Webinar]. Retrieved from https://sas.elluminate.com/site/external/playback/artifact?psid=2014-07-30.1318.M.A809AE0B7C37F89C820D3BDFD76C72.vcr&aid=115080

Oliver, K., Kellogg, S., Townsend, L., & Brady, K. (2010). Needs of elementary and middle school teachers developing online courses for a virtual school. *Distance Education, 31*(1), 55–75.

Oliver, K., Osborne, J., & Brady, K. (2009). What are secondary students' expectations for teachers in virtual school environments? *Distance Education, 30*(1), 23–45.

Texas Virtual School Network

Deep in the Heart of Distance Education

Rolando R. Garza

INTRODUCTION AND HISTORY

According to Barbour, Grzebyk, and Eye (2014), over "the past decade, the number of K–12 students engaged in online learning has increased from between 40,000 and 50,000 to more than 2 million" (p. 114). Texas has pushed

Rolando R. Garza,
President-elect, Texas Distance Learning Association, Instructional Designer II, Texas A&M University-Kingsville, MSC 197, 700 University Blvd., Kingsville, TX 78363-8202.
Telephone: (361) 593-2860.
E-mail: rolando.garza@tamuk.edu

education through distance education. In 2007 the Texas Legislature established the Texas Virtual School Network to provide students across Texas with quality online courses. "Since its inception in January 2009, the TxVSN has provided Texas students and schools with a valuable avenue for interactive, collaborative, instructor-led online courses taught by state certified and appropriately credentialed teachers" (TxVSN About Us, 2015). The Texas Education Agency (TEA)

> offers state-supported online learning opportunities to students across the state through the Texas Virtual School Network (TxVSN) using a network approach that works in partnership with districts. TEA, under the leadership of the commissioner of education, administers the TxVSN, sets standards for and approves TxVSN courses and professional development for online teachers, and has fiscal responsibility for the network. (TxVSN Resources FAQ, 2015)

The Education Service Center Region 10 is the central point of operations for the TxVSN. Region 10 oversees the day-to-day operations of the network as well reviews the courses submitted. TxVSN is comprised of two units: the TxVSN statewide course catalog and the online school program. One of the missions of TxVSN is to provide high-quality electronic courses.

The TxVSN took many years to come to fruition. The following is a brief history of the programs that make up the TxVSN (TxVSN History, 2015):

- 2001—SB 975 (77th Texas Legislature) authorizes the Commissioner of Education to establish an electronic course pilot program. 2001–2002 The Virtual School Pilot programs take place in fall 2001 and spring 2002.
- 2004–2005—The initial Electronic Course Pilot (eCP) Application to Participate is released. Three Local Education Agencies (LEAs) participate in the eCP: Houston ISD, ResponsiveEd, and Southwest Schools.
- Spring 2006—Students are first served through the eCP.
- 2007—SB 1788 (80th Texas Legislature) establishes the state virtual school network.
- April 2008—Contracts are awarded for TxVSN Central Operations and TxVSN Course Review.
- 2008–2009—The eCP becomes the Electronic Course Program.
- January 2009—The TxVSN course catalog opens with courses from three TxVSN provider districts.
- 2009—HB 3646 (81st Texas Legislature) creates the state virtual school allotment and incorporates the eCP into the Texas Virtual School Network.
- 2009–2010—The TxVSN course catalog begins offering dual credit courses.
- January 2010—The number of districts receiving courses through TxVSN course catalog exceeds 300.
- May 2010—The TxVSN course catalog offers all courses required for graduation on the Recommended High School Program.

- June 2010—Fifteen TxVSN provider districts participate in the TxVSN statewide course catalog.
- Summer 2011—Southwest Schools withdraws from the TxVSN OLS. 2011 SB 1 (82nd Texas Legislature, first-called session) repeals the state virtual school allotment.
- 2011–2012—The Electronic Course Program becomes the TxVSN Online Schools (OLS) Program. Texarkana ISD begins participating in the TxVSN OLS. Virtual Learning Scholarships are made available to districts enrolling students in courses through the TxVSN course catalog. TxVSN dropout recovery pilot is implemented. Three Local Education Agencies (LEAs) participate in the pilot: Pasadena ISD, Santa Fe ISD, and Spring ISD
- 2012–2013—The TxVSN OLS will serve students in all Grades 3 to 12 for the first time.

PROVIDER REQUIREMENTS

To become a provider within TxVSN, requirements (Texas Education Code Chapter 30A and Texas Administrative Code 19 Chapter 70 Subchapter AA) have been set in place for schools. A school district or open-enrollment charter school fall under this act; as a course provider it is only acceptable under the state accountability system. Students seeking a course provider have options within their service area.

A nonprofit entity, private entity, or corporation is eligible to act as a course provider under this chapter only if they: (1) comply with all applicable federal and state laws prohibiting discrimination; (2) demonstrate financial solvency; and (3) provide evidence of prior successful experience offering online courses to middle or high school students, with demonstrated student success in course completion and performance, as determined by the commissioner. An entity other than a school district or open-enrollment charter school is not authorized to award course credit or a diploma for courses taken through the state virtual school network (TxVSN Provider Requirements, 2015).

A school district or open-enrollment charter school is eligible to act as a course provider under this chapter only if the district or school is rated acceptable under the state accountability system. An open-enrollment charter school may serve as a course provider only to a student within its service area; or, to another student in the state through an agreement with the school district. An entity other than a school district or open-enrollment charter school is not authorized to award course credit or a diploma for courses taken through the state virtual school network; as a result, it may not operate as a TxVSN online school. An entity other than a school district or open-enrollment charter school may collaborate with a school district or open-enrollment charter school to provide support services including curriculum for a TxVSN online school (TxVSN Provider Requirements, 2015).

STUDENTS GETTING STARTED

Learning opportunities for students across the state of Texas have been made possible through TxVSN. The first step is the students must know their rights when enrolling in a TxVSN course. The student's district or open-enrollment charter school needs to make all reasonable effort to accommodate the students' needs.

Students need to speak with their school's counselor for developing a graduation plan and to explain the procedures and polices for their school. Not all schools are part of TxVSN and the student is encourage to seek assistance from TxVSN for any questions pertaining to registration procedures. TxVSN provides an online orientation course, CLUE IN; this helps the students experience learning online and

understand expectations for students taking online courses.

TxVSN courses have a cost factor and students are encouraged to seek if the course provider's cost is listed in the course catalog. Students' browse through course catalogs to check availability. The course provider is usually responsible for the course cost, but in some cases the school has requested that the student or parent pay. An important process for the student is to confirm campus support. Each learner has a campus mentor designated by the school to increase the likelihood of success. Communication is key in education, especially so in distance education. The campus mentors provide communication between the student and TxVSN teacher and the school.

TxVSN STANDARDS

TxVSN follows high standards for all online courses provided to Texas students:

- The State Board of Education (SBOE) has legislative authority to adopt the Texas Essential Knowledge and Skills (TEKS) for each subject of the required curriculum. SBOE members nominate educators, parents, business and industry representatives, and employers to serve on TEKS review committees.
- The TxVSN provides TEKS alignment documents for current and potential providers to complete an internal review of courses prior to submitting the courses for review by the TxVSN.
- TxVSN online course materials and activities must be designed to provide appropriate access to all students. Courses developed with universal design principles in mind, conform to the U.S. Section 504 and Section 508 provisions for electronic and information technology, as well as the W3C's Web Content Accessibility guidelines. To assist current and potential providers in completing an internal review of

courses, the TxVSN Accessibility Guidelines were developed. It is the expectation that courses offered through the TxVSN statewide catalog or online school (OLS) program meet these guidelines.

- The National Standards for Quality Online Courses were designed to provide states, districts, online programs, and other organizations with a set of quality guidelines for online course content, instructional design, technology, student assessment, and course management. In Version 2 of the standards, reviewer considerations have been added for each indicator. Additionally, a TxVSN rubric is included to assist in the review of online courses based on this new version. It is the expectation that courses offered through the TxVSN statewide catalog or online school (OLS) program meet these standards.
- The TxVSN provides students throughout the state with access to online courses that address all of the Texas Essential Knowledge and Skills (TEKS) and meet national standards for quality online courses. The state virtual school network includes the TxVSN statewide catalog of supplemental online courses for Grades 9 through 12 and the full-time virtual TxVSN Online Schools (OLS) program for Grades 3 through 12. (TxVSN Standards, 2015)

ONLINE TEACHING PROFESSIONAL DEVELOPMENT

Davis and Roblyer (2005) noted that, given "the increasing demand for virtual courses and the rapid expansion of schools to meet the demand, it is apparent that there will be a parallel need for teachers who are prepared to teach at a distance from their students" (p. 401). Every online TxVSN teacher must be (1) "Texas certified in the course subject area and grade level taught, and (2) Have successfully completed approved professional development" (TxVSN Professional Development, 2015). It is the responsibility of the course provider to verify the eligibility of its teacher. Every online teacher must:

- Have successfully completed a professional development course or program approved by TxVSN; or
- Have a graduate degree in online or distance learning;
- Have two or more years of documented experience teaching online courses for students in Grades 3–12; and
- Successfully complete continuing professional development specific to online learning every 3 years (TxVSN Professional Development, 2015).

Quality professional development is key for teachers to continue to learn and maintain the idea of teaching online. All teachers are required to keep records of their professional development documentation. "Teachers should be aware that individual TxVSN Provider Districts may have additional policies and requirements when hiring online teachers. Quality professional development for online teachers is important to ensure quality teaching and learning" (TxVSN Professional Development, 2015).

It is evident that research demonstrates online teaching is different from face to face. The online environment requires special tools and techniques for communication and collaboration, content management, and assessment. TxVSN professional development focuses on the K–12 Online Learning (iNACOL) National Standards for Quality Online Teaching. TxVSN teachers are required to maintain the highest standards of professional development to pursue learning in the field of online teaching.

TxVSN approved professional development is presented in Table 1.

Table 1.   TxVSN Approved Professional Development

Provider	PD Audience	Service
Connections Education	Beginning Online Teachers	Statewide
Education Development Center, Inc.	Beginning & Experienced Online Teachers	Statewide
ESC Region 4	Beginning & Experienced Online Teachers	Statewide
ESC Region 11	Beginning Online Teachers	Statewide
ESC Region 16	Beginning Online Teachers	Statewide
Florida Virtual School	Beginning Online Teachers	Statewide
Harris County Department of Education	Beginning & Experienced Online Teachers	Statewide
The Academy of Blended and Online Learning	Beginning Online Teachers	Statewide
Texas A&M University	Beginning Online Teachers	Statewide
Texas A&M University-Corpus Christi	Beginning Online Teachers	Statewide
Texas Connections Academy @ Houston	Beginning Online Teachers	Local
University of Houston Clear Lake	Beginning & Experienced Online Teachers	Statewide
University of Texas at Brownsville	Beginning Online Teachers	Statewide

CONCLUSION

Texas has recognized that education is changing, and deep in the heart of distance education is the Texas Virtual School Network. Since its founding, TxVSN has provided "Texas students and schools with a valuable avenue for interactive, collaborative, instructor-led online courses taught by state certified and appropriately credentialed teachers" (TxVSN About Us, 2015).

The momentum of K–12 distance education, along with research in innovation in online teaching, has brought forth change in Texas education. Since 2013, TxVSN has served approximately 10, 581 high school and dual enrollment students. TxVSN is growing along with the innovative teachers moving forward education across the state of Texas.

REFERENCES

Barbour, M. K., Grzebyk, T. Q., & Eye, J. (2014). Any time, any place, any pace-really? examining mobile learning in a virtual school environment. *Turkish Online Journal of Distance Education, 15*(1), 114–127.

Davis, N. E., & Roblyer, M. D. (2005). Preparing teachers for the "schools that technology built": Evaluation of a program to train teachers for virtual schooling. *Journal of Research on Technology in Education, 37*(4), 399–409.

TxVSN About Us. (2015). Texas Virtual School Network. Retrieved April 23, 2015, from http://txvsn.org/about-us/

TxVSN CLUE IN. (2015). Texas Virtual School Network. Retrieved April 23, 2015, from http://cluein.txvsn.org/

TxVSN Enrollments. (2015). Texas Virtual School Network. Retrieved April 23, 2015, from https://catalog.mytxvsn.org/enrollments

TxVSN First steps for students. (2015). Texas Virtual School Network. Retrieved April 23, 2015, from http://txvsn.org/first-steps-for-students/

TxVSN History. (2015). The Official Site of The Texas Senate. Retrieved April 23, 2015, from http://www.senate.state.tx.us/75r/Senate/commit/c530/handouts12/1008-MonicaMartinez-3.pdf

TxVSN Professional Development. (2015). Texas Virtual School Network. Retrieved April 23, 2015, from http://txvsn.org/providers/online-teaching-eligibility-reqs/

TxVSN Provider Requirements. (2015). Texas Virtual School Network. Retrieved April 23,

2015, from http://txvsn.org/provider-eligibility-requirements/

TxVSN Resources FAQ. (2015). Texas Virtual School Network. Retrieved April 23, 2015, from http://txvsn.org/resources/faq/

TxVSN Standards. (2015). Texas Virtual School Network. Retrieved April 23, 2015, from http://txvsn.org/providers/standards/

The South Carolina Virtual School Program

Opportunities for South Carolina's Students

Robin M. Clinton

INTRODUCTION

Middle and high school students in South Carolina now have additional educational opportunities beyond attending traditional "brick and mortar" schools. The development of the South Carolina Virtual School Program (SCVSP) has provided these opportunities for South Carolina's students. This article will examine the development and purpose of the SCVSP.

Robin M. Clinton,
Library Media Specialist, York Middle School,
1010 Devinney Road, York, SC 29745.
Telephone: (803) 818-6164.
E-mail: rclinton@york.k12.sc.us

Student and teacher perceptions of the program are also discussed, as well as the future of the program.

The South Carolina Department of Education (SCDE) launched a pilot program for virtual schooling in May 2006. This pilot program allowed the SCDE to determine the level of need for a virtual school program in the state, and it also presented the opportunity to test the registration and course management systems that would be used for the program. Research on other state virtual school programs was conducted and information and feedback was gathered during this time in order to continue to develop, revise, and refine the policies and procedures for the program. By partnering with local school districts and other groups, the SCDE operated the pilot program through July 2007 (South Carolina State Department of Education, 2013a).

In May 2007, one year after the launch of the pilot program, the South Carolina legislature passed Act 26, which established the South Carolina Virtual School Program at the South Carolina Department of Education. The State Board of Education was given the responsibility of developing program guidelines, which were subsequently approved in December 2007 (South Carolina State Department of Education, 2013a).

The SCVSP was established with the goal of helping to improve the graduation rate in South Carolina by having a focus on graduation requirements and credit recovery. The focus of the program has shifted to encompass offering more courses that meet the needs of many different types of learners. Legislation originally restricted the number of credits that students could earn in one school year, as well as the total credits that could be earned during a student's entire high school career. In June 2013, legislation lifted the cap on the number of credits that could be earned. Students may now earn an unlimited amount of credits through the SCVSP (South Carolina State Department of Education, 2013a).

The SCVSP is just that—a program. It is supplemental in nature; therefore, diplomas are not awarded by the SCVSP. Diplomas may only be granted by the student's sponsoring institution, which may include any public, private, or home school in the state.

SOUTH CAROLINA VIRTUAL SCHOOL PROGRAM

The vision of the SCVSP is "to become the premier provider of innovative online learning opportunities to prepare South Carolina students to lead in a global society" (South Carolina State Department of Education, 2013b, para. 1). In order to work toward this vision, the program strives to offer a variety of online options to meet students' needs. The objectives for the program are to supplement the traditional high school curriculum, to provide access to courses that may not be offered to students in traditional schools, and to provide options for students to recover credit (Lee, Sanders, Mitchell, Childs, & Zais, 2012). All of the courses offered by the SCVSP go through a quality review process to make sure that each course is aligned with state and national standards. The program and its courses are continually evaluated to ensure that students' needs are indeed being met.

LEADERSHIP

The SCVSP is supervised by the SCDE's Office of Virtual Education. The director of this office oversees the operation of the SCVSP. In addition to the director, a five-person administrative team assists in the operation and implementation of the SCVSP. Positions on the administrative team include the team leader, two student services coordinators, a blended learning coordinator, and a curriculum coordinator (South Carolina State Department of Education, 2013a). Even with the growth of the SCVSP, no additional administrative positions have been added. However, according to survey results from SCVSP teachers, all agreed that the administrative team needs additional staff (Lee et al., 2012).

TEACHERS

SCVSP has a full-time faculty of 18 teachers, six of whom were hired in the 2011-2012 school year in response to the growth of the program. In addition to the full-time teachers, 47 adjunct instructors are employed during various terms during the school year to meet enrollment needs (Lee et al., 2012).

One SCVSP teacher explained her reasons for wanting to teach with the virtual school program. She indicated that she had gotten burned out by teaching at traditional school, but was not sure if she wanted to teach from home either. After deciding to give the virtual school program a try, she loves the experience (S. Carrigan, personal communication, November 20, 2013).

TEACHER TRAINING

SCVSP teachers must be certified to teach in the state of South Carolina and must also be considered highly qualified in the content area. In addition, teachers must have an online teaching endorsement from the state of South Carolina. Online teaching experience in place of the online teaching endorsement is acceptable. SCVSP teacher Shannon Carrigan had never taught online before being hired to teach with SCVSP. She describes the initial training as overwhelming, but she also says that she gained the most knowledge by working with other online teachers.

Not only do teachers have to go through the initial training in order to teach online, but they are also required to complete day-long, monthly professional development, either online or face-to-face. Suzette Lee (personal communication, November 18, 2013), SCVSP Team Leader and Instructional Manager, says that the professional development that is provided to SCVSP teachers is a strength of the program. Training is provided to teachers on every new technology that they are expected to use.

COURSE OFFERINGS

SCVSP offers courses only for high school credit. Courses for middle school students are not offered at this time, but seventh- or eighth-grade students may enroll in courses for high school credit with approval from the sponsoring institution.

Many initial credit and credit recovery courses are offered through the SCVSP. Six Advanced Placement (AP) courses are offered: English language and composition, English literature and composition, statistics, United States history, art history, and Latin. For rural and small school districts in the state, these AP offerings give students an opportunity to take courses that cannot be offered in those districts. In addition to the AP courses that are offered, 17 career and technology courses are offered.

Credit recovery courses make up a large part of the SCVSP course offerings. Students who have not received credit for courses they have already taken or who appear unlikely to earn credit for a current course are the students who benefit from credit recovery. In the 2011-2012 school year, SCVSP began to use a new credit recovery model. Instead of using the self-paced program that employed the teacher as a monitor, SCVSP teachers developed their own credit recovery courses that use a feature that allows students to take unit pretests and then move on to the next unit if they pass with a score of 80 or better. After moving to this new model, the successful completion rate for credit recovery courses improved from 83.7% to 100% (Lee et al., 2012).

Credit recovery courses are also now offered by rolling enrollment. Instead of having to enroll on certain dates, students can now enroll in credit recovery courses at any time. Classes begin on Monday of each week (South Carolina State Department of Education, 2013a).

SCVSP courses are also designed by SCVSP faculty. A course development team works to outline course offerings and to help design courses. Currently, SCVSP teachers are beginning to adapt their courses to align with Common Core Standards. The SCVSP ensures the quality of its courses by reviewing courses for alignment with standards. Courses may be taught asynchronously, synchronously, or through blended learning. For new teachers, SCVSP has a bank of previously designed courses that they can use and make changes. Some school districts also contract with SCVSP directly to tailor specific courses to meet the particular district's needs or to offer a special project for students. Districts can opt to pay a $3,500 fee for an entire class to take a course from the SCVSP (Adcox, 2013).

TECHNOLOGY

SCVSP uses Virtual School Administrator (VSA), the same system used by Florida Virtual School, as the student information system. This system is used for registration, posting grades, accessing transcripts, and storing and accessing all other student information. For course management, the SCVSP has recently moved away from Blackboard and is now using Moodle as the learning management system. Teachers are also using a variety of delivery methods that incorporate several technology tools such as Blackboard Collaborate. Skype has been used a method of communication between students and teachers in the past, but soon a new messaging system will be used that will replace Skype.

Students are responsible for making sure that they have access to the needed technology for SCVSP courses. This could include access at home and at school. Many districts provide the access to technology for students who are completing coursework during normal school hours. Students also have access to a technical support through the program's website. The 2012 program evaluation report indicates that additional staff members are needed for technical support (Lee et al., 2012).

STUDENTS

Any public, private, or homeschooled student under the age of 21 who is a legal resident of the state of South Carolina is eligible to enroll, tuition-free, in courses with the SCVSP. Students, however, must have a connection to a diploma-granting, sponsoring institution. In order to enroll in a course, students must first create an account in VSA, and then they will be allowed to request courses. Once courses have been requested, students must then have their parent or guardian and their guidance counselor sign the course request form for approval. The student's parent or guardian and the guidance counselor must also submit an online approval for the course. Students are then responsible for logging in to VSA to check their enrollment status for requested courses. Once students have enrolled in a course, they must complete an online student orientation program before beginning the course (South Carolina State Department of Education, 2013a).

During the 2011-2012 school year, the SCVSP served 88 school districts in the state of South Carolina. The SCVSP processed 20,466 enrollment requests that same year (Lee et al., 2012) compared to 10,298 (see Figure 1) in the 2008-2009 school year (Southern Regional Education Board, 2009).

Students who enroll have a variety of reasons for enrolling. Students may need to supplement their education if desired courses are not offered at their school. They may need to work around scheduling issues with other classes or with work schedules. Some students may even be nontraditional students who have children themselves or who are adult education students. The needs of all of these learners can be met with the SCVSP (Lee et al., 2012).

Morgan (personal communication, November 18, 2013), a student in the SCVSP, is one learner who indicated that she had scheduling issues at her traditional school that did not allow her to take a particular course at school. She talked to her guidance counselor who mentioned the SCVSP as an option. Morgan decided to enroll and has had a very good experience with the SCVSP. She points out her teacher's willingness to help and her prompt feedback as pluses for the program. According to Morgan, other advantages of online learning are that there are no distractions from other students and the course is mostly self-paced. However, she also recognizes that students need to have a high level of self-discipline and maturity to successfully complete an online course with the SCVSP.

HOW IS SCVSP PERFORMING?

SCVSP Team Leader, Suzette Lee, reports that students enrolled in the

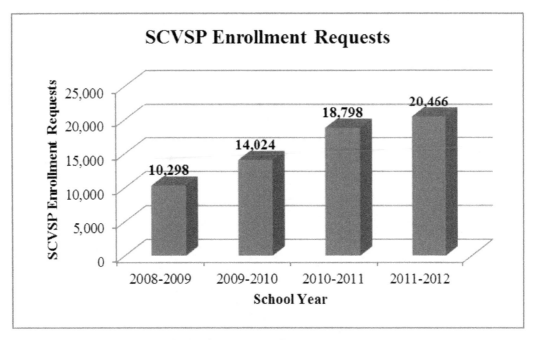

Figure 1. South Carolina Virtual School Program enrollment requests continue to grow each year.

SCVSP are consistently performing better than state averages. The course completion rate has also continued to climb since the program began. In the 2008-2009 school year, the completion rate for SCVSP courses was 68% (Southern Regional Education Board, 2009). By the end of the 2011-2012 school year, the completion rate for SCVSP courses was 93.3% (Lee et al., 2012) (see Figure 2).

One SCVSP teacher noted that she sees about the same amount of student interaction in the SCVSP courses as she saw in the traditional classroom. Some students perform better than average and stay in contact with the teacher, and other students have no contact or interaction until it is time for an assignment to be due. The SCVSP has found that in general, students perform better when they have more frequent contact with their teachers (Lee et al., 2012).

In order to gain feedback about the SCVSP, students, teachers, parents, and guidance counselors are surveyed each

year. The surveys are used to determine how well needs are being met and for those groups to offer suggestions for improvement. While the SCVSP received an adequate number of student responses in 2012 to draw conclusions about the program, the SCVSP did not receive an adequate number of responses from parents or guidance counselors. One concern is that this lack of response and communication from these groups may hinder the enrollment process and support for some students (Lee et al., 2012).

The State Board of Education is also required, as part of Act 26 that established the SCVSP, to provide an annual report to the legislature that includes information about the program. Each year, the following information must be reported: the SCVSP course offerings, the number of districts and students participating in the SCVSP, the private schools and number of private school students participating, the number of homeschool students participating, course success rates for students,

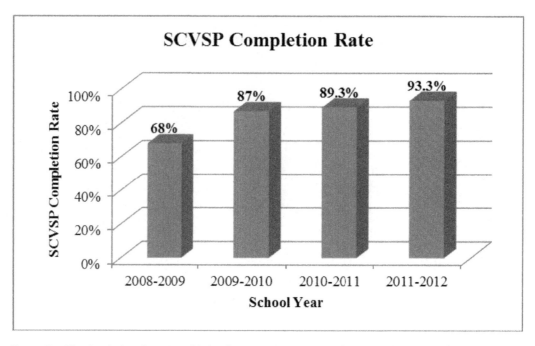

Figure 2. The South Carolina Virtual School Program course completion rate has continued to rise.

the number of students who dropped a course and the reason, budget items, and the number of students who could not enroll because of limited space.

THE FUTURE OF THE SCVSP

According to the Keeping Pace report (Watson, Murin, Vashaw, Gemin, & Rapp, 2012), South Carolina ranks third nationally in growth among state funded virtual school programs. South Carolina would like to continue this trend of growth for the program. In the fall of 2014, the SCVSP will have a completely new look that includes a new website and a new name for the program. The program is seeking a new name because it has often and easily been confused with the South Carolina Virtual Charter School. This new look for the program is being referred to as a rebranding of the program. In addition to this rebranding, a request for proposal process is soon to be started for an open student information system. The VSA system that is currently used was created for the

Florida Virtual School, and the SCVSP would like to have a system that is tailored to this specific program.

The course development team would also like to continue to work to have more course offerings for students. Some new courses that will be offered are math and English language arts intervention courses for sixth-, seventh-, and eighth-graders. Beginning in 2014, a keyboarding pilot program for third- through sixth-graders will be launched in anticipation of preparing those students for online standardized testing. The SCVSP would also like to explore the option of expanding online learning to the lower grades.

CONCLUSION

What began as a strategy to help improve South Carolina's graduation rate has now evolved into an opportunity to meet the educational needs of various types of learners in South Carolina. Whether students need to recover credits or want to take a course not offered at their traditional schools, the tuition-free South Carolina Virtual School Program is providing those opportunities for students. The opportunities for South Carolina's students are almost limitless; it is hoped that students will continue to take advantage of them.

REFERENCES

Adcox, S. (2013, July 10). S.C. expanding students' online course offerings. *Anderson Independent Mail.* Retrieved from http://www.independentmail.com

Lee, S., Sanders, T., Mitchell, B., Childs, C., & Zais, M. (2012). *South Carolina virtual school program: 2011-12 program evaluation.* Retrieved from https://scvspconnect.ed.sc.gov/sites/default/files/SCVSP_2012_AnnualReport_FINAL.pdf

South Carolina State Department of Education. (2013a). South Carolina virtual school program. Retrieved from https://scvspconnect.ed.sc.gov/

South Carolina State Department of Education. (2013b). South Carolina virtual school program: Mission. Retrieved from https://scvspconnect.ed.sc.gov/index.php?q=mission

Southern Regional Education Board. (2009). *State virtual school survey: SREB educational technology cooperative.* Retrieved from http://publications.sreb.org/2009/SVSsurvey-SC09B1.pdf

Watson, J., Murin, A., Vashaw, L., Gemin, B., & Rapp C. (2012). Keeping pace with online & blended learning: An annual review of policy and practice. Retrieved from http://kpk12.com/cms/wp-content/uploads/KeepingPace2012.pdf

Learning at Georgia Virtual School

Courtney L. Teague

INTRODUCTION

Hearing school bells ring, lockers closing, and school bus engines running are becoming sounds of the past. Classrooms are no longer four-wall rooms filled with uniformed learners sitting in desks and chairs. Learners are no longer wearing backpacks filled with heavy and outdated textbooks. Learners are now using mobile devices, tablets, smartphones, desktops, and laptops. Georgia's educational system includes learners with diverse needs: 1,639,077 enrolled in 2,289 schools (Georgia Department of Education, 2011). In 2005-2006, an estimated

Courtney L. Teague,
Educational Technologist, C7 Enterprises LLC,
P.O. Box 290, Hiram, GA 30141.
Telephone: (678) 499-3521.
E-mail: Courtney@CourtneyLTeague.com

700,000 K-12 learners were enrolled in online courses (Picciano & Seaman, 2007). In 2009, more than 3 million K-12 learners have taken an online course (Horn & Staker, 2011). Research suggests that by 2019, more than 50% of high school courses will be offered online (Christensen & Horn, 2008). Georgia Virtual School, established by Georgia Department of Education, is set up like a Georgia public school without a physical location. The address is a web URL (Hawkins, 2013).

This article will discuss Georgia Virtual School's (GaVS) background, mission, strategic learning plan, course offerings, program accreditation and evaluation, and instructional technology. GaVS was established in 5 years, demonstrating the diffusion of innovation theory. Diffusion of innovation is described as, "the process by which an innovation is communicated through certain channels over time among members of a societal system" (Rogers, 2003, p. 5). Elements of diffusion include communication, a mission, evaluations and assessments by experts.

GEORGIA VIRTUAL SCHOOL

In 2001, the Georgia State Board of Education approved the virtual learning business plan to endorse online Advanced Placement courses. The virtual learning plan addressed the needs of Georgia's learners. Georgia learners need to be prepared to compete with their global counterparts. In 2001, Georgia was a second-year AP Nexus recipient, a United States Department of

Education Advanced Placement Test free program grant that focused on at-risk learners (Georgia Department of Education, 2007). The online courses provided course options for learners in rural areas, in areas with a lack of highly qualified teachers, scheduling conflicts, and limited curricular offerings (Georgia Department of Education, 2007).

BACKGROUND

GaVS is the child organization of Georgia Virtual Learning. GaVS courses are created based on the following factors: program need, Department of Education requirements, fund availability, graduation requirements, and public request (Georgia Department of Education, 2007). Each of the courses is designed to meet Common Core Georgia Performance Standards (J. Cozart, personal communication, July 29, 2013).

GaVS STRATEGIC PLAN

GaVS does not grant diplomas or course credits independently, but in a collaborative effort with local school degree awarding districts. The strategic plan includes the following vision, mission, belief statements, and goals (J. Cozart, personal communication, July 29, 2013):

Vision:

- quality learning,
- innovating opportunities, and
- elevating performances.

Mission: Serve as a stimulus for dynamic change by providing quality digital programs to strengthen teaching and learning.

Belief statements:

- change creates opportunity;
- make education work; and
- open, equitable learning.

Goals:

- learner performance exceeds the state average;
- provide opportunities for learners with annual growth of at least 20%;
- all teachers demonstrate quality teaching; and
- prepare learners for college and career readiness.

ENROLLMENT IN GaVS

For the 2012-2013 school year over 18,567 learners from 479 schools were in enrolled in 332 online courses. The overall completion rate for GaVS is 90%. GaVS total enrollments since 2005 is 67,787 (J. Cozart, personal communication, July 29, 2013). Schools can sign up their learners for whatever class period that works for them. In order to enroll in a GaVS course, a local school facilitator must approve. Home school and out of state learners will be assigned a GaVS facilitator (Georgia Virtual School, 2010). Registration is a two-phase process. Public school learners receive preferential enrollment. Phase 1 allows public school learners the right to enroll and register for courses before and the courses are available to private school learners and home school learners. Phase 2 allows private and home school learners the opportunity to enroll (Georgia Virtual School, 2010). The course start dates are flexible and the course ends before the traditional course ends because grades have to be submitted earlier.

GaVS LEARNERS' NEEDS

GaVS learners can experience individualized learning. Prior to starting an online course, the learner can complete an online course self-assessment inventory. The online inventory asks questions about the personal attitude and technology. The learner rates each question "1 = *never*, 3 = *sometimes*, 5 = *always*" (Georgia Virtual, School, 2010). The scores serve as an indicator as to whether the learner is a good online candidate. What follows are questions that the learner answers on an online self-assessment inventory (Georgia Virtual, School, 2010):

Personal Attitude

- "I stay on task when doing schoolwork."
- "I schedule my time well at school."
- "I schedule my time well outside of school."
- "I stay on task while doing work on the Internet."
- "I follow through on requests from my teachers."
- "I answer e-mail in a timely manner."
- "I turn in my assignments on time."
- "I ask teachers for help when I need it."
- "I am willing to put in extra time for a challenging class."

Technology Skills

- "I have access to the Internet at home."
- "I know how to login to my home Internet provider."
- "My home computer has a word processing program like Word, WordPerfect, or Works."
- "I know how to use a word processing program."
- "I know how to use e-mail."
- "I know how to do Internet research."
- "I know how to copy and paste text."
- "I know how to download a file from a web page."
- "I know how to attach and send a file through e-mail."

GaVS learners also complete a survey at the beginning of the course to indicate desired course length. During the fall and spring Advanced Placement learners can choose their courses to be 14, 16, or 18 weeks long. Regular learners can chose 12, 14, 16, or 18 weeks long. The summer courses can be 5 or 6 weeks long. All of the courses have the same workload and end on the same date (Georgia Virtual School, Course Information, 2010).

Learners take online courses because approximately 77 of Georgia's high schools do not offer Advanced Placement courses. Learners are placed in an at-risk category and are at a disadvantage when applying for college because they lack college level skill application that would be provided through the AP curriculum (Georgia Department of Education, 2007). Georgia has 180 public school systems. Sixty-four percent of the school districts are understaffed. There is a need for highly qualified teachers and some school districts are too small. As a result of a lack of highly qualified teachers, the schools have to limit their course selection offerings. Thirty-seven of Georgia's high schools have fewer than 500 learners enrolled. Many learners want to have a greater course selection, take advanced courses, get ahead, repeat a failed course, and manage their schedule. Learners may have transferred from another state or private school setting and require additional coursework to meet Georgia's graduation requirement (Georgia Department of Education, 2007).

GaVS learners have said:

"I'm taking Mandarin Chinese. It's always been a dream of mine to travel to Asia and be an English as second or other language teacher," Sierra said. "I feel that Mandarin would help me in a way securing my place at that job." (Benton, 2010, para. 5)

It's really different. It's very exciting, and it's a new way to challenge yourself. (Benton, 2010, para. 6)

GaVS provides accommodations for learners with disabilities. GaVS has to receive a compliant Individualized Education Program or 504 plan each semester the learner enrolls. Online courses are not for everyone, but may be the correct place for individuals with disabilities.

A mother of a GaVS learner with disabilities said:

"We have been so pleased with our experience. Kelly Walker, his special needs consultant, has been very professional and easy to communicate with," said CeCe, the mother of a 10th Grade GaVS learner. "I am impressed with his teachers and their kindness and nature to reach out to our son when he needs more time or more understanding of a lesson." (Houck, 2013, para. 4)

Virtual learning can allow learners with disabilities the opportunity to learn at their pace without anxiety (Shah, 2011). Some learners with disabilities accommodations are already incorporated into the format of an online course. Some of the learners accommodations requires a copy of notes, frequent use of modeling which could be demonstrated through the video component of the course, repeat directions that the learner could replay the audio, and information differentiated (Houck, 2013). However, not all accommodations are conducive to an online learning environment (Georgia Department of Education, 2011).

The Digital Learning Act, Senate Bill 289, focused on the essence of digital and virtual learning, requires learners entering ninth grade during 2013-2014 school year to complete at least one online class. The bill requires that all end of year core subject assessments to be offered online (Senate Press, 2011).

GaVS Courses

Course Development

Each course is designed to contain content aligned to the Georgia Performance Standards as mandated by the Georgia Department of Education. Courses are being redesigned to align to Common Core Georgia Performance Standards. Courses are developed in two phases by a development team. A development team consists of authors, test writers, content development specialists, development coordinator, and an instructional designer. The instructional

designer is an employee of Georgia Public Broadcasting Company. During Phase 1, the development team creates a course outline. The content development specialist completes a detailed development plan and timeline that has to be completed by the development coordinator. The authors will create course materials that are assessed for special education and copyright issues. In Phase 2, it is considered the testing phase (Georgia Virtual School, n.d.). The courses typically take 9 months to design (J. Cozart, personal communication, July 29, 2013).

GaVS offers Advanced Placement Courses, which are courses that will allow high school learners to be awarded college credit if they pass the College Board Advanced Placement Test (Georgia Virtual School, Course Information Advanced Placement, 2010). In addition to AP Courses, GaVS offers career and technical education, world languages, math, language arts, science, social studies, health and physical education, fine arts, and test preparation.

GaVS Course Recovery Program

Georgia Virtual School Course Recovery Program is a free chance that will allow high school learners who were not able to successfully pass a course to have an opportunity to retake courses. The learners have mastered the time requirement but not the course standard requirements (Georgia Virtual School, 2010).

GaVS Accreditation and Evaluation

GaVS is accredited by the Southern Association of Colleges and Schools (SACS). SACS evaluates the middle and high school courses (Hawkins, 2013). GaVS is evaluated through multiple evaluative tools. GaVS receives an occasional audit from Georgia's auditor's office. GaVS reports the virtual learners End of Course scores versus state average (J. Cozart, personal communication, July 29, 2013). *Digital Learning Now!* (2012), evaluated

GaVS and found the following strengths and weaknesses.

The strengths of GaVS include:

- learners have customized learning;
- learner access to high quality digital content;
- learners have access to high quality providers; and
- learner learning assessment and accountability.

The weaknesses of GaVS include:

- the infrastructure does not support digital learning;
- GaVS funding creates incentives;
- the learner progress based on demonstrated complexity; and
- all learners are not digital learners.

GaVS adopted the Southern Regional Educational Board (SREB) standards for quality online courses to establish if courses are meeting standards. The standards for quality online courses are as follows (SREB, 2006, pp. 3-8):

1. The course provides online learners with engaging learning experiences that promote their mastery of content and are aligned with state content standards or nationally accepted content.
2. The course uses learning activities that engage learners in active learning; provides learners with multiple learning paths to master the content based on learner needs; reflects multicultural education and is accurate, current and free of bias; and provides ample opportunities for interaction and communication learner to learner, learner to instructor and instructor to learner.
3. The course uses multiple strategies and activities to assess learner readiness for and progress in course content and provides learners with feedback on their progress.

4. The course takes full advantage of a variety of technology tools, has a user-friendly interface and meets accessibility standards for interoperability and access for learners with special needs.
5. The course is evaluated regularly for effectiveness, using a variety of assessment strategies, and the findings are used as a basis for improvement. The course is kept up to date, both in content and in the application of new research on course design and technologies.

GaVS End of Course Policy

During fall and spring semesters public school learners will take the End of Course Test (EOCT) at their local school at a scheduled time. Home school, private school, and out-of-state learners will take the EOCT at an assigned Educational Technology Center (ETC). During the summer semester all learners will take the EOCT at their designated Educational Technology Center (Georgia Virtual School, 2010). The following courses require the EOCT: ninth-grade literature composition, American literature composition, biology, physical science, accelerated mathematics I and II, Accelerated CCPG coordinate mathematics I and II, Accelerated CCPG algebra, analytic geometry A, CCPS coordinate algebra, GPS algebra, GPS geometry, mathematics I & II, U.S. history, and economics (Georgia Virtual Schools, 2011). The learner must have a minimum score of 70 for all subjects. For learners who were ninth grade for the first time before July 1, 2011, the EOCT counts for 15% for the learner's final grade and 20% for learners who were enrolled after the date (Georgia Department of Education, 2011).

GaVS Teacher

Teacher Certification

Online teachers must obtain a valid Georgia teaching certificate in subject area from the Georgia Professional Standards Commission (Hawkins, 2013). Teachers must complete online learning for an add-on endorsement (Georgia Department of Education, 2007). The virtual add-on endorsement requires that the teacher demonstrate competency in three areas (standards): online teaching and learning methodology, instructional technology concepts, and online assessments (Hawkins, 2012).

The online teaching and learning standard makes sure that the teacher will be able to provide a meaningful online environment with proper communication and transparent objectives while modeling good digital citizenship in a diverse setting. When teaching in a traditional face-to-face class instructors are accustom to "reading" the body language and facial cues of the learners. Therefore in an online course, it must be assumed that the learners display the same body language (Ko & Rossen, 2012).

The online assessment standards examine the effectiveness of the assessments. Teachers will create reliable assessment tools that are valid for an online environment. The instructional technology concept standard tackles the teachers' instructional technology competency. The teacher must demonstrate knowledge, skills, and understanding of instructional technology.

GaVS Adjunct Teacher Salary

The adjunct teachers' salaries are paid through Georgia Department of Education. The teachers are paid per learner each semester. The payments are the following: $130 for half Carnegie Unit Course, $155 for half Carnegie AP Unit Course, $260 for one block Carnegie Unit, $310 for one block AP Carnegie Unit (Georgia Virtual School, 2010).

Leadership

Organizational management style influences the decision making and the implementation of tasks. The top-down approach is when all guidelines, objectives, funding, and other information come from the top of the organization. A leader communicates the expectations to be achieved by the organization (Filev, 2008). The advantage of the top down approach includes clarity of expectations. The disadvantages of the top down approach includes bureaucracy, inflexibility, lack of moral motivation, and dominant control (Finzel, 2000).

In a bureaucratic organization, all tasks are divided into specialized jobs that are performed based on technical qualifications and uniform rules (Gibson, Ivancevich, Donnelly, & Konopaske, 2006). Managers with expert knowledge hold an authoritative role because it is delegated from the top of the leadership hierarchy rules (Gibson et al., 2006). GaVS is a program of the Georgia Department of Education's Office of Technology Services. GaVS' organizational structure is reflective of bureaucratic organization. All of the decisions are based on federal mandates. The federal government passes laws that the state department of education must implement and monitor. Georgia Department of Education created standards and rules for GaVS to implement and follow. GaVS' staff hires, trains, and supervises teachers.

Instructional Technology

Desire2Learn is the learning management system that Georgia Virtual School uses to host instructional content modules (J. Cozart, personal communication, July 29, 2013). The technical requirements for GaVS are essential to learners' success:

- Internet service provider with java script enabled browser plug-ins (Internet Explorer 8 not supported);

- Computer access with productivity software (Microsoft Office) and media players;
- E-mail account: learners need a valid e-mail account. After registration they will be assigned an e-mail; and
- Software downloads: Some AP classes require software downloads.

DIFFUSION OF INNOVATION

Diffusion of innovation theory has four elements innovation, communication, time, and social system. Getting an idea adopted can be difficult although there are several advantages. Many innovative ideas take time to become available (Rogers, 2003).

Effective communication is essential for an innovation to be accepted by others. In 2005, Governor Sonny Perdue signed the Georgia Virtual School bill via live Internet broadcast. He answered questions about GaVS in a virtual chat room and Internet video stream (Georgia Virtual School, 2010). In 2001, the Georgia State Board of Education approved the virtual learning program in October 2001, Georgia Virtual Learning program was transferred to technology services as information about the AP Nexus program began to spread, more schools contacted the Department of Education to ask how they could participate (Georgia Department of Education, 2007). There was a need for more course offerings for learners. Opinion leaders from 13 school systems with virtual learning initiatives experience gathered in Atlanta, Georgia to express their desires to have a state sponsored virtual school (Georgia Department of Education, 2007). The opinion leaders represented a social system. Opinion leaders are influential leaders that can help spread new ideas (Rogers, 2003). Governor Perdue was also an opinion leader who used his leadership position to initiate change in Georgia's educational system.

CONCLUSION

Online learning has become an important part of the progression of K-12 education. It is no longer considered novel (Southern Regional Education Board, 2013). Georgia has recognized the importance and has passed legislative bills to ensure that Georgia's learners are ready to compete with their global counterparts and that they receive high quality content (Southern Regional Education Board, 2013).

REFERENCES

Benton, B. (2010, March 6). Virtual school extends courses across Georgia. *Chattanooga Times Free Press*. Retrieved from http://www.timesfreepress.com/news/2010/mar/06/virtual-school-extends-courses-across-georgia/

Christensen, C. M., & Horn, M. B. (2008). How do we transform our schools? Use technologies that compete against nothing. *Education Next, 8*(3), 12-18.

Digital Learning Now. (2012). Digital Learning report card. Retrieved from http://www.digitallearningnow.com/reportcard/#grade9/GA

Filev, A. (2008). Get maximum benefits of merging top-down and bottom-up project management. Retrieved from http://www.projectsmart.co.uk/get-maximum-benefits-of-merging-top-down-and-bottom-up-project-management.html

Finzel, H. (2000). *The top ten mistakes leaders make*. Colorado Springs, CO: Zondervan.

Georgia Department of Education. (2007). The history of Georgia Virtual School. Retrieved from http://www.gadoe.edu

Georgia Department of Education. (2011). Statewide passing score. Retrieved from http://www.doe.k12.ga.us/External-Affairs-and-Policy/State-Board-of-Education/SBOE%20Rules/160-4-2-.13.pdf

Georgia Virtual School. (2010). Georgia virtual school. Retrieved from http://www.gavirtualschool.org/

Georgia Virtual School. (n.d.). Online course development and revision handbook [wiki]. Retrieved from http://web2virtualclassroom.wikispaces.com/file/view/Georgia+

Virtual+School+Development+and+Revision+Handbook.pdf

Gibson, J., Ivancevich, J. Donnelly, J. & Konopaske, R. (2006). *Organizations: Behaviors, structure, processes.* New York, NY: McGraw Hill.

Hawkins, L. (2012). Georgia schools virtually here. *Distance Learning, 10*(1), 39-44

Horn, B., & Staker, H. (2011). The rise of K-12 blended learning. Retrieved from http://issuu.com/gfbertini/docs/the_rise_of_k-12_blended_learning

Houck, L. (2013, March 14). Special needs students can benefit from virtual learning platform. [Blog post]. Retrieved from http://www.gavirtuallearning.org/blog/Home/tabid/656/EntryId/17/Special-Needs-Learners-Can-Benefit-from-Virtual-Learning-Platform.aspx

Ko, S., & Rossen, S. (2010). *Teaching online: A practical guide* (3rd ed.). New York, NY: Routledge.

Picciano, A., & Seaman, J. (2007). K-12 online learning: A survey of U.S. school district administrators. Retrieved from http://sloan-consortium.org/publications/survey/K-12_06

Rogers, E. M. (2003). *Diffusion of innovations* (5th ed.). New York, NY: Free Press.

Senate Press. (2011). Digital learning bill passes state senate. Retrieved from http://senate-press.net/digital-learning-bill-passes-state-senate.html

Shah, N. (2011, August 24). E- learning expands for special needs students. *Education Week.* Retrieved from http://www.edweek.org/ew/articles/2011/08/24/01edtech-disabilities.h31.html

Southern Regional Education Board. (2006, November). *Standards for quality online courses.* Retrieved from http://publications.sreb.org/2006/06T05_Standards_quality_online_courses.pdf

Southern Regional Education Board. (2013, February). *Trends in state-run virtual schools in the SREB region.* Retrieved from http://publications.sreb.org/2013/13T01_Trends_State-Run.pdf

ONLINE LEARNING HAS BECOME AN IMPORTANT PART OF THE PROGRESSION OF K-12 EDUCATION. IT IS NO LONGER CONSIDERED NOVEL BUT CONSIDERED AS A RECOGNIZED METHOD OF COURSE DELIVERY. GEORGIA HAS RECOGNIZED THE IMPORTANCE AND HAS PASSED LEGISLATIVE BILLS TO ENSURE THAT GEORGIA'S LEARNERS ARE READY TO COMPETE WITH THEIR GLOBAL COUNTERPARTS AND THAT THEY RECEIVE HIGHLY QUALIFIED CONTENT.

Broward Virtual School

Nova Lishon-Savarino

OVERVIEW

Broward Virtual School (BVS) delivers education to K-12 students around the world through technology and media. The school gives students the opportunity to work at their own pace and develop strong relationships with their teachers and peers while growing into productive members of society. The curriculum design and community service opportunities stimulate positive learning experiences for students in a unique way.

MISSION

The goal of BVS is to provide students with equal and excellent education. Through successful student graduation rates, the program is able to continue; students obtain quality education that prepares them for post secondary education (community colleges, universities, and Ivy League schools around the nation). BVS (2012) "offers full-time enrollment to students in Grades K-12" and "home educated students in Grades 6-12 may enroll part-time" (para. 1). BVS is an obvious choice in that "Virtual learning provides flexibility of time and location, and promotes development of the skills, attitudes, and self-discipline necessary to achieve success in the 21st century" (para. 1).

ACCREDITATION

According to the Broward Virtual School (2012) website, "the BVS administrative office is located in Davie, Florida inside the BECON TV building" (para. 5). This is the main working center for BVS where administrators, support staff, and educators report. There are also meetings and student events held within the BECON TV building. BVS is fully accredited by the Southern Association of Colleges and Schools (SACS) and the Commission on International and Trans-Regional Accreditation (CITA). All of the BVS educators meet state standard requirements to teach for BVS, even if the educator is located outside of the state of Florida.

EDUCATORS

BVS offers a wide array of courses with experienced and well-trained instructional staff. The diverse educators' expertise range from individual or a combination of knowledge in: Spanish; science; language

Nova Lishon-Savarino,
Graduate student, Instructional Technology and Distance Education, Nova Southeastern University. E-mail: lishonsa@nova.edu

arts; reading; physical education; health; critical thinking; business; social studies; mathematics; career education; world cultures; English; and Advanced Placement (AP); Grades K-5 specialty; and Exceptional Student Education (ESE) specialty. This team of educators assists in broadening the collaborative learning experience for BVS students while providing individualized attention when needed. The courses offered at BVS encompass all the subjects any traditional public school would have (math, science, history, english, reading, the arts, and elective work).

All of the educators are very knowledgeable and patient when working with their students. However, one particular educator was recognized on the Broward Virtual School (2012) website as being an outstanding educator. Math teacher Melanie McCutcheon is the "2013 Teacher of the Year." Her devotion and active involvement in her students' learning experiences is outstanding. She spends considerable time with students over the phone and via live Elluminate chats. Even though McCutcheon resides in Texas, she has the ability to meet her students' diverse needs and can personalize instruction of any mathematical concept.

ADMINISTRATION

Administrators help to engage students and provide opportunities for success. Students have the ability to communicate openly and regularly with administrative staff. The importance of the administrators is not only to communicate with students; rather they are also greatly involved in development of programs for BVS. BVS administration is constantly working to continuously improve curriculum development, delivery techniques, and manage effective budget spending for the school.

STUDENTS

The school has a unique and diverse population of students from all over the state of

Florida and beyond. Public school, private school, and home school students all have the ability to attend BVS; the students may either register as a full-time or part-time student (Broward Virtual School, 2012). The students take BVS courses as a way to accelerate, catch up if they are behind, or have a more flexible school schedule so they can participate in activities that normally wouldn't be possible in a traditional classroom setting (e.g., sports training and competitions, acting careers, running a community service organization, or just having more time to enjoy life in other ways).

The most important indication of whether or not a school is successful is apparent from completion rates. Quillen (2011) discusses that "Articles in the 'New York Times' questioned not only the academic results for students in virtual schools, but also the propriety of business practices surrounding the use of public dollars for such programs" (p. 1). BVS is a successful program and has student statistical data to prove why. The following graph, Figure 1, shows student course completion success rates over the years. The percentage of completion rates is the highest it has been within the given time frame. BVS targeted an appropriate learning strategy that enables the majority of students to complete coursework.

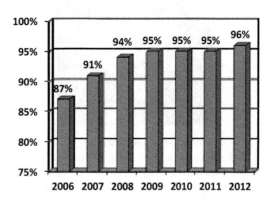

Source: McGuire (2012).

Figure 1. Student completion rates.

COST

BVS is a public school and is, therefore, free to Broward County residents. As a public school, BVS does not charge tuition fees. The school is fully online and also partners with other schools to give traditional classroom students the opportunity to experience distance education methods. The more exposure that students have to varying modes of communication and technology tools, the better prepared they will be for future studies and/or job related responsibilities.

ATTENDANCE

There is a strict student contact policy that encompasses continuous contact between students, parents/guardians, and educators. "Only through continuous communication can students be successful in an online course. Within each course the instructor outlines the weekly minimum work requirements. There is an essential component to a successful course completion that the student and instructor maintain regular contact" (2012, para. 1). If policy is not followed, there are follow-up procedures in place to deal with inconsistent contact. Communication is essential to student success in a distance education program such as BVS.

COMMUNICATION DELIVERY

BVS communicates with its students in the classroom in a variety of ways. Lishon-Savarino (2012) discusses the concept of Coldeway's Quadrants in accordance with the varying modes of communication technology that BVS utilizes. BVS incorporates three of the four delivery methods. As opposed to a traditional classroom that delivers at the same time and in the same place, BVS delivers via: a learning center, same time and different place; synchronous distance education, different time and same place; or asynchronous distance education, different time and different place (Lishon-Savarino, 2012).

The successful understanding of the material being covered is dependent upon what modes of communication are utilized in the virtual classroom. Belair (2012) concluded that "a variety of communication methods must be employed in order to facilitate effective virtual schooling" (p. 26). Prerecorded lessons are good for students to be able to review, while live chats give students the opportunity to collaborate with one another and ask their instructors questions to define their understanding of the concepts. Discussion boards are also used so that students can openly respond and discuss topics amongst themselves. In another perspective, a learning center might give a student a better ability to focus and easily ask for help from facilitators. Every student's learning style is different, so the approach to teaching educational material should be just as customized and personalized based on the students' needs.

STUDENT ACTIVITIES

A common misconception among the general public is that distance education programs lack collaborative efforts and extracurricular opportunities. BVS offers many opportunities for students to collaborate with one another and experience life as traditional classroom students do. The following "face-to-face" extracurricular activities are offered to BVS student (Broward Virtual School, 2012): Broward Teen News Internships; National Honor Society membership (for qualifying students); National Junior Honor Society membership (for qualifying students); Key Club; Florida Future Educators of America; monthly enrichment activities; student talent show; field trips; academic competitions; college planning seminars; junior and senior prom; and formal graduation ceremony for seniors. These events allow students to collectively work with one another, engage in constructive programs, raise awareness for good causes, enrich their personal learning experience, and actively participate in community services activities.

PARTNERSHIPS WITH ORGANIZATIONS

According to the Broward Virtual School (2012) website, "Broward Virtual School is a franchise partner of Florida Virtual School for middle and high school curriculum" (para. 4). Florida Virtual School developed a thriving distance learning program; serving students all over the state of Florida. Broward Virtual School caters specifically to Broward County students. As a result of the customized education Broward County residents receive, "BVS is proud to be the top performing Florida Virtual School franchise in Florida" (Broward Virtual School, 2012, para. 4). In addition to the strong middle and high school grades program, BVS has a K-5 program as well; the school is partnered with K12 Inc. (Broward Virtual School, 2012).

BVS also has aligned itself with schools that participate in videoconferencing sessions. These videoconferencing sessions have students from various schools in the district in one online classroom; students can see each other and their instructor via a television screen. Microphones are set up in the rooms to pick up audio spoken by students and teachers as to keep a steady pace and allow active participation amongst the schools. The students enjoy engaging with one another and obtaining quality education from some of the best teachers in the state.

TECHNOLOGY REQUIREMENTS

Students who take online courses must have access to the technology needed to view and complete coursework. High speed Internet is required so the students can log onto the website and access their courses in a secure account. Additional computer hardware requirements are an efficient high powered processor, Windows XP (or higher), and 256 MB RAM (Broward Virtual School, 2012).

Flash Player is another technical need for students so they can view multimedia presentations and the lessons for each section. The students must also have a safe and secure way of saving their coursework such as a jump-drive or removable disk. Audio equipment is needed for assignments, presentations, live chats, and so on; the computer must have a sound card, reliable speakers (to hear lessons, instructors, and peers), and a microphone or headset (to speak into for recording assignments or live active participating chats). If a student has a Macintosh computer then a comparable setup is required (Broward Virtual School, 2012).

TECHNOLOGY UTILIZED

The courses are comprised of interactive multicomponent lessons organized into easily navigated modules. Depending on the type of course a student is taking will depend on what type of technology is utilized. For example, in a Spanish course, the use of video and audio is required to illustrate and equip students with what is being said and how to say it. The students must record themselves orally saying things as per assignments and writing simple sentences to long papers in that language.

Technological skills of how to access special symbols specific to that language are also taught to students. The verbal, reading, and writing skills are equally important; therefore, all skills are taught via multimedia presentation delivery. A reading course, on the other hand, may have more assignments related to writing and utilizing synchronous and asynchronous chats for in depth discussions on required reading literature. A geometry class may require students to utilize graphic drawing tools to show shapes and related properties (e.g., labeling a triangle's angles and sides as per congruency theorems).

TECHNOLOGY SUPPLEMENTS AND SUPPORT

BVS has a user-friendly support system for parents and students. The E-Resource Library on the BVS (2012) website provides links to orientation presentations, downloadable software (e.g., Cute PDF Writer and OpenOffice Software Suite). Students and parents have access to the FLVS Technical Support Center to address any technical issues hindering the ability of a student to complete coursework. Another form of support is supplemental resources available for instructional purposes, such as BrainPop (activity page with interactive videos), Florida Virtual School Math Help Pages (tutorial sessions), Khan Academy (tutorial sessions), and Lit2Go Audiobooks.

VIDEOCONFERENCING

Videoconferencing is a very valuable tool in distance learning. BVS utilizes videoconferencing so students, educators, and administrators can collaborate with one another. The students and educators have the ability to see, hear, and communicate with each other easily. In addition, software may be downloaded for utilizing an e-board; the educator can write on the blank board so the student can follow along with verbal commands or steps of a problem. The setup is required in every room that has videoconferencing classes. The network system expands so that schools from across the district can communicate with one another. Latency is very small, only 1-3 seconds.

At Coconut Creek Elementary School, fifth grade students learning mathematical concepts via videoconferencing are given dry erase boards and markers. The television screen is set up in the front of the classroom, microphones pick up speech, and a camera is set up to show the entire classroom.

Multiple schools may be videoconferencing at one time. The educator is set up in one of the classrooms, in this case Coconut Creek Elementary. The reason the educator is actually in a classroom is to assist the educator in knowing if the pacing of the lesson is appropriate. Students enjoy seeing each other on the television screen and actively participating in completing mathematical problems. The students compare answers to every problem and then the educator reviews how to obtain the answer to the question. Students also participate in other activities such as art projects (making geometrical shapes) and utilizing creative ways to learn more difficult concepts. The classes are divided based on the level of the students (grade level and cognitive abilities).

STATISTICS

Videoconferencing is an effective way to distribute effective educational material on a massive scale. Educators who participated in videoconferencing courses were asked a series of questions related to lessons plans and the overall effectiveness of the instructor from BVS providing the lesson. McGuire (2012) provided numerical data that indicated the number of educators that agreed or disagreed with specific statements. The relevancy of the lessons with integrated videoconferencing is indirectly analyzed from the results of the surveys.

The lesson plans were evaluated by educators present in classrooms during videoconferencing sessions. The majority of educators strongly agreed that the course objectives were met with quality planning and implementation. Very few respondents of the entire polled population sample disagreed that the videoconferencing course lesson plans were effective. The colleagues appear to be in

Table 1. Video Conference Course Lesson Plans

Answer Options	Strongly Disagree	Disagree	Neutral	Agree	Strongly Agree
The lesson plans reflect a correlation to the Sunshine State and/or Next Generation Standards.	5	0	2	26	151
The lesson plans contain measurable objectives.	4	0	3	28	148
The lesson plans introduce concepts measured on the FCAT.	4	0	20	23	137
The lesson plans include student activities that address a variety of learning styles.	4	0	5	34	141

Source: McGuire (2012).

Table 2. Instructor of Video Conference Course

Answer Options	Strongly Disagree	Disagree	Neutral	Agree	Strongly Agree
The instructor reflected knowledge of appropriate instructional strategies for the subject taught.	6	0	0	21	156
The instructor displayed knowledge of appropriate learning activities for the subject taught.	6	0	0	22	155
The instructor actively engaged students.	6	1	1	26	149
The instructor maintained student interest.	6	0	2	35	138
The instructor effectively integrated technology into lesson presentation.	5	1	2	28	146
The instructor's pacing during lesson presentation was effective.	5	3	4	33	137

Source: McGuire (2012).

strong agreement that videoconferencing lesson plans are very good for students and meet the needs of the standards set by the schools, state, and testing requirements (see Table 1).

The instructor implementing the videoconferencing lesson was evaluated by educators present in classrooms during videoconferencing sessions. The majority of educators strongly agreed that the instructor was knowledgeable and enhanced the students' learning experience. A relatively small amount of the polled population sample disagreed that the instructor was effective in implementing lessons via videoconferencing. The data show a clear indication that many educators feel the videoconferencing instructor is well equipped to handle diverse classroom environments and keep the students actively engaged (see Table 2).

AWARDS AND RECOGNITION
The standards for BVS are high, as it "was the first and only district virtual school to

be rated as an 'A' school by the Florida Department of Education in 2010. BVS offers courses and a diploma approved by the NCAA" (Broward Virtual School, 2012, para. 1). BVS has achieved many special recognitions and partnerships with programs. Last year BVS was very active in expanding their program academically and via extracurricular activities. McGuire (2012) discussed the following BVS achievements:

> EOC (End of Course) exam results (100% passed Algebra, 100% passed Biology, 97% passed Geometry); trained 56 students and staff in CPR; partnered with Atlantic Technical Center to provide every ninth grader an opportunity to earn online learning credit (Reading for College Success); partnered with 10 elementary schools and 3 middle schools to offer acceleration opportunities. (p. 4).

In 2010, BVS was the recipient of the International Association for Online Learning (iNACOL) Outstanding Online Learning Practice award (Broward Virtual School, 2012). This award encompasses the ideals of a distance education program. The focus is on the students and the best deliveries for the students. Since this particular award was international, this shows the versatility and capabilities that BVS has in distributing good, quality education. The curriculum is the same to that of a traditional school setting; however, the delivery system is different.

GOALS

Broward Virtual School has ideas for projects and programs to be implemented for the future. McGuire (2012) discussed that BVS would like to see the percentage of their students rise in ability to pass with higher scores of 3 or above on the Florida Comprehensive Assessment Test (FCAT), maintain a 95% student course completion rate, and that 95% of students and parents

will have verbal communication with their instructors at least once a month.

CONCLUSION

In terms of accountability, McGuire (2012) outlined important aspects BVS considers: "student learning; successful course completions; school improvement plan goals; graduation rate; customer surveys; and student success act (Marzano Evaluation System)" (p. 10). With these goals and measurable objectives at the foundation of BVS, the room for growth is limitless. BVS is a good option for students seeking a flexible learning environment that considers their individualized needs.

Broward Virtual School (2012) states that "Our courses engage students in real-life projects, requiring the use of critical thinking, problem-solving skills, and the ability to apply the knowledge they have acquired" (para. 9). BVS keeps a few main stakeholders in mind: administrators, educators, students, and parents. Funding is necessary to keep BVS operational; new programs and partnerships are constantly being formed to expand and enhance the distance education program for students. Broward Virtual School is revolutionizing distance education by providing students with opportunity to complete school studies with a fully online program utilizing the latest and greatest technology available.

REFERENCES

Belair, M. (2012). The investigation of virtual school communications. *TechTrends, 56*(4), 26-33.

Broward Virtual School. (2012). *BVED*. Retrieved from http://www.bved.net/

McGuire, C. P. (2012). *Earning the gold*. Davie, FL: Broward Virtual School.

Lishon-Savarino, N. (2012). *Coldeway's quadrants lesson*. Retrieved from https://itdenova .wikispaces.com/

Quillen, I. (2011). Virtual ed. faces sharp criticism. *Education Week, 31*(13), 1.

Georgia Schools
Virtually Here

Lynn M. Hawkins

INTRODUCTION

The appearance of Georgia schools is changing. No longer are all Georgia students heading off to school each morning on the traditional yellow school bus. Some students are heading to the Internet via smartphone, tablet, laptop, or desktop.

This is not the only change taking place around the state of Georgia. Georgia citizens made a historical decision on November 6, 2012. The state's voters ratified an amendment to the Georgia Constitution in favor of charter schools. Local school districts no longer hold the power; a state commission will now approve these institutions.

Couple the virtual concept with a charter school and the new product on the market in Georgia is virtual charter schools. Brick and mortar move over; cyber city is virtually here.

This article examines the culminating historical timeline of online learning's birth in the state of Georgia. By examining the two current parties involved in Georgia's cyber learning (Georgia public schools and Georgia charter schools), Georgia's certification process for teaching online, and the recent turn of events in legislature, explanations for how and why Georgia's e-learning environments were founded will be presented, in conjunction with a look of what's to come.

GEORGIA'S VIRTUAL CERTIFICATION

To make the transition from brick-and-mortar teaching to cyber instructing smoother, the state of Georgia offers teachers an online certification. Starting in 2006, Georgia became the first state to offer certification for online teachers. This certification, according to the PSC Rule 505-3-.85, is in effect to prepare educators to teach in an online environment.

Prior to teaching in the state of Georgia, all Georgia teachers must hold a certificate from the Georgia Professional Standards Commission (PSC). This document from the PSC certifies the teacher's qualifications and classifications.

To receive the online endorsement, candidates must hold a valid teaching certificate and complete an online preparation program. The preparation program or practicum focuses on three standards: instructional technology concepts, online teaching and learning methodology, and online assessments.

The first standard addresses the teacher's knowledge, skills, and understanding of instructional technology concepts. In addition to the instructional technology terminology, candidates are expected to be competent with technology pertaining to online instruction.

The second standard tackles the ins and outs of online teaching and learning methodologies. Through this preparation process, teachers will be able to provide an active, meaningful online learning environment with prompt feedback and clear expectations, while modeling appropriate online behavior. In addition, the teacher will be prepped to be considerate of students with disabilities and aware of cultural differences, all the while encouraging cultural diversity and inclusive learning.

The third standard examines effective online assessments. Here, candidates will demonstrate the creation (and implementation) of valid and reliable assessments in an online environment.

Using this virtual certification, teachers can transition from the little red schoolhouse to the cyber portal. Combine this certification with the training that most online institutions require (and provide) and the virtual instructor is born.

GEORGIA VIRTUAL LEARNING FOR PUBLIC SCHOOLS

HISTORY

Virtual instruction or Georgia's e-learning took shape in August of 2001, when a need for high school Advanced Placement (AP) classes and core curricular classes arose. With a shortage of qualified staff, the absence of course offerings and scheduling conflicts, the Georgia State Board of Education made provisions for these courses by establishing the Virtual Learning Business Plan.

In October of 2001, the Virtual Learning Business Plan was transferred to Georgia Department of Education's (GaDOE) Technology Services. However, GaDOE tech services had its hands full with the AP Nexus grant. This grant, sponsored by the U.S. Department of Education (USDOE), was designed to increase the number of low-income, disadvantaged students who took AP classes. In collaboration with South Carolina, Tennessee, and Apex Learning (an online AP course provider), Georgia hoped to increase the availability of these AP courses to this specific group of students by offering an online setting.

During the next several years, several school districts in Georgia created their own online learning community, 13 of which convened in Atlanta and worked with Governor Sonny Perdue to produce the first statewide online program called Georgia Virtual School (GaVS). This cyber school was officially signed into law in May of 2005.

Governor Perdue conducted the first live broadcast after signing the bill. He spoke face to face to an AP class at Winder Barrow High and online to 18 other classes and libraries across the state. The entire event was broadcast live by Georgia Public Broadcasting (GPB).

GEORGIA VIRTUAL SCHOOL (GaVS)

GaVS does not have a physical location, but it does have an address. That address is, however, a URL. And just like any other school, there are host of intricate details. But because the Georgia Department of Education established this entity, the school's set-up is exactly like a Georgia public school, with the exception that it is fully online.

GaVS ACCREDITATION AND CERTIFICATION

Accredited by the Southern Association of Colleges and Schools (SACS), Georgia Virtual School offers middle school and high school level courses across the state in a virtual classroom setting. Equipped with an online media center, guidance support and online teachers, GaVS offers more than 100 courses in core curricular (math, language arts, science, social studies); foreign languages; electives; career, technical and agricultural education (CTAE); and AP studies.

In line with the Georgia PSC, GaVS teachers must possess a valid Georgia teaching certificate and be certified in the appropriate subject area. Teachers must complete a training program hosted by GaVS, as well.

GaVS TIMES AND TUITION

The schedule for GaVS high school is summer, fall, and spring semester courses, while middle school is summer semester only. Students enrolled in a course during fall or spring may have their tuition covered by their local public schools, while full time equivalent (FTE) monies can be used to cover private and home school students. Tuition for high school is $500 per Carnegie unit, while middle school costs $250 per course. All students pay tuition during summer semesters and out of state students must pay full tuition.

CREDIT RECOVERY

Another online experience offered by the GaDOE is the Credit Recovery Program. Here, high school students have an opportunity to retake courses online that they previously failed.

COURSEWORK/SCHEDULE

Core curricular classes and limited electives, mainly health, are offered in a 26 week completion time, with the focus being on fulfilling graduation requirements. Each course contains the Georgia Performance Standards (GPS) content, as laid out by the Georgia Department of Education.

The schedule is flexible and not facilitated by a teacher, with the exception of test monitoring. Through the use of web-based learning activities and unit assessments, credit recovery is designed to help students complete state requirements for graduation.

GRADING

A pretest sets the wheels in motion. The results of this exam determine a student's direction. If a score of 85% of higher is attained at the beginning of each unit, the student is allowed to test out, with the unit posttest. But if the pretest score is lower than 85%, the student must review every content item in the entire unit before the posttest is made available again.

To complete a course, students must score 70% or higher on the posttest and final exam (or EOCT). Upon this final grade, credit for the course will be granted and students will then earn credits based on their proficiency and competency of the state standards.

COST

This program is provided free of charge to participating Georgia public high schools. However, no money has been designated for the test proctors or monitors. As such, this cost may be passed on to students.

EXPRESS

ExPreSS is another online learning environment established by GaDOE. It is not a school, per se, but rather a free online tutorial program set-up to help students who were unsuccessful in passing the Georgia High School Graduation Test. This program consists of self-paced modules based on the GPS content areas (science, social studies, English language arts, and mathematics).

GEORGIA VIRTUAL CHARTER SCHOOLS

GEORGIA CHARTER SCHOOLS

Switching gears from public schools to charter schools, the Georgia Charter Schools Association (GCSA) was established in 2001, as a nonprofit corporation whose mission is to advocate and serve all Georgia charter schools. By increasing awareness of charter schools; communicating with state and local officials; networking Georgia charter schools; and advancing the cause of charter schools, GCSA supports school choice, student achievement, collaboration, innovation, communication and accountability (GCSA, 2012).

There are over 100 charter schools in Georgia. These schools are considered public schools, as they receive public funding, have open enrollment, and serve all populations of students (GaDOE, n.d.).

Although similar to public schools, charter schools are different on two main fronts—governance and accountability. The charter school is run by an independent board of directors, as opposed to the public school's board of education. The other difference is in their flexibility with state and local rules/regulations. This flexibility comes at a price, as charter schools are held to a higher standard of accountability.

As for online charter schools, GCSA lists three as virtual charter schools: Georgia Connections Academy Charter School, Georgia Cyber Academy, and Provost Academy. A brief examination of each follows.

GEORGIA CONNECTIONS ACADEMY CHARTER SCHOOL

Georgia Connections Academy Charter School is a tuition free K-12 virtual school. Approved by GCSA in 2011, the school served K-8 in its first year and expanded to K-12 in the 2012-2013 school year.

This cyber school provides highly qualified, state-certified staff; social and community events; and Connexus, their very own education management system (Connections Education, 2012).

GEORGIA CYBER ACADEMY

Established in 2008 as a program of the Odyssey School, the Georgia Cyber Academy served grades K-9 for 3 years. Then in February of 2011, the state board unanimously agreed to expand the school to Grades K-12 (Georgia Education News, 2011).

The head of the school has referred to Georgia Cyber Academy as an "education support system" for students (Georgia Cyber Academy, 2012). However, recent allegations regarding failure to provide services to special education students could prove otherwise (O'Connor, 2012).

PROVOST ACADEMY

Approved in 2010 by the Georgia Charter Schools Association, Provost Academy did not open until July 2012. As this is their first year in business, they have not yet been accredited. This institution serves Grades 9-12 online through a student portal. Monitoring of student access to coursework is recorded and attendance is taken through this portal.

Coursework at Provost Academy is based on Georgia Performance Standards, but additional focus is given to electives. Science, technology, engineering, and mathematics (STEM) are offered to students to "develop the skills necessary to succeed in today's high-tech world" (Edison Learning, 2012).

Included in the Provost Academy package is a supplemental software subscription that is offered to all students. The program is called Study Island and is designed to help students master Georgia Performance Standards.

GEORGIA'S AMENDMENT 1

Charter virtual instruction may be closer to the norm in the years to come, as Georgians passed Amendment 1 in November 2012. Amendment 1 asked the question, "Shall the Constitution of Georgia be amended to allow state or local approval of public charter schools upon the request of local communities? (Horne, 2012).

THE CHANGE

In the past, charter schools were approved or disapproved by the local school board. If disapproved, the group could go to the State Board of Education. The problem was that if the group was granted the charter by the State, the new charter school could not receive local tax money. It would receive only state and federal funds (Krache, 2012).

With this new law, charter schools will be approved by a state commission; a charter school that had been denied by the local school board or State Board of Education could be approved.

SUPPORT

Support for the Georgia Amendment came from some unexpected folks, such as Alice Walton, the daughter of Wal-Mart founder Sam Walton. Also, the Koch brothers, billionaires who founded the Tea Party organization Americans for Prosperity, donated support in favor of Georgia Amendment 1. Others that gave included companies that manage charter schools, like K12 Inc., which supports the Georgia Cyber Academy.

HISTORICAL SIGNIFICANCE

What does this amendment mean for Georgia? Georgia voters who supported the amendment believed that "charter schools give parents more opportunities to be actively involved in their child's education" (Patel, 2012). As such, the idea is that the power of choice was given to the people/parents in deciding what is best in educating their children.

WHY E-LEARNING IN GEORGIA

As technology advances and allows for more user-friendly devices and applications, the thinking is that everything else in life should follow suit. Hence, teaching and learning should move from sticks and bricks to virtual worlds and cyberspace.

Originally the online learning community in Georgia was developed to fill a need. AP classes, core curricular, scheduling conflicts and lack of qualified staff were just some of the reasons named by the Georgia Department of Education for the development.

Team these needs with an individualized education and charter schools surface in the state of Georgia. Charter schools give parents and students an alternative to public schools, by filling the need of quality education on an individual instruction plan.

Establishing "online" charter schools was sure to follow suit. These cyber schools add one more ingredient to the pot—freedom to choose. As these establishments are accessible anywhere/anytime, that convenience adds spice to any student educational life.

CONCLUSION

What happens now? The ratification of the charter school amendment was just the beginning. Freedom comes with a price; it is never free. Parents want the freedom to choose the best education plan for their children. What will it cost?

Will there be a surplus of charter schools, virtual and the like, all clamoring for parents' attention? Are too many choices a bad thing? Let's ask the lunch ladies who serve our students on the five different lunch lines.

REFERENCES

Bennett, J. (2012, March 28). Virtual schools expanding in Georgia. Retrieved from http://www.gpb.org/news/2012/03/28/virtual-schools-expanding-in-georgia

Connections Education. (2012). Free public cyber school in Georgia. Retrieved from Georgia Connections Academy website: http://www.connectionsacademy.com/georgia-school/home.aspx

Davis, M. R. (2012). New laws, programs expand K-12 online-learning options. *Education Week, 32*(2), S3-S5.

Edison Learning, Inc. (2012). Learning technology. Retrieved from http://ga.provostacademy.com/how-it-works

Evergreen Education Group. (2011, December 19). Georgia data & information. Retrieved from http://kpk12.com/states/georgia/

Flanigan, R. L. (2012). Virtual ed. begins addressing teacher-certification questions. *Education Week, 32*(2), S10-S11.

GaDOE. (n.d.). General frequently asked questions (charter schools). Retrieved from http://www.doe.k12.ga.us/External-Affairs-and-Policy/Charter-Schools/Pages/General-Frequently-Asked-Questions.aspx

GaPSC. (2006, December 15). 505-3-.85 Online teaching endorsement program. Retrieved from http://www.gapsc.com/Rules/Current/EducatorPreparation/505-3-.85.pdf

Georgia Charter Schools Association. (2012). Virtual. Retrieved from http://www.gacharters.org/tag/virtual/

Georgia Cyber Academy. (2012). Who we are. Retrieved from K12 Inc. website: http://www.k12.com/gca/who-we-are

Georgia Department of Education. (2012). Accreditation & history. Retrieved from http://www.gavirtualschool.org/About/AccreditationHistory.aspx

Georgia Department of Education. (n.d.). Georgia virtual learning. Retrieved from http://www.doe.k12.ga.us/Technology-Services/Pages/GAVS.aspx

Georgia Education News. (2011, February 23). Georgia Cyber Academy unanimously approved by State Charter Commission. Retrieved from http://gaeducation.blogspot.com/2011/02/georgia-cyber-academy-unanimously.html

Goss, M. (2011). Georgia Virtual School. *Distance Learning, 8*(3), 41-45

Horne, C. (2012, November 6). Georgia amendment ballot question results. Retrieved from http://www.13wmaz.com/politics/article/203054/318/Georgia-Amendment-Ballot-Question-Results

Krache, D. (2012, November 6). All eyes on Georgia, Washington as voters consider charter school initiatives. Retrieved from http://schoolsofthought.blogs.cnn.com/2012/11/06/all-eyes-on-georgia-washington-as-voters-consider-charter-school-initiatives/

O'Connor, J. (2012, November 26). Georgia threatens to close K12-run online charter school. Retrieved from http://stateimpact.npr.org/florida/2012/11/26/georgia-threatens-to-close-k12-run-online-charter-school/

Patel, V. (2012, October 13). Amendment 1: Charter schools—A closer look. Retrieved from http://unionrecorder.com/election/x688425111/Amendment-1-Charter-Schools-a-closer-look

Quillen, I. R. (2010). States eye standards for virtual educators. *Education Week, 30*(4), S3-S5.

Vocus PRW Holdings. (2011, January 11). Connections Academy virtual school comes to Georgia—Approved to open for 2011-2012 school year. Retrieved from http://www.prweb.com/releases/2011/1/prweb8057679.htm

Washington, W. (2012, November 6). State's voters approve charter amendment. *The Atlanta Journal-Constitution*. Retrieved from http://www.ajc.com/news/news/charter-school-amendment-heading-toward-passage/nSy2J/

Meeting the Shifting Perspective

The Iowa Communications Network

John Gillispie, Joseph Cassis, Tami Fujinaka, and Gail McMahon

The educational world operates in many dimensions. Population, learning expectations, resources, and technology all contribute to today's shifting perspectives on how to deliver curriculum to students. In 1989, when the Internet was unheard of and "global economy" was not in our regular vernacular, the state of Iowa was already starting a giant technology shift. With the creation of the Iowa Communications Network (ICN), our predominantly rural state was ahead of its time by using fiber optic telecommunications to bring video distance learning opportunities across the miles to Iowa students.

Today, over 6,400 miles of fiber cable, 3,100 owned by the network and 3,300 leased, allows Iowans to access education, health, and government through the network's authorized users—secondary and postsecondary schools, libraries, hospitals, National Guard armories, state agencies, and federal offices (see Figure 1). Standard

John Gillispie, Executive Director, Iowa Communications Network, Grimes State Office Building, 400 E. 14th Street, Des Moines, IA 50319.
Telephone: (515) 725-4707.
E-mail: john.gillispie@iowa.gov

Joseph Cassis, Deputy Director, Iowa Communications Network, Grimes State Office Building, 400 E. 14th Street, Des Moines, IA 50319.
Telephone: (515) 725-4600.
E-mail: joseph.cassis@iowa.gov

Iowa Communications Network Video Classrooms

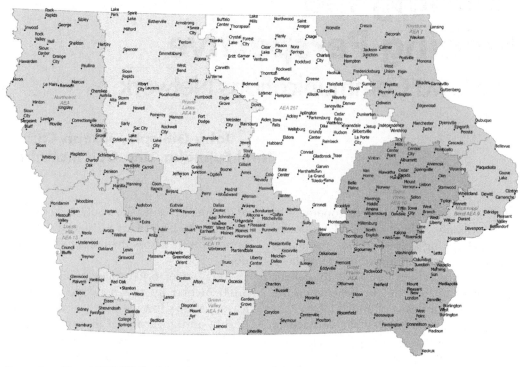

Figure 1. Almost 75% (518) of the classrooms are in the education system.

Tami Fujinaka, Government Relations Manager, Iowa Communications Network, Grimes State Office Building, 400 E. 14th Street, Des Moines, IA 50319. Telephone: (515) 725-458. E-mail: tami.fujinaka@iowa.gov

Gail McMahon, Public Relations Manager, Iowa Communications Network, Grimes State Office Building, 400 E. 14th Street, Des Moines, IA 50319. Telephone (515) 725-4713. E-mail: gail.mcmahon@iowa.gov

ICN video classrooms are based on Asynchronous Transfer Mode (ATM) connectivity with Motion Picture Experts Group-2 (MPEG-2) video compression.

Those who had the bold vision to think outside brick-and-mortar met the ICN with open arms. Some who did not see the need, now have a new perspective, while those who had the vision, now need and want more; and the ICN is shifting its perspective to deliver.

TIME SHIFT

Any time, anywhere—a unique concept just a few years ago—is now an expectation among much of society. Today's traditional students have grown up in the instantaneous world of technology, where time is based on how long it takes to upload or download information from the Internet, not how long it takes to travel somewhere.

A constant challenge facing the ICN throughout its young life has been the issue of school bell schedules. With over 350 school districts, and an almost equal number of differing bell schedules, the need for a shift in perspective regarding time and education is ever increasing.

Bell schedules are often cited by school districts as an obstacle to using the ICN, but the fact remains that where there is a will, there is a way. Some Iowa K-12 administrators look past bell schedules and work together to bring classes to their students. For example, Brooklyn-Guernsey-Malcom (BGM) High School Principal Rick Radcliffe faced losing a Spanish teacher and another foreign language option for students. So, he created a model to entice the Spanish teacher to stay and, as word spread about BGM Spanish classes over the ICN, requests to participate came in from other districts. Conflicting bell schedules posed a challenge, but nothing insurmountable. One school even changed its schedule and calendar to match that of the BGM district. With flexibility and a shift in perspective, four school districts retained the possibilities for almost 200 Iowa students to meet foreign language requirements by using the ICN video services.

The ICN is not just video; the network also provides bandwidth to authorized users. A growing trend toward time-saving online and hybrid courses, a desire for

Figure 2.   BGM HS Spanish instructor Nicki Maestre teaches to her students and others via a traditional MPEG-2 ICN video classroom.

more access to online curriculum content, and increased movement of content via Internet Protocol (IP) have all created a dramatic increase in the need for bandwidth.

Through a strong collaborative effort forged by the network and Iowa Public Television (affiliated with the Iowa Department of Education), pre-K-12 students, teachers, administrators, and school personnel benefit from distance learning opportunities delivered over the ICN. During the 2006-07 school year, more than 50,000 students and teachers came together "virtually" through *K-12 Connections*. This IPTV project, designed to provide curriculum-enhancing opportunities for students, educators, and school personnel, provided almost 7,000 hours of full-motion, interactive video learning sessions to Iowa students, teachers, or schools.

One university professor sees *K-12 Connections* as a way to educate and spark students' interest in science and teaching in a field where demand is high. Iowa State University professor Dr. Larry Genalo is the host of the "Science Fun: What's Hot and What's Not" ICN sessions, which focus on the atomic structure of materials and the effects of changing these structures through heating and cooling. His ICN sessions are full of activity and lively demonstrations. Metal, glass, and rubber objects are melted, frozen, bent, broken, and shattered by using fire and liquid nitrogen. In addition to the demonstrations, Dr. Genalo has constant interaction with the students and explains real-world examples, such as the space shuttle Challenger and the Titanic, which bring home the lesson.

Current *K-12 Connections* sessions are scheduled via a reservation system, as are all ICN video sessions, which provides little time flexibility. With a shift in perspective, *K-12 Connections* is progressing into online streaming and more video rebroadcasts of popular ICN sessions, for easier access by teachers, students, and administrators, via Internet connectivity made possible through the ICN.

PLACE SHIFT

The "anywhere" mentality of today's distance learner is a shift from the centuries-old face-to-face delivery of classes. The ICN's MPEG-2 infrastructure calls for video classrooms at most public school districts and certified public schools that were willing to purchase the classroom equipment, as well as community colleges, regent universities, and private colleges. Today, ICN video classrooms are within 15 miles of every Iowan.

The American mindset no longer accepts the excuse that if you live in rural Iowa you have to give up the opportunity for advanced classes or a field trip to the capital in exchange for valued rural culture. The ICN was built on the premise of equal access to educational opportunities for all Iowans—in 1994, one of the first classes shared was a high school Russian class. The mantra for many of today's parents is, "If it's there, I want it for my child." If course content is available, a student should be able to access it, no matter where he or she lives. Parents and their children expect to be able to access curriculum like Chinese, Russian, statistics, and physics. Busy schedules, including academics, sports, jobs, and family activities underscore the need for nomadic learning.

However, the debate over virtual versus face-to-face classes still plays a part in distance education and for the ICN. Some educators, administrators, parents, and others believe that the most effective way to learn is with face-to-face communication between the student and the teacher. Even in today's technological world, some still consider online classes, with electronic interaction via e-mails and chat rooms, to be less effective than face-to-face interaction. The ICN helps bridge the two factions. The traditional ICN video high school course, offers MPEG-2 broadcast

Figure 3. ILO physics instructor Terry Frisch demonstrates a concept to students over ICN from the Johnston High School video classroom, which is Voice over IP capable.

quality video, providing many of the elements that educators believe are missing in online courses. Students can access classes not available at their location, there is live interaction with an instructor, and the push-to-talk microphones are similar to having students raise their hands to ask a question. Students can ask questions and instantaneously receive an answer.

Online offerings have surpassed the traditional video classroom courses; however, the ICN video classroom remains an important tool for Iowa's small schools and communities. The ICN delivered more than 184,000 hours of video to K-12 districts and higher education institutions around Iowa in fiscal year 2006-07. High school students continue to benefit academically from high school, college-credit, and Advanced Placement classes offered over the ICN, which was the original intent of the network. Foreign languages outweigh other topics in the number of session hours, coming in last year at just over 5,000. On the college level, traditional and nontraditional students also have opportunities to participate in videoconferencing classes. Some community college consortiums have as many as 13 high school locations with students joining via video in career-focused coursework. Northeast Iowa Community College had

Figure 4.   Jim Christensen (right) of Northwest AEA and Sioux City Police Officer Chad Sheehan visit over the ICN with Wales Police Officer Lucy Bennet and Welsh students.

more than 200 students in the fall of 2007 taking classes through a health careers consortium. The University of Northern Iowa led the higher education usage last year and offers 15 programs over the ICN, including undergraduate and graduate programs, and one certificate program, to nontraditional students around the state, along with two online graduate programs.

Iowa Learning Online (ILO), an initiative of the Iowa Department of Education, offers several hybrid online/MPEG-2 videoconference classes, allowing the conflicting beliefs to come together while serving students. Location and accessibility factors are addressed, but the face-to-face factor remains. ILO offers classes to school districts for free or at a discounted rate. During the current school year, one ILO chemistry class has 31 students participat-

ing from South Page, Russell, Mormon Trail, Schaller-Crestland, Ankeny, Belmond-Klemme, and Waterloo School Districts. Students explore the central ideas of chemistry through online discussions, readings, online and kitchen labs, and problem-solving scenarios. Teachers use the ICN video classroom to discuss and view classroom demonstrations and laboratory experiments and to hold regular office hours. Students spend considerable time working on real-life problems in chemistry, and required regional labs are an integral part of the learning experience. Each student also has a student coach in his or her school. The districts participating in just this one chemistry class represent a diverse geographic and demographic populace of the state, further adding to the learning experience.

Today, we assume that students in a geographic area want to learn together. With the power of the Internet, geographic boundaries disappear and allow students to collaborate anywhere around the world. However, this is nothing new to the ICN, which has carried Iowa students to worlds outside their school corridors since 1995.

After his sixth grade class in the Galva Holstein School District (population just over 1,000) became the first elementary students to use the ICN in the fall of 1993, Jim Christiansen was hooked on using the network, and was determined to take his students to all corners of the world and then some. He created an interactive project linking middle-level students in schools across the state with NASA planetary exploration experts. Christensen then developed his Virtual Interaction Project Planning Model from which projects such as the AstroVIP emerged—interactive videoconferences conducted between Iowa students and astronauts at Johnson Space Center. He conducted the first videoconference between students and the crew of the International Space Station. Iowa students continue to connect to astronauts in flight and under water today.

During this time, Christensen also developed an international program linking students across the United States with students in the United Kingdom. To this day, oceans apart, enthusiastic third graders in two school communities regularly come together thanks to this project and ICN technology. Students in Sioux City, Iowa, and the country of Wales have created a tool for collaboration and international understanding by using the ICN. Their visits include topics such as holidays, sports, the cost of living, and the weather in Iowa. The Sioux City students even participated in a question and answer session with an American astronaut and Russian cosmonaut who were guests at the Welsh school.

Wales Halfway School Principal Colin Evans says the students play an integral part in the success of the program, helping decide the content of the conference at least 3 months in advance, allowing plenty of time for practice. In 6 years, they have streamlined the international exchange to involve two yearly ICN videoconferencing sessions, an "e-pal" program, and report sharing.

Another video session over the ICN brought together 29 students and faculty from four community colleges in Florida, Wisconsin, Illinois, and Washington, as well as one in Ecuador, so they could meet before a "Transcultural Nursing" study-abroad program, sponsored by Community Colleges for International Development. Headquarters for CCID are at Kirkwood Community College, in Cedar Rapids, Iowa, which hosted the meeting.

Numerous other sessions have crossed borders and brought students of all ages together, such as the 2006 National High School Mock Trial championship team from Valley High School in West Des Moines. The team was honored by their school in a celebration with their peers over the ICN, while the team was still in Oklahoma. The championship team beat 43 competing schools at the national competition in Oklahoma.

The anywhere concept does not just apply to K-12 or higher education students working together in the name of distance learning. Professional development and training have been prevalent over the ICN, and the network's role in the community has become even stronger. In telemedicine, the Midwest Rural Telemedicine Consortium (MRTC) is successful in educating health care professionals and specific patient groups across the ICN. The MRTC reaches out to hospital administrators, employees, patients, and the general public through accredited and nonaccredited programs and education classes, such as diabetes, pain management, and coping with cancer. The group reaches a wide audience, while saving time and mileage for all involved. The consortium has also sponsored international educational opportunities, such as connecting a doctor in Des Moines with a dermatological society in the Philippines.

The state library system relies heavily on the ICN to educate librarians and the public. Some examples include local and city government representatives learning how to help the U.S. Census Bureau prepare for the 2010 census, Public Library Management 1 and 2 courses, required for public librarian certification, and satellite downlinks of teleconferences provided by the College of DuPage in suburban Chicago. The state library also relies on the network as the backbone of its Web sites providing Iowans access to a wide range of learning resources, including library catalogs, databases, census data, patent information, and consumer health information.

In Iowa's far northeast corner, the ICN video classroom at Waukon High School has become an integral part of the community. The school led the way in room usage in fiscal year 2007, providing additional learning opportunities for the community. For 6 to 7 hours a day, high school students and adult learners took college credit classes ranging from medical related to statistics to entrepreneurship and marketing. Younger children participated in educational, interactive sessions offered by IPTV and educational and community professionals received training without the high costs of travel. The room has been so successful for the school and community that district officials asked Northeast Iowa Community College to include an ICN classroom in their satellite campus being built across the street from the high school.

MENTAL SHIFT

The days of students sitting in classrooms is rapidly changing. Student learning methods can be customized to their specific learning patterns with current technology advances. The adoption of new technologies by students is almost an innate process, but administrators and instructors struggle to keep up the pace. The next generation of tools allows collaboration without the need to be a technical wizard. Video over IP, Wikis, chat boards, discussion groups, and social networking sites—all are tools in the public domain making a rapid crossover into the educational arena and making time and place even less important factors in the decision process students and teachers use to seek out learning. All of these tools require non-blocking bandwidth, something the ICN has had to do since its early days.

Observing the social patterns of the multithreading next generation learners promotes the viewpoint that collaboration using technology is a more natural process for them than any preceding generation. These tools, with their ease of use, make collaboration a natural for even the most technically challenged person, and creating a mental shift that can push aside the factors of time and place.

The call for collaboration resounds throughout Iowa. More schools are coming together to offer courses in a collaborative manner as teaching resources become an increasingly scarce commodity. In the case of the BGM School District, Principal Radcliff used the ICN as a way to provide a monetary incentive for the teacher and maintain an academic option for his students and those in four other districts. More districts are looking at collaborative class sharing with other districts for fall 2008, as they grapple with the challenges of high fuel prices, teacher shortages, and meeting students' needs in rigor and standards.

For the ICN, collaboration in creating formats to deliver content created by partners that are valuable to students has been a priority over the last 4 years. A partnership with IPTV ensures the *K-12 Connections* virtual field trip program continues to operate and provides valuable professional development opportunities for all levels of school personnel. The innovation shown

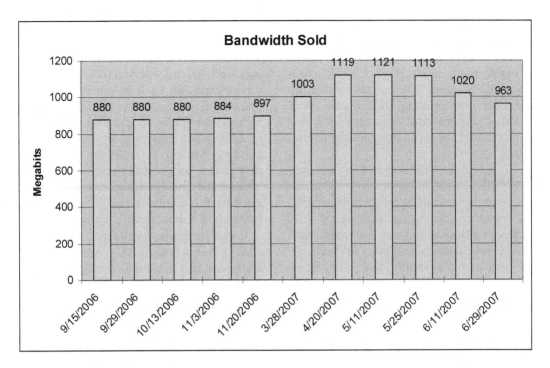

Bandwidth Sold

Figure 5. Educational entities use 74% of the Internet provided by the ICN. Downward trend reflects K-12 school year ending for the summer.

by the partnership has resulted in reaching large-scale, diverse audiences not reached before, such as school nurses and school food service professionals.

Iowa Learning Online continues to gather momentum, but increasingly uses Video over IP and Internet-based course software to deliver on the promise of distance learning. These initiatives use a mixture of technologies to deliver their content, and the ICN remains an essential piece of the whole solution delivered.

The shift in the expectations of students, parents, and the next generation of teachers is not happening; it has already happened. A mental shift among administrators and educators is slowly, but surely, kicking into gear. Time, space, soaring fuel costs, and financial resources have schools rethinking access to technology, and the rapidly evolving marketplace brings resource constraints to the forefront. Many Iowa school buildings do not have ICN video classrooms,

cannot afford a dedicated classroom, some of the rooms are already fully booked, and some have rooms being used for other purposes.

For the ICN, the shift from the video classroom to streaming content is taking place rapidly. The growth of Internet services has happened exponentially in a very short period. This shift is putting pressure on the ICN to adapt and adopt with its own mental shift. While the traditional video classroom usage has remained about the same over the last few years, the demand by schools for big Internet "pipes" has increased dramatically (see Figure 5).

IP has dynamically changed the way people interact in education, business, social networking, safety, and in health. Videoconferencing is one of those capabilities that is significantly changing through IP; providing a greater number of people access to communicate interactively as an alternative to face-to-face. ICN recognizes the need for a shift in delivery to provide schools, and other authorized users, greater access to videoconference—not as a replacement of its current video classroom MPEG-2 service, but one that compliments this service and, in the end, benefits students and educators by filling the voids felt in technology, budgets, and space.

In the early 1990s and before the commercialization of Internet, over 750 classrooms truly gave ICN the "WOW factor." Videoconferences using the legacy ICN video classrooms remain hallmark with broadcast-quality connections and reliability consistently averaging five 9s or higher. The quality of Video over IP does not equate to broadcast MPEG-2; however, users are adapting to their expectations over convenience, similar to cell phones versus landline phones. With the sleek, multipurpose, credit card-sized phones of today, do we still expect to have a call drop or to hit a dead spot, once in a while? Absolutely. Nevertheless, the benefits of convenience, access, and mobility outweigh those occasional frustrations with quality, lack of cell towers, and multitudes of plans. So much so, that many people have dropped their landlines completely. Such is the conundrum of tradition (ICN MPEG-2 video) versus advancement (Video over IP).

Students at Edgewood-Colesburg Elementary School can not learn from IPTV's *K-12 Connections* programs. They are 12 miles from the ICN video classroom at Edgewood-Colesburg High School—same district, different town, which is often the case in Iowa. Participation would mean transporting young children to the high school to participate. With Video over IP, the mobility and access of the equipment means a teacher can use it anywhere there is an Internet connection via a laptop or mobile PC. There is no dependency on a specific classroom.

A high school in northwest Iowa has an ICN video classroom, that is a "receive-only" site. However, they want to originate sessions, too, so they can have their teachers teach to other schools, possibly boosting a course or department struggling to stay afloat due to low enrollment. The costs of upgrading their current ICN classroom could significantly outweigh the cost of adding a Video over IP system in the building. Mobility and access come in to play again, as the equipment can move throughout the building, allowing more teachers the ability to use it for teaching curriculum enhancement or class sharing.

Connecting sites by using Video over IP takes a well-coordinated effort, since IP addresses and availability of participants need to be known. Congestion of Internet traffic may further impact the quality and sound of the videoconference. Various forms of equipment among schools might cause problems with the connections, and local Internet service providers may have different levels of quality of service that might affect the sessions. All that being noted, the fact remains that Video over IP addresses the void that schools face, given their constraints in access to technology, budgets, and space resources, while reflecting the world's shift in technological expectations.

SHIFTING GEARS

A high school principal receives a phone call from a seventh grader's parent, wanting to know if the student will have access to Chinese in 5 years when he reaches high school. A college freshman laments to her former high school counselor about the lack of access to advanced science and math classes, which would have better prepared her for college. Teachers request to teach in their school's ICN video classroom because it has more technology available to them than their regular classroom ... including something as simple as a CD or DVD player. New teachers yearn for more accessibility to the latest and greatest technology.

Technology continues to whittle away at the arguments of time and place in the Iowa classroom, where students and upcoming teachers have already shifted into high speed and are cruising in overdrive. The ICN is shifting, too, bringing these new technologies to current and future generations, with a focus on the new expectations and standards of today's educational world—mobility, access, and collaboration.

Just as technology has supported the increasing globalization of business, the ICN remains, and will continue to play, an integral part of the shifting solutions delivered for the globalization of Iowa education—transporting knowledge, instead of students.

Designing the "Perfect" Online *Program*

Michael Simonson

"The Perfect Online Course" was described by Orellana, Hudgins, and Simonson (2009). This book of readings clearly presented issues central to course design such as time, organization, production, evaluation, and accreditation. It is an important planning document for the distance educator.

Since then, best practices for course design have become much more widely understood. However, Orellana, Hudgins

Michael Simonson, Editor, *Distance Learning,* and Program Professor, Programs in Instructional Technology and Distance Education, Fischler School of Education, Nova Southeastern University, 1750 NE 167 St., North Miami Beach, FL 33162. Telephone: (954) 262-8563. E-mail: simsmich@nsu.nova.edu

and Simonson's book did not explain how to design the "perfect online *program.*" Developing an entire program to be offered at a distance is considerably more complex than designing an online course.

Schools, universities, and organizations are moving quickly to offer classes, programs, and training at a distance. Most seem to be gradually making the transition from traditional offerings to distance education by first trying parts of classes, then individual courses, next blended courses, and finally entire distance-delivered programs.

Documenting the process of transitioning from traditional offerings to distance education has not been a priority of those involved in this process. It seems that "trial and error" is the favored approach, rather than a more reasoned process supported by applied research. There are some guides available, if not all in one location. For example in 2005, Simonson wrote about the eight steps for transforming an organization, with the primary purpose of the transformation being the move to distance delivered offerings. And, in 2012, the development of distance education policy and plans was described. What is missing is a combination of the two approaches—the process of distance education implementation and the artifacts needed to support the move. Certainly, research is needed in this area.

At this point it has become clear that the following two components are needed when an organization plans to infuse distance education as a mission-central approach:

1. First, an academic technology/distance education plan is needed. This plan includes the following components:

   - vision statement;
   - mission statement;
   - guiding principles;
   - definitions;
   - goals;
   - policy development processes;
   - timeline;
   - policy review and faculty guidance;
   - references; and
   - resources.

2. Next, a process for diffusion and implementation of distance education is needed. This process includes these components:

   - development of a sense of urgency by the organization's leaders;
   - identification and empowerment of a powerful planning group;
   - identification of a clear, widely understood and agreed-on vision
   - identification of those willing to act on the vision;
   - development of plans to guarantee short term successes—successes that are widely publicized;
   - agreement on the process to combine successes; and
   - development and adoption of successes into models for additional implementation.

At the heart of the plan and process is the role of stakeholders, especially teachers, professors, and trainers. Certainly, leaders can and must support the transformation process, but those expected to implement changes—the teachers, professors, and trainers—are the groups who will promote or limit success.

The ingredients of a successful, distance delivered academic program include:

- committed and strong organizational leader;
- assessment and statement of need;
- technology plan with a detailed program for implementation of distance education;
- steering committee led by faculty that includes stakeholders such as students, staff, administrators, and alumni;
- detailed timeline;
- formative and summative evaluation plan;
- course design model, such as the unit-module-topic approach;
- full-time faculty person to implement the plan;
- instructional designer with media production skills;
- provision for a help desk for students and faculty;
- distance education policy manual for use by students, faculty, and most important, support staff;
- course management system and media production facilities and equipment;
- templates for syllabi and course components;
- budget.

And finally, it is important not to be overly worried about the many small decisions that must be made, for as Thoreau said, "Our life is frittered away by detail … simplify, simplify."

REFERENCES

Orellana, A., Hudgins, T. L., & Simonson, M. (Eds.) (2009). *The perfect online course*. Charlotte, NC: Information Age.

Simonson, M. (2005). Distance education: Eight steps for transforming an organization. *Quarterly Review of Distance Education*, 6(2), vii-viii.

Simonson, M., & Schlosser, C. (2012). Institutional policy issues. In M. Moore (Ed.), *Handbook of distance education* (3rd ed.). Mahwah, NJ: Erlbaum.

Part II
Institution-Based Applications of Distance Education

Michigan Virtual University
Providing Online Learning Opportunities

Sophia Lafayette

INTRODUCTION

Founded in 1998, Michigan Virtual University (MVU) is a 501(c)3 corporation that provides a variety of services to Michigan's K–12 education community focused in the area of online learning. This article will outline the historical context in which Michigan Virtual University was created and how it has transformed to its current state. MVU is

Sophia Lafayette,
Doctoral student, Nova Southeastern University, 4345 Livernois, Troy, Michigan 48098. Telephone: 248-343-4441.
E-mail: SBMWL91@gmail.com

not an actual university. Rather, it provides services focused on Michigan's K–12, not postsecondary environment. Furthermore, MVU does not issue diplomas. Examining the origins of MVU will help clarify why the organization's name includes the term "university."

THE ORIGINS OF MICHIGAN VIRTUAL UNIVERSITY

HISTORICAL CONTEXT

Michigan Virtual University can trace its roots to 1996. At that time, representatives from three of Michigan's major state universities—Michigan State University, the University of Michigan, and Wayne State University—met with the Michigan Economic Development Corporation (MEDC) to talk about how to successfully provide education and training to employees of the auto industry, Michigan's largest manufacturing industry and the main economic engine for the state. As a result of these conversations, which also included the big three auto companies of Michigan—Ford, Chrysler, and General Motors—and funding provided by MEDC, the Michigan Virtual Automotive College (MVAC) was created. The focus of MVAC was to provide training to employees of the automotive companies on topics that were considered nonproprietary, and would be beneficial to employees of all the companies. Some specific areas they focused on were leaner manufacturing and workplace safety (J. Fitzpatrick, personal communication, April 7, 2015).

After a few years, MEDC started to consider building capacity beyond the automotive industry and specifically utilize the Internet for broader workforce development. It was determined that MVAC was too narrow in its focus and that it was important to look at how training could be provided to other industries and fields in Michigan. Furthermore, MEDC recognized that they needed to consider how they could deliver this training in which time and distance were not a barrier to people located throughout Michigan (J. Fitzpatrick, personal communication, April 7, 2015).

CREATION OF MICHIGAN VIRTUAL UNIVERSITY

MVU was born in 1998 with the primary mission of providing workforce development to help improve economic development in Michigan. Interestingly enough, the K–12 education environment was not part of the initial focus for MVU. At that time MVU looked at training for adults in other major core workforce areas, including: manufacturing, healthcare, tourism, and small business development. Although MVU called itself a virtual university, it never had the intention of actually awarding diplomas or degrees. Its primary focus was always to provide supplemental training (J. Fitzpatrick, personal communication, April 7, 2015).

Another important focus of MVU in its original state was to help Michigan colleges and universities develop the ability to provide online learning opportunities to college students. Most of the universities at that time did not have the infrastructure or systems in place to offer online courses. MVU worked with universities to develop the infrastructure as well as provide training to faculty on how to design and teach online courses. Fitzpatrick states that he believes that "MVU was a catalyst for changing online learning in the state of Michigan," as a result of the conversations that were generated with universities throughout the state about the future of education and the inclusion of online learning as an integral component of that future (J. Fitzpatrick, personal communication, April 7, 2015).

In late 1999, conversations began to take place between the president of the Michigan Association of School Administrators, MVU, the business community, and then-Governor of Michigan, John Engler, regarding the idea of MVU sponsoring a school that focused more on K–12 education. At that time, approximately 40% of Michigan's schools had no AP offerings, so the focus of the school would be to provide Advanced Placement courses to high school students throughout Michigan. In 2000, Engler put a recommendation in the state budget to fund the concept of the Michigan Virtual School (MVS). The governor also recommended passage of Public Act 230 of 2000: legislation that would allow for the creation of MVS, operated by MVU (Michigan Virtual University, 2014a). The first major subdivision of MVU was born.

Although MVU was created with the intent of focusing on workforce development, after several years of the existence of the MVS, MVU determined in 2004 it was time to undergo a major reorganization. Under the direction of new leadership, the organization determined that it needed to shift its focus from higher education and the workforce and instead concentrate exclusively on K–12 education (J. Fitzpatrick, personal communication, April 7, 2015).

Since 2004, MVU has held true to its commitment to focus on K–12 education and has expanded significantly to include two additional subdivisions. Michigan

LearnPort provides online professional development and training to K–12 educators, and the Michigan Virtual Learning Research Institute engages in research activities to examine how to effectively implement online learning in K–12 schools.

ORGANIZATIONAL STRUCTURE OF MICHIGAN VIRTUAL UNIVERSITY

MVU is a 501(c)3 corporation funded in part by the state's general fund, but also brings in revenue through tuition, grants, and contracts. It is governed by a board of directors who represent a variety of industries, businesses, educational institutions (K–12 and postsecondary), and the state government. Michigan Virtual University provides governance, management, and fiscal oversight for all three of its subdivisions: MVS, Michigan LearnPort, and MVLRI (Michigan Virtual University, 2015a). Jamey Fitzpatrick serves as the president and chief executive officer of MVU. Table 1 outlines the leadership structure of Michigan Virtual University. The four levels of leadership of MVU provide governance, management and support for all three major subdivisions (Freidhoff, 2014).

MICHIGAN VIRTUAL SCHOOL, A DIVISION OF MICHIGAN VIRTUAL UNIVERSITY

MVS was established in 2000 with the passing of Public Act 230 of 2000. In the beginning, MVS focused on providing high school students access to online AP courses that were not available in their local schools. However, over the years MVS has expanded its course offerings and now provides over 200 different courses to students in multiple areas including academic core subjects, Advanced Placement courses, and credit recovery options (Michigan Virtual University, 2014b). MVS employs 17 full-time teachers and approximately 200 contract teachers to teach these courses. Although MVS course designers develop some of the course content, much of the content is purchased through third-party content providers. MVS hires highly qualified and certified teachers to teach its courses.

During the 2013–2014 school year MVS had over 21,000 course enrollments and since MVS's inception they have had approximately 170,000 total course enrollments (J. Freidhoff, personal communication, April 6, 2015). Table 2 shows the breakdown of the content areas where the majority of the course enrollments were focused in 2013–2014.

As shown in Table 2, the majority of enrollments are in core content areas, with the exception of foreign language and literature. MVS also has enrollments in areas such as business and marketing; physical, health, and safety education; fine and performing arts; and computer and information sciences. However, each of these other categories represent less than 5% of the total enrollments (Michigan Virtual University, 2014b).

Table 1. Leadership Structure of Michigan Virtual University

Level 1	One person serves as president and chief executive officer
Level 2	Four officers —One of which is the chief executive officer
Level 3	Executive Leadership Team (ELT) —Consists of four officers and four additional executive directors
Level 4	Leadership Team (LT) —Includes all members of the ELT plus 11 middle management-level personnel

Table 2. Michigan Virtual School 2013–2014 Course Enrollments by Subject Area

Subject Area	Total Enrollments (21,142) 2013–2014	
	Percentage	Number
1. Foreign Language and Literature	21.4%	4,522
2. Social Sciences and History	16.1%	3,396
3. Mathematics	14.7%	3,101
4. Life and Physical Sciences	11.7%	2,473
5. English Language and Literature	7.8%	1,653

One key point to understand about MVS is that it is not a stand-alone cyber school and it does not issue diplomas. MVS would be more accurately described as a supplementary online learning program. Typically most students who enroll in courses take one or two courses to supplement the courses they take from their traditional brick-and-mortar school. Most courses cost in the range of $270–$300 (Michigan Virtual School, 2015a). However, today most students can take online courses from Michigan Virtual School for free due to legislation passed in 2013.

In 2013, the Michigan legislature passed Section 21f of the State School Aid Act, which provided that any student in 6th–12th grade enrolled in a public school was eligible to enroll in up to two online courses per academic semester and that the district in which the student is enrolled is obligated to pay the cost for the course(s) using a portion of its state per-pupil foundation allowance. One key point regarding this provision is that the district is responsible only for paying for courses that replace courses the student would take as part of a normal course load. In other words, students in a traditional high school typically take six classes as a full course load. They could take four of their classes at their traditional school and then enroll in two online courses that the district would be responsible for paying for. Student who wants to take a larger course load than traditionally offered by their

local school would be required to pay for those courses. Section 21f also allows for local school districts to create their own online courses that students can enroll in. All districts must advertise their courses through the Michigan Online Course Catalog and any student from any district can enroll in any course listed in the state catalog. By the 2013–2014 school year, there were over 319,000 virtual enrollments by 76,000 students across the state. Approximately 95% of those course enrollments were not provided by MVS, but through local school districts, cyber schools, and charter schools in the state (Freidhoff, 2014).

MICHIGAN LEARNPORT, A DIVISION OF MICHIGAN VIRTUAL UNIVERSITY

In the 2003–2004 school year, 3 years after Michigan Virtual School was established, Michigan LearnPort, an online professional development portal, was created. According to Jason Marentette, professional services manager for Michigan LearnPort, at the time it was established, LearnPort was funded entirely by the federal Elementary and Secondary Education Act Title II for the purpose of improving teacher effectiveness (J. Marentette, personal communication, April 6, 2015). By the 2008–2009 school year, Michigan LearnPort had over 45,000 user accounts and more than 300 courses in its course catalog (Michigan LearnPort, 2015).

In 2008, a needs assessment survey was given to educators throughout the state to help determine the areas in which educators felt they needed online professional development the most. The Michigan LearnPort Content Needs Assessment Survey had 600 people provide feedback about the type of courses they felt Michigan LearnPort should offer to help them grow professionally. The top five areas were: curriculum alignment and development, technology integration, assessment, differentiated instruction, and instructional strategies. At the time of the survey, Michigan LearnPort was already offering courses in all of the areas except assessment (Michigan LearnPort, 2008). By the school year of 2010–2011, Michigan LearnPort had over 60,000 user accounts.

A significant change occurred with Michigan LearnPort during the 2011–2012 fiscal year, when LearnPort began to be funded entirely by the State of Michigan's General Funds (Michigan LearnPort, 2008). Marentette explains that this was a key turning point for the organization, as it allowed LearnPort to expand course offerings to a larger K–12 professional constituency beyond teachers. Offerings were created and made available to school employees at all levels, including administrators, counselors, paraprofessionals, food and nutrition workers, custodians, and other service providers (J. Marentette, personal communication, April 6, 2015). Courses expanded beyond teacher content, incorporating compliance training topics such as food safety, sexual harassment, and blood-borne pathogens training. Online courses in LearnPort are offered through a variety of means including self-paced study, instructor-led, and on-demand webinars.

Not only could teachers take courses to benefit themselves professionally, but teachers could also utilize many of these courses towards the renewal of their Michigan teacher certification. Additionally, in the 2013–2014 school year, Michigan legislation went into effect that changed the teacher certification renewal process to include teacher attendance on professional development days as an activity they could use towards that renewal. Since then, Michigan LearnPort has been working with school districts to see how it can better service the districts' mandated professional development days with a blend of face-to-face training sessions and presentations and the online resources available through the Michigan LearnPort catalog. As of 2013–2014, LearnPort had over 81,000 user accounts and over 800 offerings in its catalog and it continues to grow (Michigan LearnPort, 2015). Marentette explains that LearnPort is now considering how the division can offer services and support for teachers and administrators on the state's educator evaluation process (J. Marentette, personal communication, April 6, 2015).

MICHIGAN VIRTUAL LEARNING RESEARCH INSTITUTE, A DIVISION OF MICHIGAN VIRTUAL UNIVERSITY

Michigan Virtual Learning Research Institute is the most recent addition to the Michigan Virtual University organization. It was established in 2012 when the state legislature approached MVU with the idea of creating an institute to help provide quality control and distill best practices of online and blended learning through scholarly research. The legislature passed Public Act 201 of 2012 that officially established Michigan Virtual Learning Research Institute (MVLRI) as the third division of Michigan Virtual University (Michigan Virtual University, 2014a). According to the MVLRI website the primary goal of the division "is to expand Michigan's capacity to support new learning models, engage in active research to inform new policies in online and blended learning, and strengthen the state's infrastructures for sharing best practices" (Michigan Virtual Learning Research Institute, 2015).

Through a memorandum of understanding with the Michigan Department of Education and the Center for Educational Performance and Information, MVLRI uses student data to produce an annual effectiveness report. The findings from the most recent *Michigan's K–12 Effectiveness Report* (Freidhoff, 2014) provided some important findings regarding online learning in Michigan, including:

1. Michigan students accounted for 319,630 virtual enrollments in the 2013-14 school year, an increase of over 134,577 virtual enrollments from the prior year. Only 5% of those enrollments were delivered by MVS.
2. Although almost 90% of enrollments were by secondary students (Grades 7-12), elementary level students had the highest year-over-year percentage growth.
3. Fifty-seven percent of virtual enrollments from virtual students ended with a completion status of "completed/passed." Those same virtual students, however, passed their non-virtual courses 71% of the time. In contrast, non-virtual learners passed their traditional courses 87% of the time.
4. Of the virtual learners taking courses, those taking courses through MVS had a passed/completed rate of 72%, while cyber schools had a rate of 54%, and local districts rate was 57%.
5. Students who tend to have lower levels of academic success are being directed to take virtual courses, primarily in core content areas.

According to Freidhoff (2015), these findings offer questions for MVLRI to consider as they look at research about best practices for online and blended learning implementation. For example, what types of support are local districts and cyber schools providing to students who take online courses? Although the 21f legislation includes a provision that local districts

must provide a mentor for each student in their local district taking online courses, questions arise as to the quality and consistency of how those mentors provide support to students. The results of the most recent effectiveness report will help MVLRI determine where additional research and leadership efforts should be focused.

MVLRI has played a key role in developing and offering support for schools and students involved in online and blended learning. It has developed several publications to provide best practices and guidance on how to successfully implement or take advantage of online and blended learning courses. It developed a 21f "Implementation Guide" (Michigan Virtual University, 2014c) tool kit to help schools through the process of implementing the 21f legislation that allows students to take up to two online courses in place of courses taken in their local school. Another important publication that MVLRI was key in helping to develop was a parent guide (Michigan Virtual University, 2014e) that helps parents determine if online learning is best for their child and how to support their child through the process of successful completion of online courses.

MVLRI has also partnered with the International Association for K–12 Online Learning (iNACOL) for several other efforts that the institute is involved in. This includes working with iNACOL to manage the Research Clearinghouse for K–12 Blended & Online Learning (Michigan Virtual Learning Research Institute, 2015). The clearinghouse was established in February 2013, but contains articles predating 2013 (Research, 2015). Finally, MVLRI also maintains Michigan's Online Learning Course Catalog and the Online Learning Orientation Tool (Michigan Virtual Learning Research Institute, 2015). The addition of MVLRI as the latest division of Michigan Virtual University has clearly been beneficial to supporting the

Table 3.   Michigan Virtual University Goals

Goal Name	Goal Description
1. Market awareness	1. MVU will increase awareness of its products and services and their value.
2. Capacity building	2. MVU will grow its professional competencies as well as those of Michigan school districts and professional organizations.
3. Management of outcomes	3. MVU will improve outcomes from the uses of its products and services.
4. Financial sustainability	4. MVU will implement strategies to promote financial sustainability.
5. Data driven decision making	5. MVU will collect and use data in decision making throughout the organization.

Source: Michigan Virtual University (2014a, p. 9).

implementation of online learning in the State of Michigan.

THE FUTURE OF MICHIGAN VIRTUAL UNIVERSITY

Michigan Virtual University has established itself as the key organization in the state to support online learning initiatives through its three major subdivisions: Michigan Virtual School, Michigan Learn-Port, and Michigan Virtual Learning Research Institute. MVU was founded on the idea of building the capacity of people in the state of Michigan to support and improve the economy. Jamey Fitzpatrick, chief executive officer and president, says that MVU is really all about "teaching more people how to fish" (J. Fitzpatrick, personal communication, April 7, 2015). Fitzpatrick and those who support the efforts of MVU believe the best way to do this is to leverage technology to provide personalized learning opportunities for all students and educators in Michigan (J. Fitzpatrick, personal communication, April 7, 2015).

In an effort to plan for the future of MVU and its continued endeavors to support online learning in the state, the organization commenced a strategic planning process in the summer of 2013. Through that planning process, MVU developed five key goals (Michigan Virtual University, 2014a). Those goals are displayed in Table 3.

For each of the goals created, MVU has begun developing action strategies to support the attainment of those goals. Although MVU has served as a catalyst for implementation of online learning opportunities in Michigan, it recognizes there is much work still to be done to improve the quality and success of online learning delivery throughout the state. MVU's current strategic plan has laid the groundwork for helping it achieve its vision of being "Michigan's digital learning leader advancing personalized education for all learners" (Michigan Virtual University, 2014a, p. 8).

REFERENCES

Freidhoff, J. (2014). *Michigan's K–12 virtual learning effectiveness report 2013–2014.* Lansing, MI: Michigan Virtual University.

Michigan LearnPort. (2008). *2008 content needs assessment survey: Summary report.* Lansing, MI: Michigan Virtual University.

Michigan LearnPort. (2015). Michigan Learn-Port history: Serving Michigan educators and organizations since 2003. Retrieved from http://www.learnport.org/About-Us/History

Michigan Virtual Learning Research Institute. (2015). Michigan Virtual Learning Research Institute: A division of MVU. Retrieved from http://www.mvlri.org/

Michigan Virtual University. (2014a). *Strategic decisions: A framework for the future.* Lansing, MI: Michigan Virtual University.

Michigan Virtual University. (2014b). *A report to the legislature.* Lansing, MI: Michigan Virtual University.

Michigan Virtual University. (2014c). *Implementation guidelines: Section 21f of the state school aid act, Version 2.* Lansing, MI: Michigan Virtual University.

Michigan Virtual University. (2014d). *Mentor fundamentals: A guide for mentoring online learners.* Lansing, MI: Michigan Virtual University.

Michigan Virtual University. (2014e). *Parent guide to online learning.* Lansing, MI: Michigan Virtual University.

Michigan Virtual School. (2015a). Pricing information. Retrieved from http://www.mvhs.org/Parents/Pricing-Information

Michigan Virtual University. (2015b). MVU at a glance. Retrieved from http://www.mivu.org/About-Us/MVU-Facts

Michigan Virtual University. (n.d.). *Planning guide for online and blended learning.* Lansing, MI: Michigan Virtual University.

Research Clearinghouse for K–12 Blended & Online Learning. (2015). Retrieved from http://k12onlineresearch.org

Navy College Program for Afloat College Education

Christopher Bergeron

INTRODUCTION

The U.S. Navy has ships deployed around the globe, which brings with it the unique needs regarding delivering a quality college education to the sailors aboard on active duty. The purpose of this article is to outline the U.S. Navy's distance learning programs for supporting sailors at sea.

The Naval Education and Training Command is responsible for the education and training of naval personal. Under their command is the Center for Personal and Professional development, which has the mission "to develop the Navy's workforce by providing education and training opportunities that build personal, professional, and leadership competencies in support of mission readiness" (U.S. Navy, 2013c, para. 3). Offerings under the Center for Personal and Professional Development are broken into three categories: personal development, professional development, and voluntary education. Personal and professional development courses are delivered online via the Navy Knowledge Online portal or by CD-ROM as well as classroom format at established sites and via mobile training teams (U.S. Navy, 2013a) The different components to the voluntary education program is targeted to provide a different set of services to its respective customers (McLaughlin, 2010)

Under the volunteer education program sailors have the opportunity to take correspondence courses or online courses through the navy's distance learning partnerships and use a combination of the Navy's tuition assistance program and the Montgomery GI Bill where 43 partner institutions deliver courses via internet, CD-ROM, USB drive, and paper to complete degree requirements. Sailors at sea also have the opportunity to take distance learning courses from the Navy College Program for Afloat College Education, where ten partner institutions have partnered with the U.S. Navy to target their program for sailors deployed in areas where Internet access cannot be guaranteed.

The tuition assistance program offered through the Navy College Distance Learn-

Christopher Bergeron,
39 Cinnamon Ridge Road,
Somersworth, NH 03878.
Telephone: (603) 842-0407.
E-mail: cb1808@nova.edu

ing Partnership and the Navy College Program for Afloat College Education are the two programs that more than allow for sailors to pursue college degrees in their off duty time while deployed but require participants to be actively working toward a college degree to be eligible (U.S. Navy, 2013a)

NAVY COLLEGE PROGRAM DISTANCE LEARNING PARTNERSHIP

The Navy College Program Distance Learning Partnership was piloted in 1999 with five distance learning partners. Initially the sailors were required to choose a program that was directly related to their rating or field (McLaughlin, 2010). The partnership approach was chosen to allow "greater flexibility, as well as a more open approach to generating ideas," according to one of the Navy commanders on the project (Carr, 2000, p. A60). But the Navy was interested in more than just online courses since "The education environment of our sailors includes frequent deployments, infrequent or intermittent Internet connectivity, and a mobile lifestyle," said the commander. "Thus, not only is the number of distance-learning courses offered important, but also a variety of distance-learning formats" (Carr, 2000, p. 60). As a result, the agreement's memorandum of understanding specifically includes the requirement that courses must be available without Internet access (Carr, 2000; McLaughlin, 2010).

In 2004 the program was expanded to cover all of the Navy's ratings with 96 degree choices and 17 partner institutions (McLaughlin, 2010). In 2007 the Navy College Program Distance Learning Partnership removed the requirement that sailors take a course of study directly related to their Navy rating or field. The increased flexibility allowed for both wider participation and the opportunity for a wider variety of degrees to be pursued. By 2010 the program had grown to 34 fully accredited

academic institutions offering a total of 264 degree programs at the associate and baccalaureate level (McLaughlin, 2010). There are currently 43 institutions participating in the program (U.S. Navy, 2013b).

Participation in distance learning courses grew steadily between 2000 and 2007; the number of sailors taking distance courses with the tuition assistance program grew tenfold, while face-to-face enrollment fell by 29% in the same time period, with distance learning enrollment exceeding classroom enrollment in 2006 (Mehay & Pema, 2010).

NAVY COLLEGE PROGRAM FOR AFLOAT COLLEGE EDUCATION

Sailors at sea also have the option of using the Navy College Program for Afloat College Education, which offers courses free of charge and also offers the additional benefit of master's degree programs (U.S. Navy, 2013b). Central Texas College has been contracted by the U.S. Navy to administer the Navy College Program for Afloat College Education (NCPACE) and offers the opportunity for sailors to continue their education while on sea duty assignments. The program offers instructor delivered and distance learning courses. The distance learning courses are offered by a consortium of 10 colleges that have service-member opportunity agreements to ensure that the credits are transferable. Because NCPACE tuition is covered by the Navy, sailors pay only for textbooks and materials.

NCPACE is specifically targeted for service members who would otherwise have difficulty gaining access to college courses due to physical isolation, a lack of reliable Internet access, and unpredictable work schedules (Park, 2011). Distance learning courses are delivered via CD-ROM, PDA, and MP4 methods since ships at sea cannot guarantee reliable and consistent Internet access. A total of 287 distance learning courses are offered at the associate's degree, bachelor's degree, and master's degree levels. There are currently 42 associate's degrees, 24 bachelor's degrees and six master's degrees available via the program.

In order to participate in the program sailors need permission from their command to register, they need to have completed an individualized education plan with their ship's education service officer to outline the list of courses needed to complete a degree and to ensure that the sailor understands the requirements of the degree path chosen. Prospective students must take an ACT ASSET test to assess math and English skills (can be administered by Navy College or by the ship's education service officer) or have proof of prior college level coursework and complete a distance learning assessment for distance learning courses as a way to stem previously lower distance learning completion rates.

Sailors then register with their education service officer and buy books. Surface Sailors have 14 days from the start date to drop the course without penalty, and Submarine Sailors have 30 days from the term start date to drop without penalty by seeing their educational service officer to drop the course. The course terms run 90 days and sailors are advised to pace themselves in the distance learning program with a midterm at six weeks and a final at 12 weeks which are proctored by the ship's education service officer.

Ninety-seven percent of program participants are enlisted sailors, with 82.5% falling within the pay grades of E3-E6. Higher ranked sailors had higher rates of success, with E6's three times more likely than E1's to be successful. With the high demands of active duty at sea, only 48.1% of first time technology course students were successful at completing their first course, while 79.5% first-time instructor-led students were successful (McLaughlin, 2010).

The difficulty of taking classes during off-duty time demonstrates that sailors who enroll in distance learning classes may have higher ability and motivation levels than those who do not enroll in courses (McLaughlin, 2010). With active duty on a naval vessel being more than a full-time job, first-time distance learners are limited to a single course and returning distance leaners are limited to two simultaneous courses.

DISTANCE DEGREES OFFERED VIA NCPACE

42 ASSOCIATE'S DEGREES

- Associate of applied science from Central Texas College (Not intended as the first two years of a bachelor's degree): applied management, applied technology, business management, and criminal justice
- Associate of Arts in General Studies From Central Texas College
- Associate degrees from Coastline Community College (each can transfer 100% into a bachelor's degree with several universities): American studies, administrative manager, arts and humanities, business administration, communications, computer networking: Cisco, computer network: Microsoft, computer networking: security, electronics, emergency management/Homeland security, financial manager, general accounting, general business, general office manager, gerontology, health and fitness, healthcare management, history, human resources management, human services, management, marketing, psychology, science and math, small business management, social and behavioral science, sociology, spanish, supervision and management, and supply chain management
- Associate in arts general education/ undergraduate transfer from Dallas Colleges Online

- Associate in science general education/undergraduate transfer from Dallas Colleges Online
- Associate of science in computer and information science from ECPI University
- Associate of science from Vincennes University in law enforcement, administration of justice, criminal justice, and corrections

24 BACHELOR'S DEGREES

- Bachelor of science in business administration from ECPI University
- Bachelor of arts in interdisciplinary studies from Governors State University
- Bachelor of science in engineering technology from Old Dominion University
- Bachelor of arts in Criminal Justice from Saint Leo University
- Bachelor of arts from Thomas Edison State College in liberal studies, social sciences, humanities, natural science/mathematics, history, and psychology
- Bachelor of science in business administration from Thomas Edison State College
- Bachelor of science in applied science and technology for air traffic control, electronics engineering technology, nuclear medicine, biomedical electronics, electrical technology, nuclear energy engineering technology, clinical laboratory science, medical imaging, nuclear engineering technology from Thomas Edison State College
- Bachelor of arts in administrative leadership from the University of Oklahoma

6 MASTER'S DEGREES

- Master of engineering management from Old Dominion University (for graduates of Navy's Officer Nuclear Power School)
- Master of business administration from Saint Leo University
- Master of science in criminal justice from Saint Leo University
- Master of science in critical incident management from Saint Leo University
- Master of arts in administrative leadership from the University of Oklahoma

REFERENCES

Carr, S. (2000). Navy picks institutions for online-learning effort. *Chronicle of Higher Education, 47*(12), A60.

McLaughlin, J. P. (2010, March). *A statistical analysis of the effect of the Navy's tuition assistance program: Do distance learning classes make a difference?* (Master's thesis). Graduate School of Business and Public Policy, Naval Postgraduate School, Monterey, CA.

Mehay, S. L., & Pema, E. (2010). *Analysis of the tuition assistance program: Does the method of instruction matter in TA classes?* (Report). Monterey, CA: Naval Postgraduate School.

Park, S. C. (2011, March). *Effectiveness of voluntary education in operational environments: An analysis of the Navy College program for afloat college education (NCPACE).* (Master's thesis). Naval Postgraduate School, Monterey, CA.

U.S. Navy. (2013a). Navy College Program. Retrieved from https://www.navycollege.navy.mil

U.S. Navy. (2013b). NETC homepage. Retrieved from http://www.netc.navy.mil

U.S. Navy. (2013c). Center for Personal and Professional Development. Retrieved from https://www.netc.navy.mil/centers/cppd/

UMassOnline

Online Education
at the University of Massachusetts

Eileen B. Perez

INTRODUCTION

This article presents an overview of UMassOnline, the online learning organization within the University of Massachusetts. The article begins with an overview of three distance education models commonly found in higher education. Next a brief history of the University of Massachusetts system sets the stage for the introduction of UMassOnline. The organizational and reporting structures of both the university system and UMassOnline follow. A discussion of enrollment figures, programs, and degrees offered online is covered. Once an understanding of the

Eileen B. Perez,
Assistant Professor and Developmental Mathematics Program Director, Worcester State University, 486 Chandler Street, Worcester, MA 01602-2597.
Telephone: (508) 929-8977.
E-mail: eileen.perez@worcester.edu

online learning program has been established, the findings of a 2012 online education report requested by the president of the university are detailed. The article concludes with a discussion of the potential future direction of UMassOnline based on the report's findings.

DISTANCE EDUCATION MODELS

Online learning programs in higher education tend to follow one of three models: standalone, integrated, or consortium. Standalone programs are those programs only offering online courses such as Westerner Governors University (Eastmond, 2013). An integrated online learning program is one where online is embedded alongside an institute's traditional campus based programs, for example Nova Southeastern University. A consortium-based model is formed from an association of institutes that share resources to deliver online programs. UMassOnline is a consortium-based online learning program bringing together the vast resources on each of the University of Massachusetts campuses under the state's Department of Higher Education. A history of the evolution of the university systems precedes the introduction of UMassOnline.

UNIVERSITY OF MASSACHUSETTS HISTORY

The University of Massachusetts was founded in 1863 with 56 students and four faculty members as a land-grant agricultural college named Massachusetts Agricultural College. The college was set in Amherst, a town located in the western, rural region of the state (UMass Amherst History, n.d.; Office of the Chancellor, n.d.). Due to growth in both programs and size, in 1931 the state renamed the institution Massachusetts State College. With more growth fueled by the influx of GI Bill funded soldier-students after World War II the institution achieved University status in 1947. Growth continued with the baby-boomers generation during the 1960s and 1970s. The focus of the university shifted to research, the academic standing improved, program offerings increased, admissions standards rose, and prestigious faculty arrived, all leading to the designation of the Amherst site as the Research University and the flagship campus of the UMASS system in 2003. Enrollment over time grew from 1,263 in 1941, to 7,600 in 1963; by 1993 there were over 18,000 students, and nearly 28,000 undergraduate and graduate students as of 2013.

The Boston campus was formed in 1964 by an act of the state legislature to meet the growing needs of the urban and commuter student (UMass Boston History, n.d.). The college relocated to the present Dorchester campus in 1974. Boston State College, founded in 1852 as a teacher's normal school, was incorporated into University of Massachusetts Boston in 1982. Today the Boston campus serves over 16,000 students across its eight colleges.

The Worcester campus was established by act of the state legislature in 1962 to create the only public medical school in the state (UMass Worcester History, n.d.). The first class of 16 medical students entered the accredited program in 1970. The teaching hospital was established in 1976. Today the educational campus includes the School of Medicine, the Graduate School of Biomedical Sciences, and the Graduate School of Nursing. The campus has expanded to include dozens of buildings, a large teaching hospital serving the central region of the state, and a research complex. The Medical School consistently ranks in the top 10% of medical schools, and a 2006 Nobel Prize in physiology or medicine was won by a researcher at the affiliated research center, demonstrating the prestige of the site.

The Lowell campus has its roots in two institutions (UMass Lowell History n.d.). First, the Lowell Normal School, founded in 1894 to train teachers and later known as Lowell State. The second, the Lowell Textile School, which trained technicians and managers for industry and was later known as Lowell Tech. Lowell State and Lowell Tech merged in 1975, forming the University of Lowell which subsequently joined the UMass System in 1991. Today the University of Massachusetts Lowell campus serves over 16,000 undergraduate and graduate students, offers 120 undergraduate, 39 master's, and 33 doctoral degrees across its six colleges. The Lowell campus today focuses on high technology.

The Dartmouth campus also grew from two earlier institutes, the New Bedford Textile School and the Bradford Durfee Textile School in Fall River (UMass Dartmouth History, n.d.). As textile manufacturing left the area, the institutes expanded to serve the needs of students under the GI Bill. In 1962 the state legislator joined these two institutes to form the Southeastern Massachusetts Technological Institute and began building the centrally located Dartmouth campus. Southeastern Massachusetts Technological Institute expanded and was renamed Southeastern Massachusetts University in 1969 to reflect expanded program offerings. Southeastern Massachusetts University joined the UMass Family in 1991 and became known as University of Massachusetts Dartmouth. Today the campus serves over 9,000 students and is home to the new and only public law school in the state.

In 2001 the University of Massachusetts welcomed its newest member, UMassOnline (UMassOnline About, n.d.). The division began with the dual goals of meeting the needs of online learners in higher education through accredited programs and giving the University of Massachusetts a presence in the growing field of online learning. An objective was to leverage the reputation of the university system as an outstanding public research focused university system for the newly formed online branch.

ONLINE LEARNING AT THE UNIVERSITY OF MASSACHUSETTS

REPORTING STRUCTURE

Before discussing UMassOnline in detail, an understanding of the multilayered reporting structure within the state educational system is beneficial. Two state level departments reporting to the governor are responsible for education, the Department of Elementary and Secondary Education (DOE) and the Department of Higher Education (DOHE) (DOE, n.d.; DOHE, n.d.). The Board of Higher Education governs higher education and the DOHE and consists of members appointed by the governor. Staff of DOHE report to a commissioner and are charged with implementing the policies of the Board of Higher Education and the day-to-day administration of higher education. Three divisions fall under the Board of Higher Education and the DOHE. The 15 community colleges, nine state universities, and the University of Massachusetts are each a division. A board of directors oversees each of the community colleges and state universities, but not the University of Massachusetts campuses.

The administration of the entire University of Massachusetts system resides with the president and a common board of directors overseeing the entire university system. The board of directors, comprised of lay trustees, governs the system and sets policy on matters including budget and tuition, while the president and his office are responsible for operations (BOT, n.d.). In addition, each of the five University of Massachusetts campuses has a local Chancellor and an administration overseeing local operations (UMass System, n.d.). Unlike the University of Massachusetts campuses, which are led by individual chancellors, UMassOnline is led by a chief executive officer who reports to the office of the President of the University of Massachusetts. This reporting structure had caused conflict with the campuses regarding the autonomy and role of UMassOnline (Mellenbrook Policy Advisors, 2012).

UMASSONLINE ORGANIZATIONAL STRUCTURE AND FUNDING

Being a consortium means UMassOnline has a small staff supporting marketing and technology (UMass Online Team, n.d.). In 2013 the staff numbered less than a dozen full time members. The organizational staff remains small because all teaching staff reside on one of the five campuses and reports to their campus.

Financial obligations include covering the operational budget, repaying a loan for startup costs to the Trustee's Loan Pool, and returning net revenues to the five campuses (Mellenbrook Policy Advisors, 2012). For fiscal year (FY) 2010 major expense categories were marketing and business development, technology, and administration. Funding for the organization comes from three sources: an assessment for each of the five campuses, technology hosting for third parties, and the University of Massachusetts President's Office. The contribution from the President's Office covers expenses related to state funded programs within the system. Up until 2007 UMassOnline ran a budget deficit. Annual budget details can be found in Table 1. The data shows a profit of over $1.2 million for FY 2010, but this figure needs to be regarded with caution due to $680,000 in FY 20110 expenses deferred to FY 2011. The organization has paid off its loans and completed on time several tech-

Table 1. Annual Budget

Fiscal Year	Revenue	President's Contribution
2007	45,000	1,150,000
2008	13,900	1,150,000
2009	4,000	850,000
2010	1,256,724	700,000
2011	Not available*	500,000

Note: *Data from early 2012.

nology related one-time payments, putting the organization in position for continued profitability from FY 2011 on.

ONLINE LEARNING FUNDING

Online learning on each of the five physical campuses falls within the continuing education division (Mellenbrook Policy Advisors, 2012). Having online learning within continuing education has financial implications due to the way the state educational budget operates. For day classes, tuition at all of the institutions of higher education is retained by the state, while fees are kept by each institution. This distinction often leads to fee increases while keeping tuition constant. This structure leads to confusion on actual cost of courses for students. Unlike day courses, both tuition and fees are retained locally within continuing education divisions, which are seen as self-supporting and an area of financial growth on campus. For this reason online learning was placed in continuing education when the decision was made to expand online learning with the introduction of UMassOnline in 2001.

UMASSONLINE ENROLLMENT, PROGRAMS, AND DEGREE OFFERINGS

UMassOnline enrollment grew from 5,009 in its first year, 2001, to about 59,000 in its 10th year, 2011-2012 (About UMassOnline, n.d.; Facts 2012-2013, 2013). Details for annual enrollment can be found

in Figure 1. Program offerings have expanded to included 113 online programs as of 2011, including degrees from the associate level to the doctoral level. Several certificate and professional development programs are also offered. A detailed breakdown of programs by campus can be found in Table 2. In FY 2011 online learning within the University of Massachusetts System brought in over $65 million in tuition while serving 51,097 students (President's Office, n.d.).

ONLINE EDUCATION AT THE UNIVERSITY OF MASSACHUSETTS REVIEWED

In 2012 the president of the University of Massachusetts engaged Mellenbrook Policy Advisors to review online education (Mellenbrook Policy Advisors, 2012). The goal of the Mellenbrook study was to provide a complete overview of the opportunities for online education within the system. To do this the study discussed the political, educational, financial, and institutional settings that influence online learning in the state system. The evaluation was to explore online learning at each of the five campuses and UMassOnline. Interviews were conducted, documents reviewed, and comparisons with online models at others schools made. The relationship between the five campuses and UMassOnline was explored, as was the validity of UMassOnline as implemented.

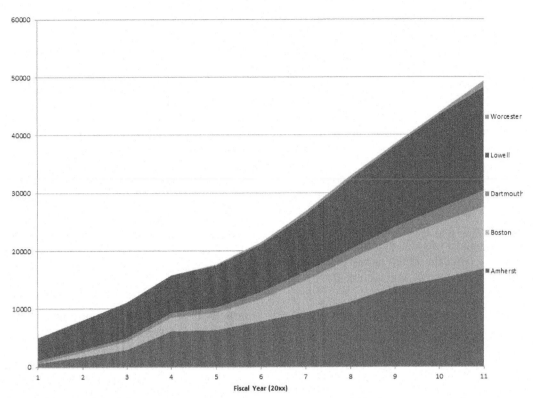

Figure 1.   Online enrollment.

Table 2.   Programs by Campus

Program Type	Amherst	Boston	Dartmouth	Lowell	Worcester
Noncredit Certificate	3	0	1	0	0
Certificate	5	13	10	23	1
Bachelor's	12	2	3	5	0
Master's	5	10	1	9	0
Doctoral	1	1	0	0	0
Professional	1	5	0	0	0
Continuing Ed Units	0	0	0	0	1
Total	27	31	15	37	2

ONLINE LEARNING AND THE FIVE CAMPUSES

In exploring online learning at each of the campuses, the reviewers found two campuses, Amherst and Lowell, fully engaged in online learning with strong faculty support. Boston showed small but growing online offerings and further growth is anticipated due to the creation of the online-centered University College within the Boston campus. Dartmouth and Worcester were nearly absent in online learning, according to the study. Additionally, the program offerings at the Amherst campus were concentrated in one area, business administration and the Isenberg School of Management. The offerings at Lowell concentrated on more fields, including technology, psychology, and business. The study also found more faculty support and engagement for online learning at Amherst and Lowell. This finding was attributed to funding and support. Faculty fellows from Amherst developed a handbook called *Teaching and Learning Online: Communications, Community, and Assessment* to help faculty transition to online teaching (Feldman & Zucker, 2011). The creation of the handbook received funding from the office of the President of the University of Massachusetts and is public.

UMassOnline

The goals for UMassOnline when founded were to meet the needs of online learners in higher education through accredited programs and giving the University of Massachusetts a presence in the expanding field of online education. The three roles originally defined to meet these goals for UMassOnline were (a) technology leadership for online learning including learning management system (LMS), (b) marketing and branding of online learning for the university system, and (c) to identify programs areas with a demand for online learning and possibly develop online programs.

The role of technology leadership was evident in the selection of a new LMS. According to UMassOnline leadership the process of evaluation and selection was open and transparent, although some of the campuses do not concur. According to Mellenbrook (2012), the selection of a single LMS for the university system achieves significant cost savings, including support costs. Additionally, having a common LMS enables cross campus collaboration. Generally campuses are pleased with the technology leadership role UMassOnline has

achieved, but there is some dissention. With the recent selection of a new LMS issues arose. Some campuses report having little input to the decision process, that the decision was predetermined, and that the review period was just a formality.

Regarding marketing and branding, the study findings report mixed results. A strong brand has been established and achieved name recognition. UMassOnline markets to create awareness of all online educational offering at the five campuses, while individual programs are not directly marketed by UMassOnline. A portal containing all programs at all campuses allows students to look at the offerings collectively and select the program that best meets their needs. Widespread confusion exists with much misunderstanding of the distinction between the marketing of online learning collectively versus the marketing of individual programs. Additionally, too many marketing efforts exist, including those of UMassOnline, campus continuing education offices, departments, and schools within campuses. The report found coordination among the existing efforts lacking. In fact, these organizations were found to operate as vertical silos with little communication and few joint efforts.

The third role of the organization was to identify programs areas with a high demand for online learning and possibly develop online programs. According to the report this goal has not been met. Early discussions of UMassOnline becoming another campus have been abandoned.

Another area found lacking was data reporting in several key areas. First, the study found data related to the use of the LMS for blended courses difficult to obtain. Additionally, data for the role of the LMS in face-to-face course were not available. Without these data it was difficult to assess the value added by both UMassOnline and the LMS. Another area lacking data collection was the tracking of student leads. Feedback on UMassOnline-generated leads is limited and hampers measuring the effectiveness of UMassOnline.

UMassOnline and the Five Campuses

The report found the relationship between UMassOnline and the five campuses often fraught with conflict. UMassOnline staff reported experiencing open hostility from some on the five campuses. Communication channels are lacking or broken. UMassOnline reporting directly to the President's Office, but with less oversight than any other organization with a similar reporting structure, has caused concern. Additionally, the lack of a well-defined governance structure generates concern. No formal service agreements or communication channels exist between the five campuses and UMassOnline leading to conflicts and misunderstandings.

Recommendations of the Reviewers

In order to address the issues discussed in the study, the reviewers made the following recommendations

- establish formal governing structures for UMassOnline;
- make online education a priority at all campuses;
- expansion of online offerings by the five campuses;
- development of online programs addressing the needs of state workforce and economic development;
- update and improve communication methods between all parties;
- increase cooperative marketing efforts and the development of strategic marketing plans;
- continue and expand the role of UMass-Online in technology selection;
- create a clear delineation of technology support roles;

- do not expand the mission of UMass-Online to include the development of standalone programs;
- improve data systems for better tracking and reporting;
- address financial issues regarding faculty compensation for blended and online; and
- resolve issues with the UMassOnline funding model.

Conclusion

In the last 12 years, the new organization UMassOnline succeeded in increasing online enrollment, program and course offerings, and created a brand that capitalized on the strengths of the University of Massachusetts system. As outlined in the assessment of the program, to continue to have a strong presence in online learning requires organizational and fiscal changes for UMassOnline, and continued growth in online learning offerings at each of the five campuses. Continued prioritization of online learning by higher education leaders in the state of Massachusetts is critical to continued success.

References

About UMassOnline. (n.d.). About UMassOnline. Retrieved from http://www .umassonline.net/about-us

BOT. (n.d.). The board of trustees. Retrieved from http://www.massachusetts.edu/bot/index.html

DOE. (n.d.). Massachusetts department of elementary & secondary education. Retrieved from http://www.doe.mass.edu/

Eastmond, D. (2013). Education without boundaries: The Western Governors University story. In M. Simonson (Ed.), *Distance education statewide, institutional, and international applications: Readings from the pages of Distance Learning Journal* (pp. 21-33). Charlotte, NC: Information Age.

Facts 2012-2013. (2013). *Facts 2012-2013.* Retrieved from http://media.umassp.edu/massedu/ir/facts2012-2013.pdf

Feldman, R., & Zucker, D. (n.d.) *Teaching and learning online: Communications, community, and assessment.* Retrieved from University of Massachusetts, Amherst, Office of Academic Planning and Assessment website: http://www.umass.edu/oapa/oapa/publications/online_handbooks/Teaching_and_Learning_Online_Handbook.pdf

Mellenbrook Policy Advisors. (2012). Online education at the University of Massachusetts a report to the president. Retrieved from http://www.umass.edu/senate/News%20and%20Updates/2012-2013/MEL-LENBROOK_REPORT_FEB12.pdf

Office of the Chancellor. (n.d.). Office of the chancellor. Retrieved from http://www.umass.edu/chancellor/

President's Office. (n.d.). UMassOnline. Retrieved from http://www.massachusetts.edu/po/umassonline.html

UMass Amherst History. (n.d.). 150 Years of UMass Amherst history. Retrieved from http://www.umass.edu/150/timeline

UMass Boston History. (n.d.). History of UMass Boston. Retrieved from http://www.umb.edu/the_university/history

UMass Dartmouth History. (n.d.). History of UMass Dartmouth. Retrieved from http://www.umassd.edu/about/historyofumassdartmouth/)

UMass Lowell History. (n.d.). University quick facts. Retrieved from http://www.uml.edu/About/quick-facts.aspx

UMass Online About. (n.d.). About UMassOnline. Retrieved from http://www.umassonline.net/about-us

UMass Online Team. (n.d.). UMass Online team. Retrieved from http://www.umassonline.net/staff

UMass System. (n.d.). The University of Massachusetts system. Retrieved from http://www.massachusetts.edu/system/about.html

UMass Worcester History. (n.d.). An introduction to UMass Medical School. Retrieved from http://www.umassmed.edu/about/index.aspx

IN THE LAST 12 YEARS, THE NEW ORGANIZATION UMASSONLINE SUCCEEDED IN INCREASING ONLINE ENROLLMENT, PROGRAM AND COURSE OFFERINGS, AND CREATED A BRAND THAT CAPITALIZED ON THE STRENGTHS OF THE UNIVERSITY OF MASSACHUSETTS SYSTEM.

Tribal Colleges and Universities

Rebuilding Culture and Education Through Distance Education

Ayasia Hampton

INTRODUCTION

Today the phenomenal excitement about education is learning at a distance. Distance education is making revolutionary changes to the pedagogical processes of learning and teaching at a distance. Distance education bridges the instructional gap between teacher and student when various technologies are used for teaching and learning. Historically, education has changed based on new technologies; more than ever it is steadily providing a new direction for many higher institutions such as tribal colleges and universities (TCU).

In 1998, Sanchez, Stuckey, and Morris noted that distance education is a promising phenomenon that is preserving, maintaining, and revitalizing traditional native languages and cultures. In addition, Moore (2007) reminds that distance education has many elemental parts such as distributed learning, tele-learning, e-learning, open learning, blended learning, and flexi-learning. Each of these applications hold true to allowing many tribal colleges and universities to offer distance education programs. These motivated programs create opportunities for those who find it impossible to attend traditional colleges and universities because of family obligations. Tribal colleges and universities and community programs are collectively encouraging sustainable adoption of broadband use and services so that underserved American Indians can learn how to become digital citizens.

Ayasia Hampton,
Science Teacher, Thomson High,
McDuffie County School District,
1160 Whiteoak Rd., Thomson, GA 30824.
Telephone: (706) 389-0357.
E-mail: aqhamp@gmail.com

BRIEF HISTORY OF AMERICAN INDIAN EDUCATION

Let's take ride on an imaginary time machine that takes us back centuries before colonial settlements, and the beginnings of formal education in America. Here we will find American Indians who relied on the nature, morals, and values of their culture to educate their children. American Indians' educational methods were historically family based, and learning was not as traditional as we know it today. Legacies of inspiration came from nontraditional classrooms that were operated by observing and respecting tribal elders (Rifkin, 1992). According to Reyhner and Elder (2004), and Oesch (1996), American Indians used stories, ceremonies, and apprenticeships as educational tools. The accumulating purpose of these tools were to guide the student "to that indescribable moment when information and insight clash, and the proverbial 'light bulb' [was] illumined" (Oesch, 1996, p. 3). Through these educational tools, American Indians made self-discoveries that opened doors to understanding.

However, as the government emerged and mandated new policies, their way of life started to diminish. Various tribes sent their children to government-funded Indian boarding schools with the promises that their children would have a new, better vision of the world through education, and their success would echo across America for their cultures' greater good (Osech, 1996). The way they lived was their educational journey, and as their livelihood changed at the boarding schools their education did also. This was just the beginning of the American Indian culture being ripped away from them, and the powerful weapon the "new" Americans were using against them were their own children. Parental influences ceased when American Indian children attended boarding schools. Overall, the ideology of the American society was to uplift the natives to "civilization from a savage state" (Stokes, 1997, p. 576). Researchers agree that the "blinding confusion" of the American Indians contributed to the genocide of their culture (Oesch, 1996, p. 6). Moreover, the struggles the American Indians endured over the centuries are evident in the history of their education. For years, American Indians have had the highest dropout rates, and are the poorest among other minority groups in America today (Bowker, 1992). However, distance education is starting a chain reaction that is helping American Indians crystallize an identity once lost survive the ages to come.

TCU, CULTURE, AND DISTANCE EDUCATION

The American Indian Higher Education Consortium (1999) reminds us that tribal colleges and universities were created to meet the higher educational needs of American Indians. In response, Dine College (originally Navajo Community College) became the foundational start of tribal colleges and universities when it was founded in 1968 by the Navajo Nation (Dine College, 2013). The American Indian College Fund (2013) states that there are 34 fully accredited tribal colleges and universities throughout the United States. Since the beginning of the first TCU, an array of organizations and policies has been established to create conditions of opportunity for American Indians. For instance, the Tribal Controlled Community College Act of 1968 was authorized to federally fund community colleges operated by tribes located on reservations. This created a domino effect, which brought into existence more tribal colleges and universities. Moreover, in 1989 the American Indian College Fund was created to raise money for scholarships (American Indian College Fund, 2013). Tribal colleges and universities are mostly centralized in the middle of the United States. They are nestled in Alaska, Arizona, Kansas, Michigan, Minnesota, Montana, North Dakota, Nebraska, New Mexico, Oklahoma, South Dakota, Washington, and Wisconsin with each ranging from 1-7 TCU respectively. Most Indian Americans attending college are the first generations to enroll, and most of those are single mothers in their early thirties (American Indian Higher Education

Consortium, 1999). Tribal colleges and universities are seeing enrollments increase, especially in their distance education programs.

Tribal colleges and universities are significantly regenerating tribal culture and education through the use distance learning services. Culture and education are two priorities for American Indians. Through the prodigious efforts of tribal leaders grew the tribal college movement, and from there tribal colleges and universities are adhering to strengthening tribal culture and education without assimilation, but through the importance of regaining a cultural identity (American Indian Higher Education Consortium, 1999).

THE IMPORTANCE OF CULTURE

Culture is defined as the integrated pattern of human knowledge, belief, and behavior that depends upon the capacity for learning and transmitting knowledge to succeeding generations. With that in mind, only through education can culture be preserved for future generations, but historically the mentoring system of tribal communities have dissolved. So, how is distance education rebooting American Indian culture and education?

Culture allows individuals to feel a connection with those who are familiar; hence, social awareness is recognized. Gentry and Fugate (2012) outline the importance of cultural elements that need to be embedded in American Indian education so that cultural integration is experienced in classrooms. The methodology of this approach signifies the survival of American Indian culture and language, which is essential to rejuvenating the feeling of belonging for American Indians. Opportunities are put in place so that cultural perspectives and experiences are catalysts to increasing American Indian graduation rates. Ambler (1999) of the *Tribal College Journal* states that Haskell Indian Nations University is offering telecourses through the American

Indian Higher Education Consortium telecommunications project. One course allows students to communicate with native elders who are relics of American Indian history. Providing ideal avenues such as this emphasizes the critical connection between culture and distance education. Sanchez et al. (1998) insists that through distance education

> The tribe can maintain cultural sensitivity by deciding who will be teaching, and what they will be teaching. Given the severe shortage of American Indian teachers, this technology can be used to increase the numbers of American Indian students who are taught by people who share their cultural and tribal values. (para. 25)

Many tribal colleges and universities educational philosophies are grounded in their cultural traditions. The importance of culture is echoed throughout tribal colleges and universities distance education courses.

A GLANCE AT DISTANCE EDUCATION AT WORK

Distance education brings with it opportunity. There are at least 29 tribal colleges and universities that offer some form of distance education (Ambler, 2004). Gerald "Carty" Monette, Lori Lambert, and Mark Trebian are noted as being pioneers of distance education for tribal colleges (Ambler, 2004). Each of them has brought inspiration to thousands who have entered and graduated from tribal colleges and universities. There are many challenges that come with learning at a distance such as cultural sensitivities, but tribal colleges and universities and tribal leaders are taking the challenge head-on so that precautions are taken to protect precious tribal information (Sanchez et al., 1998). Tribal colleges and universities recognize authentic identities of the American Indian, which allows students to define themselves in a positive manner.

United Tribes Technical College (UTTC) is just one of many tribal colleges that is participating in the forthcomings of what distance education has to offer by partaking in the North Dakota interactive video network system. In 1990, the North Dakota interactive videoconferencing system was established to provide higher education opportunities for those who are underserved (Williston State College, 2010). Today tribally controlled colleges and universities located in North Dakota are using the interactive video network. Through this system United Tribes Technical College was the first tribal college to offer full online degree programs. Today, United Tribes Technical College offers eight associate of applied science degrees through their distance education division (United Tribes Technical College, 2013). Although 6% of the American Indian population has completed four or more years of college, distance education is reaching more American Indians than ever.

Northwest Indian College is located in Washington, but has eight campuses that serve not only Washington but also tribes from Idaho and Oregon. As of 2011, 75% of Northwest Indian College's students were served via distance education (Northwest Indian College, 2011). Salish Kooten College (SKC) is another TCU that is has had a successful run with distance education by designing and implementing its own distance learning program. Today, SKC offers over 125 courses and is continuing to design more courses. Stein and Jetty (2002) mention that the success of the SKC distance education program lies in the constant training of faculty members; in addition, the interaction the faculty is building with students. With the help of the Native American Higher Education Initiative, SKC has "built a strong, high quality" distance education program (Stein & Jetty, 2002, para. 28). SKC is also connecting with communities by being the first to offer a degree in Tribal Historic Preservation.

Mobile technologies like tablets and smartphones are offline technological tools that distance education students can take advantage of when Internet access is not available. Bates (2012) explains these "smart" gadgets can extend distance learning beyond Internet access by allowing students to preserve their native languages through recording applications originally placed or downloaded on the device. In other words, "previously limited access to language and the cultural stories and related contexts that contribute to the unique learning styles of many tribal communities is being captured and shared throughout a variety of communities and learning environments" (Bates, 2012, para. 26).

BROADBAND CONNECTING AND TRANSFORMING AMERICAN INDIANS

Broadband refers to high-speed Internet access that is faster than dial-up. There are many advantages to having broadband access, for broadband can help promote economic develop, facilitate medical care to those who are underserved, help promote pubic safety, and break geographical barriers so that individuals can have access to educational and cultural opportunities (Broadband, n.d.). The government is working hard to bring the nation up to date. Broadband is unlocking new possibilities for many, but for tribal colleges and universities it is redefining the tribal nation. Broadband "accelerates online learning by enabling the creation of digital content and learning systems, and removes regulatory barriers and promotes digital literacy" (Broadband, para. 12). The government's National Broadband Plan, in conjunction with the Broadband Technologies Opportunities Program, is maximizing all efforts to set standards to optimize the innovative richness broadband has to offer.

THE DIGITAL DIVIDE AND THE BROADBAND TECHNOLOGIES OPPORTUNITIES PROGRAM (BTOP)

It is true that American Indians are among those who are engulfed by the digital divide. The ambiguous and influential parameters of the digital divide revolve around the aspects of access, skills, economic opportunity, and democratic avenues (Choemprayong, 2006). Therefore, not only are tribal colleges and universities stepping up to loosen the constraints of the great divide, tribal community programs are being governmentally funded to bring American Indians closer to digital citizenship. The Department of Commerce's National Telecommunications and Information Administration heads BTOP (National Telecommunications and Information Administration, n.d.). BTOP's overall objective is to provide and support the development of broadband infrastructure, provide public computer centers, and encourage sustainable adoption of broadband service and use (National Telecommunications and Information Administration, n.d.). Through these measures the program has awarded millions of dollars to projects so that they can expand and extend broadband access to individuals and organizations. The College of Menominee Nation and ZeroDivide Tribal are just two examples of programs using BTOP funds to further tribal communities broadband access and connection.

THE COLLEGE OF MENOMINEE NATION (CMN)

The CMN has two campus locations in Wisconsin: the Keshena campus and the Green Bay/Oneida campus each offering numerous educational opportunities through distance education. The college is going beyond campus grounds, and is expanding its computer services to the public, especially for the Menominee Indian Tribe. The comprehensive computer center will provide high speed Internet access so that the disadvantaged and rural area receive public Internet use, technology based community education, and job training (BTOP, 2010a). CMN documents that 15% of enrolled CMN participants have Internet access. Consequently, many of them have never used social networks to communicate with family and friends, done online banking, or ever used the Internet at all. Barriers such as these put restrictions on individuals who live in limited and underserved niches. The CMN computer center provides various training programs ranging from video game design to Menominee language. General equivalency degree preparation programs are also set in place to help boost graduation rates. The ongoing efforts of the program will rejuvenate the Menominee Indian Tribe.

ZERODIVIDE TRIBAL

ZeroDivide Tribal represents the Tribal Digital Village (TDV) Broadband Adoption Program, which is another BTOP participant that is leapfrogging the digital divide in 19 tribal communities across Southeastern California by providing digital literacy training (BTOP, 2010b). The purpose of TDV is to raise the current 17% baseline of tribal residents that have access to broadband, training, and awareness up to 70% of the 8,900 tribal community members living in the southern California area (BTOP, 2010b). Based on a 2007 survey by the United States census, TDV reports that American Indians and Native Alaskans had the lowest broadband adoption rate. Consequently, TDV is working hard to bring broadband access to the Southern California Tribal Chairman's Association tribal communities. TDV has also established a platform called the Tribal Digital Shadow Project called the Young Native Story Tellers to mentor and train the local youth in the TDV infrastructure and technology; 15 of the participants will be graduating from the program this year. Since their start TDV has calculated that 1,236 individuals has accessed broadband through subscriptions to the TDV services with Southern California Tribal Chairman's Association (BTOP, 2010b). TDV is a representation of a program that is developing skills and knowledge by recognizing individuals of minority groups need to learn how to function successfully in a digitized global society.

CONCLUSION

From the early efforts to eradicate tribal culture and education, tribal leaders and the government have had an unstable relationship that has suppressed American Indians over the years. The 21st century brings about change and new innovations; therefore, distance education is illuminating the readiness and motivation of American Indians as they embrace cultural traditions in a modernized and evolving society. The ideology of tribal education involves both societal and tribal colleges and universities' goals that comprise of cultural pluralism and equal opportunity. According to Sleeter and Grant (2007) cultural pluralism "includes the maintenance of diversity, a respect for difference, and the right to participate actively in all aspects of society without having to give up ones unique identity" (p. 152). American Indians are modifying stereotypes and misconceptions about their culture and education by embracing cultural identities. The government is building new relationships with tribal leaders by not only improving educational opportunities, but also promoting sustainable economic development and touching issues of healthcare and public safety within tribal communities. The bruises are slowly healing, but these monumental steps that tribal colleges, distance education, and community programs are revitalizing American Indian education and culture.

REFERENCES

Ambler, M. (1999). Educating the native student at a distance. *Tribal College Journal of American Indian Higher Education, 10*(3). Retrieved from http://www.tribalcollegejournal.org/archives/14068/2

Ambler, M. (2004). Distance education comes home. *Tribal College Journal of American Indian Higher Education, 15*(4). Retrieved from http://www.tribalcollegejournal.org/archives/10720

American Indian College Fund. (2013). Tribal colleges. Retrieved from http://www.collegefund.org/content/tribal_colleges

American Indian Higher Education Consortium. (1999). Tribal colleges: An introduction. Retrieved from http://www.aihec.org/colleges/documents/TCU_intro.pdf

Bates, R. (2012). Distance learning for special populations. *Online Journal of Distance Learning Administration, 15*(2). Retrieved from http://www.westga.edu/~distance/ojdla/summer152/bates152.html

Bowker, A. (1992). The American Indian female dropout. *Journal of American Indian Education, 31*(3).

Broadband. (n.d.). Executive summary. Retrieved from http://broadband.gov/plan/executive-summary/

Broadband Technologies Opportunities Program. (2010a). College of Menominee Nation. Retrieved from http://www2.ntia.doc.gov/grantee/college-of-menominee-nation

Broadband Technologies Opportunities Program. (2010b). Zerodivide tribal. Retrieved from http://www2.ntia.doc.gov/grantee/zerodivide-tribal

Choemprayong, S. (2006). Closing digital divides: The United States' policies. *Libri, 56*, 201-212.

Dine College. (2013). Retrieved from http://www.dinecollege.edu/index.php

Gentry, M., & Fugate, M. (2012). Gifted native American students: Underperforming, under-identified, and overlooked. *Psychology in the Schools, 49*(7), 631-646. doi:10.1002/pits.21624

Moore, M. (Ed.). (2007). Preface. In *Handbook of distance education* (pp. ix-xiii). Mahwah, NJ: Erlbaum.

National Telecommunications and Information Administration. (n.d.). Retrieved from http://www2.ntia.doc.gov/about

Northwest Indian College. (2011). Weaving our communities, one student at a time: Our journey. Retrieved from http://www.nwic.edu/content/nwic-capital-campaign

Oesch, D. (1996). *Accommodating difference: Native American English education-reexamining past assumptions and recognizing socio-political influences.* Milwaukee, WI: CCCC Roundtable.

Reyhner, J., & Eder, J. (2004). *American Indian education: A history.* Norman, OK: University of Oklahoma Press.

Rifkin, J. (1992). D-Q college campus succeeds on the Soboba reservation. *Hispanic Times Magazine, 13*, 16-17.

Sanchez, J., Stuckey, M. E., Morris, R. (1998). Distance learning in Indian country: Becoming the spider on the web. *Journal of American Indian Education, 37*(3). Retrieved from http://jaie.asu.edu/v37/V37S3dis.htm

Sleeter, C., & Grant, C. (2007). *Making choices for multicultural education: Five approaches to race, class and gender* (5th ed.). Hoboken, NJ: Wiley.

Stein, W., & Jetty, M. (2002). The story of distance learning at Salish Kootenai College. *Journal of American Indian Education, 41*(2). Retrieved from http://jaie.asu.edu/v41/V41I2A3.pdf

Stokes, S. (1997). Curriculum for Native American students: Using native American values. *The Reading Teacher, 50*(7), p. 576-584.

United Tribes Technical College. (2013). Center for educational outreach. Retrieved from http://www.uttc.edu/distance/

Williston State College. (2010). Interactive video networking. Retrieved from http://www.willistonstate.edu/Current-Students/Online-Campus/Interactive-Video-Networking.html

DISTANCE EDUCATION BRIDGES THE INSTRUCTIONAL GAP BETWEEN TEACHER AND STUDENT WHEN VARIOUS TECHNOLOGIES ARE USED FOR TEACHING AND LEARNING. HISTORICALLY, EDUCATION HAS CHANGED BASED ON NEW TECHNOLOGIES; MORE THAN EVER IT IS STEADILY PROVIDING A NEW DIRECTION FOR MANY HIGHER INSTITUTIONS SUCH AS TRIBAL COLLEGES AND UNIVERSITIES.

Maximizing HR Professionals' Leadership Role in e-Learning for Organizational Effectiveness

Jane Waweru

INTRODUCTION

According to Cornish (2004), technology has become the "great transformation of human life"

Jane Waweru,
Senior HR Manager, PHR,
2904 Kings Chapel Road, Suite 16, Falls Church, VA 22042.
Telephone: (703) 328-3645.
E-mail: waweru@nova.edu

(p. 9). Our society's increasing dependence on technology has affected all facets of our lives to include the human resource management function. Lockwood (2006) predicted that human resources (HR) leaders will be the personnel who will do most to focus efforts on innovative and creative learning in their organizations. E-learning methods have been proposed as a key means of accomplishing the goal of fostering effective, ongoing learning within these organizations. However, it has been reported that due to a variety of barriers, HR professionals are not taking the lead in promoting the use of e-learning. More information is needed to confirm whether or not this problem exists by assessing current levels of e-learning leadership by HR professionals.

PERCEPTIONS OF INNOVATION ATTRIBUTES

Rogers (2003) discussed five characteristics that help predict how an innovation is adopted. According to Rogers, the relative advantage, compatibility, complexity, trialability, and observability are characteristics of innovations that can help predict the overall rate and extent of adoption. A study of HR professionals may help show innovative attributes that are desirable for HR professionals. Organizations may be able to use this information to hire HR professionals with competencies that would help enhance e-learning effectiveness. In addition, results from the study will help readers understand why HR professionals adopt or fail to adopt e-learning.

Society for Human Resource Management (2009) said practitioners in the HR industry reported that learning in "organizations not only promotes retention and career development, but also supports the organization's ability to innovate and remain competitive" (Advocating for Education section, para. 4). Researchers and practitioners stated that HR professionals should be cognizant of the need to lead in creating a learning environment to help meet the demands of a knowledge-based economy (Lawler & Mohrman, 2003; Society for Human Resource Management, 2009). Saghafian (2011) said that technology is associated with excellence and advancement; consequently, various stakeholders that include the management expect technology to be implemented in the training programs. Hence, there is an increase in popularity in the use of e-learning (Bell, Lee, Yeung, 2006; Forum Corporation, 2003; Long, DuBuois, & Faley, 2008). The reasons for this increase include reduced costs, the ability to manage the changes in the courseware, increased content in the course, and because employees do not have to miss work when participating in e-learning because they can take the course anywhere and at any time.

Hall (2005) supported the same perspective when he stated that every HR professional needs to know the case for e-learning, which includes cost benefits, an increase in the competitive advantage, adaptability to change, attracting and retaining the workforce, training in a new

product, and increased advantage with mergers. Hence, the increased pressure for HR professionals to produce training that meets the demands of the organizations is required by the management (Saghafian, 2011).

IMPLICATIONS OF LIMITED E-LEARNING

Because HR workers play such a key role in promoting e-learning within organizations, lack of e-learning use by HR professionals may result in a failure by organizations to take advantage of the benefits associated with e-learning. The consequences of this failure may be organizations with employees who lack the skills and insights that can contribute to innovations to make the organization more competitive. According to Lawler and Mohrman (2003), "Many companies in the knowledge economy rely on the processing of knowledge by skilled knowledge workers—on its development and utilization of human capital" (p. 4). Thus, e-learning may be a key to whether or not organizations survive in an increasingly competitive economic environment.

Most important is organizations will fail to take advantage of the convenience of learning that can be conducted at anytime and anyplace. Organizations may also fail to take advantage of the reduced costs associated with e-learning and course materials that can be edited and produced instantly. In addition, organizations may fail to take advantage of consistent and reliable data and standardized information among other e-learning advantages, all of which may contribute in the failure of organizations to compete in the global market.

According to the Society for Human Resource Management (2008), e-learning is not only useful for delivering high-quality and timely instruction and assessment of skills in formal courses, better employee performance is also supported in less for-

Table 1. e-Learning Opportunities for HR Professionals

Human Resource Management Function	e-Learning Opportunities
Recruiting and hiring	HR professionals can utilize e-learning to educate the applicants on the organization's mission, vision, and organizational values being sought.
Benefits administration	e-Learning can be utilized to educate employees on company benefits such as the Flexible Spending Account or the Family Medical Leave, not only as new hires but also on an ongoing basis.
Compensation administration	Educating employees on equal pay and Lilly Ledbetter among other pay acts through e-learning would help save the organization time while ensuring all employees are receiving similar information through e-learning (Phillips & Phillips, 2009).
Compliance and policy development	e-Learning provides an organization with the opportunity to communicate state, local, and federal regulations at the same time.
Employee relations	Managers can utilize e-learning to engage their employees on several organizational fronts, which includes educating the staff on the latest product development.
Organizational and employee development	e-Learning can also be utilized to help build effective teams.
Performance management	Performance management is enhanced by e-learning based on the fact that it enhances (a) collaboration among various stakeholders; (b) communication; (c) knowledge function by having the capability of providing analytical results; and (d) task function, which makes it possible to sieve data from various sources (Hsiao-Ya, Chieh-Chung, & An-Pin, 2008).
Safety and security	E-learning can be utilized to educate employees on a company's safety and security.

mal ways by supplying reference tools and job aids and by facilitating ongoing communications among instructors, experts, and colleagues from which they learn. These formal and informal strategies provide valuable information in a number of areas that affect organizational performance, including recruiting and hiring, benefits administration, compensation, compliance, employee relations, organizational and employee development, and safety and security.

Researchers said that the utilization of e-learning can help organizations focus more on the strategic role of HR, thereby increasing the opportunity to grow the organization (Panayotopoulou, Vakola, & Galanaki, 2005). Most importantly, organizations would fail to obtain benefits associated with e-learning as it relates to benefits administration, compensation, compliance, employee relations, and safety and security as issues from these areas of the human resource management may arise on a day to day. Failing to take advantage of such benefits would decrease learning opportunities, thereby affecting the organization's performance and production.

FOCUS GROUP QUALITATIVE DATA

In an effort to establish HR professionals' use or nonuse or e-learning and the barriers as perceived by HR professionals to the adoption of e-learning, qualitative data was collected using a pilot study and three focus groups to help better understand HR professions views and attitudes on e-learning (Gay, Mills, & Airasian, 2009). Gay et al. stated that qualitative data helps in the understanding of a "deep and holistic or complex understanding of a particular phenomenon" (p. 399). According to Fink, qualitative data "collect information on the meanings that people attach to their experiences and on the ways they express themselves" (p. 61).

Targeted HR professionals worked in various industries that included retail, technology, manufacturing, nonprofit, government, health, finance, research, education, marketing, consulting, and international. All industries were expected to be represented. Only willing HR professionals volunteered to participate. A total of 22 HR professionals participated and provided their rationale on why they do or do not participate in e-learning.

REASONS FOR USE OR NONUSE OF E-LEARNING

Common themes for HR participation in e-learning included the following:

1. Professional/personal development. Most HR professionals stated they participated in e-learning for their own professional or personal development. On professional development, participants indicated they utilized e-learning resources to recertify their credentials and take classes online, among others. Participants indicated they utilized e-learning for exploratory learning and for self-knowledge.
2. Convenience. Participants generally perceived that e-learning provides easy access to learning. Consequently, distance from a training site or even time of day was not an obstacle when training was done through e-learning. One participant stated she enjoyed the convenience of being able to be "trained at 2 A.M." Other participants cited the ability to use multiple locations for learning.

3. Compliance. Participants stated they were able to educate employees on mandated courses such as code of ethics and harassment policies among others through e-learning.
4. Facilitate/instruct/intervention. Several participants indicated they had been exposed to e-learning as facilitators or instructors or utilized e-learning as an intervention.
5. Customized training. Participants stated that e-learning provided the ability to provide customized training to employees with special needs. A HR professional stated that "different learners require unique needs which may not be met through e-learning."

POTENTIAL BARRIERS

HR professionals provided their rationale on barriers and challenges that contributed to their nonuse of e-learning. Five of the leading themes cited included the following:

1. Lack of face-to-face interaction. Participants stated that a lack of face-to-face interaction or engagement does create a barrier to e-learning. A participant was of the view that online interaction "can be strange." The participant added by stating, "I do not learn well learning on software, it is not my format." Another participant stated that "in person, one can tell a person story which is lost in e-learning, and would probably not learn very well if instruction was all online" while another stated "some people need motivation for structure to take classes online. There is need for a face-to-face to expand the network. 'You can't fax a handshake'." Another HR professional stated that although one is forced to take some certifications classes online, she preferred face to face because she "belongs to that era."

2. Accessibility and usability. Some participants were of the view that technical challenges can create a barrier to e-learning. Participants stated that, sometimes, e-learning may not be easy to use because of "terrible technology." An HR professional stated that "web-based e-learning the system is sometimes down and you cannot do anything until Information Technology team is ready to resolve the problem." Participants believed there is need for better designed e-learning content.

3. Cost. Participants stated that cost of e-learning can be a barrier to e-learning because finances are needed to support the software, people, developers, and designers of the innovation. Some believed that due to hard economic challenges, compliance issues were on the back burner. Others were of the view that capital was needed to develop and maintain e-learning. Some HR professionals said that financial cost associated with e-learning can be a challenge when trying to promote the innovation to the top management.

4. Effectiveness. Participants believed that the inability to measure the effectiveness of e-learning was a barrier to learning.

5. Lack of time. HR professionals stated they were sometimes busy and may not have had time for e-learning on the job. One participant stated that not having enough time at work made e-learning "a bother at work." Others felt that interruptions on the job presented a barrier to e-learning because they were not able to concentrate.

INTERPRETATION OF THE FOCUS GROUP RESULTS ON THE USE OR NONUSE OF E-LEARNING

Findings of this study showed that focus group members identify mainly advantages of e-learning, rather than disadvantages, thereby confirming that at least some HR professionals were aware of the advantages of e-learning. Taking advantage of professional/personal development through e-learning is a clear indication that HR professionals recognize the advantages of e-learning methods. HR professionals seem to realize that e-learning has conveniences to their professional life and that e-learning can help them assist their organization on compliance issues.

However, because these focus group participants mainly focused only on what they liked about e-learning, it seems likely the group contained only e-learning advocates/leaders. Findings indicated that given the right environment, these particular HR professionals would take charge and lead the e-learning process. However, they may not be characteristic of all HR professionals.

INTERPRETATION OF RESULTS FOR THE BARRIERS OF E-LEARNING

Previous studies showed that attitudes about innovation attributes contributed to HR decisions on whether or not to adopt, and this study was not an exception (Martin & Reddington, 2009; Vaughan & MacVicar, 2004). As an example, one focus group participant stated that taking into account that HR professionals' style is generally one that prefers face-to-face interaction, many may tend to be resistant to e-learning. This rationale was shared by Martin and Reddington (2009) who stated, "HR staff have been resistant to technology mediation because it conflicts with their view of HR as best carried out through face-to-face relationships with clients" (p. 529). Lack of a face-to-face interaction had the highest number of frequency (22) of comments on barriers to e-learning. Another participant stated that given her generation, she preferred face-to-face learning because it provides interaction. Her comments were supported by another participant who stated that a lot of people prefer face-to-face training. Another participant stated she did not want to sit at the computer all day learning. A need for a human face was cited as critical in the learning process because some employees would like someone to assist them throughout the process.

A few comments cannot be used to reflect the perception of the entire HR population but the examples provide an opportunity to show a possible connection between e-learning barriers and the perceptions of compatibility. HR professionals would like to ensure that e-learning is compatible with their personal and organizational values prior to trying it. Hassan (2007) defined *organizational values* as "beliefs and attitudes that go deep inside and constitute a collective understanding regarding norms and standards of behavior acceptable in the organization" (p. 437). Hassan reported that organizational values "set the tone" (p. 437) for how members of the organization ought to behave. Consequently, organizational values help employees bond towards a common purpose with the goal of achieving business goals (Hassan, 2007). HR professionals can use e-learning to help educate the applicants and employees of the organization's values by modeling these uses in their own work.

This study confirmed that real problems exist that may be contributing to lack of e-learning leadership by HR professionals. These include difficulties with accessibility and usability of e-learning, the cost of e-learning, challenges in measuring e-learning effectiveness, and the quality of the learning information. This indicates that HR professionals, like any people who choose to adopt a given innovation, need to see the relative advantage of the innovation (in this case, e-learning) prior to adopting it. Most importantly, HR professionals would like to ensure that e-learning is compatible with their personal and organizational values prior to trying it.

IMPLICATIONS FOR PRACTICE

This study's results indicate that much work remains to be done to demonstrate the value of e-learning for HR purposes and ensure that e-learning methods are more adopted. Suggestions for future practice include (a) publication of this research for awareness raising, (b) workshops, (c) technical support, (d) training that focuses on innovative attributes, (e) organizational synergy, and (f) communication within the organization.

PUBLICATION OF THE RESEARCH

This study provides updated information on the current state of e-learning leadership on HR Professionals. Publishing this research on e-learning leadership in relevant HR professional publications could help create awareness of the advantages and disadvantages of e-learning.

The publication of the study could help provide an important body of knowledge to HR professionals as it would introduce them to Rogers' (2003) diffusion of innovation theory and illustrate how it applies to their situation. Bauck (2002) stated that "professional development is most effective when it includes theory, demonstration, practice, feedback and coaching" (p. iv).

OFFERING WORKSHOPS

Study findings suggested that e-learning advocates should do more to increase acceptance and use of e-learning. In HR, e-learning advocates could be HR professionals themselves or the management within the organization. If workshops on e-learning benefits were offered in HR-related conferences, they could provide professional development with the assistance of opinion leaders.

Opinion leaders who advocate increased use of e-learning could help educate the HR professionals on its benefits. Consequently, conference-learning workshops could help confront and address the barriers to adoption of e-learning while emphasizing the benefits. The workshop could emphasize the relative advantage and compatibility attributes of e-learning, because HR professionals prefer seeing the advantage of e-learning, and that innovation aligns with their values and that of the organization. Opinion leaders could emphasize that using e-learning is the modern way to do things.

OFFERING TECHNICAL SUPPORT

Organizations could do much to encourage e-learning acceptance by providing increased technical support to HR professionals to help minimize challenges that were cited in the focus groups. When possible, the management could designate a technical support person in every department to help address issues related to usability of e-learning. Researchers stated that a support system and adequate support resources are needed to ensure successful diffusion of an innovation (Demuth, 2010).

Most importantly, Dublin (2007) stated that an effective integration of e-learning solutions often requires a shift in roles, responsibilities, and jobs within the organization. This means there is a need for HR professionals to wear a training hat that will enable them to take advantage of every available opportunity to educate employees on any task in the human resource management cycle. As educators, HR professionals will serve the role of being information and resource providers to the employees.

As organizational educators of e-learning, HR professionals will serve the critical role of launching new ideas within the organization and make others within the system aware of it (Rogers, 2003). Rogers (2003) said this can best be achieved if HR professionals understand the diffusion of innovation as a "process by which (1) an innovation (2) is communicated through certain channels (3) over time (4) among the members of a social system" (p. 11). Researchers stated that a trainer's desire to want to learn more and discover knowledge can result in an increase in the trainer's skill level (Boyatzis, 2008). This would eventually help improve the learning outcomes toward a desired state.

ENHANCING ORGANIZATIONAL SYNERGY

Researchers stated that the human resource management function is best achieved when evaluated as a whole (Lawler & Mohrman, 2003). The human resource management function is better placed to understand the complex and intricate organizational dynamics and ways that human capital can be used to help achieve the organization's strategic goals. Being able to see an opportunity to educate or train employees in the use of e-learning can help accelerate its use. A coordinated and systematic approach to innovative advances is needed in order to address organizational problems.

Organizational problems can best be addressed with management support. Input received from the focus group participants indicated that managerial, organizational, and technological barriers do contribute to or prevent the adoption of e-learning. According to Hung et al. (2009), "Managerial and organizational variables were all found to have a positive influence on the adoption decision, whereas technological variables were all found to have a negative influence on a hospital's decision to adopt" e-learning (p. 250). Most importantly, managerial support was found to be indispensable in the adoption of e-learning. Consequently, Hung et al. stated that for a successful adoption of e-learning, the top management would need to be educated on the benefits.

The management can help reduce the lack of adoption by providing HR professionals with the resources they need to make e-learning part of the organizational learning culture. In exchange, the management can hold HR professionals accountable, through performance management, to ensure that they provide well-designed training. Most importantly, management can set criteria that metrics be provided to link organizational strategic goals and the effectiveness of e-learning.

ENHANCING COMMUNICATION WITHIN THE ORGANIZATION

The open-ended comments from focus groups in this study represented advantages, disadvantages, barriers, and challenges of e-learning in the workforce. Failure to lead in an e-learning initiative is an area of improvement for HR professionals. They should ensure they actually have had the opportunity to lead an e-learning initiative if it is available to them as an option. This opportunity might arise if HR professionals communicated this concern with the stakeholders and helped them understand the role of HR and the importance of being able to lead e-learning initiatives.

IMPLICATIONS FOR FUTURE RESEARCH

The section recommends possible research studies that could shed more light on e-learning leadership and provide information to build on the results.

CONDUCTING STUDIES IN SPECIFIC COMPANIES

Respondents from this study were HR professionals from various industries. Further studies of this research could be conducted in specific companies with the goal of obtaining specific data on e-learning leadership and challenges experienced by HR professionals within such firms. If organizations were to conduct their own exploration of e-learning leadership on the part of HR professionals, they could obtain internal data that could help enhance organizational and employee development. Consequently, the organizations would conduct the study and report them to a larger population. Grgurovic (2010) recommended further studies in a specific organization, as a unit of analysis, in order to build on the diffusion of innovation study on technology-enhanced blended language learning in an English as a second language class. This view was supported by Tyan (2004), who stated that the size of the organization may not be issue; consequently, there is need to obtain data from specific companies in order to understand the challenges that are faced by corporations.

RESEARCH ON SPECIFIC HR MANAGEMENT FUNCTIONS

The focus group in this study focused on barriers and challenges of e-learning as a whole in the organization. There is need for further research to help understand the challenges and barriers faced by HR professionals when advocating e-learning for specific HRM job functions such as recruiting and hiring, benefits administration, compensation, employee relations, performance management, organizational and employee development, and safety and security. Research could be conducted in specific organizations with the goal of obtaining specific data on e-learning leadership on HR responsibilities and challenges that are experienced by HR professionals. Researchers recommended the need to conduct diffusion of innovation research in specific organizations (Grgurovic, 2010; Tyan, 2004). Research in this diffusion of innovation could be done in companies where they could obtain direct feedback on HR on specific area of concerns.

SUMMARY

Although it seems important that HR professionals take a leadership role in helping organizations maximize the advantages of e-learning, there were few studies that indicated how much this was happening. This study helped provide this evidence by exploring e-learning leadership among HR professionals, obstacles to adoption, and possible ways to promote higher rates of adoption.

REFERENCES

Bauck, T. (2002). Diffusion of videoconferencing using the Digital Dakota Network (Doctoral dissertation). Nova Southeastern University, Fort Lauderdale, FL.

Bell, B. S., Lee, S. W., & Yeung, S. K. (2006). The impact of e-HR on professional competences in HRM: Implications for the development of HR professionals. *Human Resource Management, 45*, 295-308. doi:10.1002/hrm.20113

Boyatzis, R. (2008). Competencies in the 21st century. *Journal of Management Development, 27*, 5-12. doi:10.1108/02621710810840730

Cornish, E. (2004). *Futuring: The exploration of the future*. Bethesda, MD: World Future Society.

Demuth, L. (2010). Accepting technology as a solution: A qualitative study investigating the adoption of technology at colleges. (Doctoral dissertation). Capella University, Minneapolis, MN. (UMI No. 3402090)

Dublin, C. (2007). *Success with e-learning*. Alexandria, VA: American Society for Training and Development.

Forum Corporation. (2003). *E-learning: Adoption rates and barriers*. Boston, MA: Forum.

Gay, R. L., Mills, G. E., & Airasian, P. (2009). *Educational research: Competencies for analysis and applications* (9th ed.). Upper Saddle River, NJ: Merrill Prentice Hall.

Grgurovic, M. (2010). *Technology-enhanced blended language learning in an ESL class: A description of a model and an application of the diffusion of innovations theory* (Doctoral dissertation). Retrieved from ProQuest Dissertations and Theses database. (UMI No. 3438697)

Hall, B. (2005). *E-learning: What every HR needs to know*. Alexandria, VA: Society for Human Resource Management.

Hassan, A. (2007). Human resource development and organizational values. *Journal of European Industrial Training, 31*, 435-448. doi:10.1108/03090590710772631

Hsiao-Ya, C., Chieh-Chung, S., & An-Pin, C. (2008). Modeling agent-based performance evaluations for e-learning systems. *The Electronic Library, 26*(3), 345-362.

Hung, S., Chen, C., & Lee, W. (2009). Moving hospitals toward e-learning adoption: An empirical investigation. *Journal of Organizational Change Management, 22*(3), 239-256.

Lawler, E. E., III, & Mohrman, S. A. (2003). HR as a strategic partner: What does it take to make it happen? Retrieved from http://ceo.usc.edu/pdf/G032430.pdf

Lockwood, N. (2006, July). Building learning cultures series Part 1: Human resource management for learning and building talent. Retrieved from http://www.shrmindia.org/building-learning-cultures-series-part-i-human-resource-management-learning-building-talent

Long, L. K., DuBuois, C. Z., & Faley, R. H. (2008). Online training: The value of capturing trainee reactions. *Journal of Workplace Learning, 20*, 21-37. doi:10.1108/13665620810843629

Martin, G., & Reddington, M. (2009). Reconceptualising absorptive capacity to explain the e-enablement of the HR function (e-HR) in organizations. *Employee Relations, 31*(5), 515-537.

Panayotopoulou, L., Vakola, M., & Galanaki, E. (2005). E-HR adoption and the role of HRM: Evidence from Greece. *Personnel Review, 36*, 277-294. doi:10.1108/00483480710726145

Phillips, J. J., & Phillips, P. (2009). Using ROI to demonstrate performance value in the public sector. *Performance Improvement, 48*(4), 22-31.

Rogers, E. M. (2003). *Diffusion of innovations* (5th ed.). New York, NY: Free Press.

Saghafian, M. (2011, March). A critical review of research on technology-based training in business organizations. *Research in Higher Education Journal, 10*. Retrieved from http://www.aabri.com/manuscripts/10632.pdf

Society for Human Resource Management. (2009, October). *Educating for advocacy, advocating for education*. Retrieved from http://www.shrm.org/Research/Articles/Articles/Pages/EducatingforAdvocacy.aspx

Society for Human Resource Management. (2008). *Introduction to the discipline of human resources technology.* Retrieved from http://www.shrm.org/hrdisciplines/employeerelations/Pages/EmpRelIntro.aspx

Tyan, K. (2004). *Diffusion barriers to e-learning in corporate Taiwan: A factor analysis of practitioners' perspectives* (Doctoral dissertation). Retrieved from ProQuest Dissertations and Theses database. (UMI No. 3133982)

Vaughan, K., & MacVicar, A. (2004). Employees' pre-implementation attitudes and perceptions to e-learning: A banking case study analysis. *Journal of European Industrial Training, 28*(5), 400-413.

The Global Campus

Examining the Initiative From the Perspective of Diffusion Theory

Kevin E. Johnson

The University of Illinois Global Campus is a rather new initiative with the mission to "become a national leader in online education, focused on innovation, quality, superior instruction, service, and accessibility" (University of Illinois Global Campus, 2007, p. 1). As a campus, The Global Campus itself is not accredited and relies on partnerships with other colleges and departments to design and develop its online programs and courses. Therefore, faculty senate buy-in and support at all three land-based campuses is essential.

Kevin E. Johnson,
CEO, The Cutting Ed, Inc.,
506 W. Florida Ave., Urbana, IL 61801.
Telephone: (217) 253-8670.
E-mail: kevin@thecuttinged.com

This unique structure has encountered its own challenges to the point of forcing The Global Campus to close its doors as a separate campus and return distance education programming to the individual campuses.

In September of 2005, a newly appointed president, Joseph B. White, made it clear in his inaugural speech that the University of Illinois should strive to become a leader in providing quality education in a more accessible and user-friendly fashion (White, 2005). Since that time, efforts ensued on creating a fourth campus: The University of Illinois Global Campus. In 4 short years, The Global Campus formed and developed distant programs, enrolled students, conducted virtual classes, and come full circle to closing its doors for restructuring.

The University of Illinois Board of Directors approved the creation of The Global Campus in March 2007. The board's decision was based on several market analyses and the president's vision for increasing the university's presence in the distance education field. The board approved the initiative based upon a proposal brought forth by a core team of professionals, headed by Chet Gardner, who was appointed special assistant to the president in 2006. The proposal included a strengths, weaknesses, opportunities, threats analysis, market analysis of initial programs, and processes and policies for registering students, designing quality courses, hiring faculty, and measuring success. Originally, it was intended that The

Global Campus would become a for-profit arm of the university as well, which ultimately was changed due to all three campus faculty senates expressing lack of support for a profit-based business model.

Once the board approved the initiative, the core team was provided with a budget and the green light to hire additional staff. The staff had less than nine months to establish its new virtual campus before going live with its first two programs in January 2008. For the next year, The Global Campus was criticized for the lack of enrollment numbers and continued lack of support by many faculty and academic units. It was decided that one possible solution was to become accredited so that the virtual campus could work toward academic independence. In November 2008, the board of trustees approved the request to seek accreditation, which was quickly added to the Global Campus project management schedule to be completed by Fall 2010. To help address faculty concerns, the board of trustees approved The Constitution for the Academic Policy Council of the University of Illinois Global Campus, which established a faculty oversight committee of Global Campus academic programs and educational policies. Despite these efforts, on April 15, 2009, the president and University of Illinois Senates Conference produced a document that outlined a redesign for the Global Campus that would return all academic responsibility over to each of the campuses and stopping all efforts of The Global Campus to become a separate campus.

So, what went wrong? Let's look at the initiative through the eyes of Rogers' (2003) elements of diffusion and try to identify components of the theory that may have helped The Global Campus initiative be more successful. According to Rogers (2003), *diffusion* is "the process by which (1) an *innovation* (2) is *communicated* through certain *channels* (3) *over time* (4) among the members of a *social system*" (emphasis added, p. 5). Let's first examine

these components one a time in order to get a picture of the entire system.

INNOVATION

Even though the University of Illinois is already comprised of three land-based campuses, only a few individual departments have implemented distance education courses within their program. For example, the Urbana-Champaign campus' Graduate School of Library and Information Science (GSLIS) offers a fully American Library Association accredited master of science degree program (http://www.lis.illinois.edu/programs/leep/). For the most part, program planning, instructional design, and delivery methods specific to distance education are foreign concepts to university faculty and college/department administration. Therefore, the innovation in our scenario is the construction of a new virtual campus that challenges the social structure of the members associated with the existing culture.

In order for faculty to adopt such an innovation, they must understand the five *characteristics of innovations*. These characteristics also help determine and individual's rate of adoption as well. They consist of *relative advantage, compatibility, complexity, trialability, and observability*. When we examine these one at a time relative to The Global Campus, we can begin to see where considering Rogers' (2003) theory in the initial planning stages may have encouraged a more successful implementation.

1. *Relative Advantage*: one's perception of how advantageous the innovation in terms of economics, social prestige factors, convenience, and satisfaction (Rogers, 2003). For a majority of the Global Campus adopters, the advantages of The Global Campus are indirectly related to the individual. Unless the individual became a course designer or an instructor, the benefit to oneself is minimal at best. One must

look at how partnering with The Global Campus benefits students, the department, and the overall university system. This is not to say this can't be achieved, but understanding this in the initial planning stages may have helped administration focus on approaches to getting more buy-in.

2. *Compatibility*: determines how compatible the individual perceives the innovation to the adopting society (Rogers, 2003). In the initial stages, The Global Campus was to be a for-profit arm of the university that relied solely on the idea of hiring subject matter experts to design courses and adjunct faculty to teach them. Faculty senates shared their concerns regarding content development and oversight of instruction being taken out of existing department and faculty responsibility. However, similarly speaking, faculty also expressed concern about their workloads and their inability to take on additional responsibilities.

3. *Complexity*: "The degree to which an innovation is perceived as difficult to understand and use (Rogers, 2003, p. 15). The starting of a new campus is always complex in nature. However, most people understand the nature of developing policies, procedures, and other technologies to create an on-ground campus. The creation of a virtual campus is something few can relate to and may be perceived as overly complex and technical simply due to ignorance. This in itself is a gap The Global Campus administration tried to close by conducting face-to-face meetings where field experts, administration, and faculty could discuss and answer questions.

4. *Trialability*: the degree to which an individual is able to practice the innovation before making a decision (Rogers, 2003). The Global Campus worked hard to meet with other successful programs such as University of Massa-chusetts, University of Phoenix, and Capella University before deciding on a model. However, no faculty were a part of these exhibitions and demonstrations. Faculty and administration, however, were invited to participate in the proposal process for deciding on a learning management system.

5. *Observability*: the degree to which the results of an innovation are visible to others. Global Campus administration provided faculty and college administrators with economic projections specific to enrollment and university income (Rogers, 2003). Other than financials, the only measurable outcome for which adopters could observe progress was enrollment numbers. Unfortunately, The Global Campus was unable to meet project enrollment numbers within its first year of operation. One the same note, Global Campus staff had only 9 months to put a campus together, which was 4 months less than expected based on the time needed to get board of trustee approval. Timing affected not only initial startup plans but program approval and marketing efforts as well, which all contributed to the campus' ability to achieve enrollment numbers.

COMMUNICATION AND COMMUNICATION CHANNELS

Specific to diffusion, *communication* occurs when some method is used to connect those with expert knowledge and experience regarding the innovation with those without knowledge and experience surrounding the same innovation (Rogers, 2003). In 2006, White appointed Gardner to lead The Global Campus initiative. Gardner, at the time, was serving as the assistant vice president for academic affairs. His first task was to develop a core team of experts to develop a proposal to submit for review by the faculty senate at all three campuses before presenting it to the board of trustees for approval. Faculty and staff were invited to campus presentations and provided the opportunity to give feedback and discuss concerns. Though this strategy provided opportunities for faculty involvement, no faculty participated on the core team.

TIME

Time with respect to diffusion reflects three measurable components of the discussion process which include (a) the time it takes for an individual to be introduced to the innovation to the time it takes the same individual to determine whether to adopt or reject the innovation, (b) the timeframe in which the innovation is adopted relative to that of other adopters, and (c) the rate of adoption by those within the system (Rogers, 2003). With regard to The Global Campus, time was of the essence. However, in its lifespan of 4 short years, too many adopters determined to reject the innovation to the point of pressuring the initiative's administration to close the doors.

SOCIAL SYSTEM

Rogers (2003) defines a *social system* as "a set of interrelated units that are engaged in joint problem solving to accomplish a common goal" (p. 23). Innovation decisions can be made based upon one of three types of choices: (a) *optional innovation-decisions* where "choices to adopt or reject an innovation that are made by an individual independent of the decisions of the other members of the system" (p. 28), (b) *collective innovation-decisions*, which are those "choices to adopt or reject an innovation that are made by consensus among the members of a system" (p. 28), and (c) *authority innovation-decisions*, which are "choices to adopt or reject an innovation that are made by a relatively few individuals in a system who possess power, status, or technical expertise" (p. 28).

It was the decision of President White to move forward with developing The Global Campus, therefore, causing the initial choice to be one of authority. However, due to the political nature of a system as large as the University of Illinois, no one person has sole authority to implement such large initiatives in a manner that rejects the input, concerns, and voices of its members. Such authoritarian introduction of The Global Campus may have been the single greatest factor in its downfall.

In order for an authoritarian approach to be successful in terms of diffusion, the authoritarian figure must require implementation and have full authority to do so. The University of Illinois, like many institutions of higher education, shares operational power among tenure-track faculty, governing boards, and advising committees. Therefore, the successful creation of a separate virtual campus would have required full autonomy and administrative control or the overall support of the faulty senates and chancellors at all three campuses.

Without an authoritarian figure dictating adoption, change must happen through the use of *opinion leaders* who serve as respectable members of the society and are early adopters of the innovation (Rogers, 2003). With no opinion leader sitting on the initial core team The Global Campus initiative could have been perceived as an us against them (faculty against administration) scenario, causing resentment and negative attitudes toward change from the onset. Michael Lindeman (personal communication, October 21, 2009), director of program and course development for The Global Campus, feels that appointing a faculty member (or other opinion leader within the system) to lead the initiative rather than an existing administrator would have earned more initial respect by the adopting community. By doing so, faculty may have felt that the existing academic oversight and rigor would have been less questionable. However, one must still wonder if things had been different, how different would they actually be? Would the mission to reach more students be successful if the university's current model had simply transferred to an online delivery modality? Would tenure-track faculty rely on adjunct faculty to help ensure multiple sections of a course could be offered? No one knows. What we do know is that due to the administration's inability to get the faculty senates' and chancellors' support, The Global Campus closed its virtual doors on December 31, 2009. Individual campus units became responsible for the creation and implementation of any distance education adventures. May The Global Campus torch not burn out, but be passed, carrying reminders of past mistakes and successes, and may each campus stay true to the original mission of The Global Campus: "become a national leader in online education, focused on innovation, quality, superior instruction, service, and accessibility" (University of Illinois Global Campus, 2007, p. 1).

REFERENCES

Kolowich, S. (2009). What doomed Global Campus? Retrieved from the Inside Higher Education website: http://www.insidehighered.com/news/2009/09/03/globalcampus

Rogers, E. M. (2003). *Diffusion of innovations.* (5th ed). New York, NY: Free Press.

University of Illinois Global Campus. (2007). *The University of Illinois Global Campus instructor policies and procedures manual.* Champaign, IL: Author.

White, J. B. (2005). *Inaugural address.* Retrieved from http://www.uillinois.edu/president/speeches/20042005/sep22.Inaugural.Address.cfm

---

"THE UNIVERSITY OF ILLINOIS GLOBAL CAMPUS IS A RATHER NEW INITIATIVE WITH THE MISSION TO BECOME A NATIONAL LEADER IN ONLINE EDUCATION, FOCUSED ON INNOVATION, QUALITY, SUPERIOR INSTRUCTION, SERVICE, AND ACCESSIBILITY."

Online Learning Opportunities for K-12 Students in Florida's Nassau County

Kari Burgess-Watkins

INTRODUCTION

Research suggests that in approximately 4 years, 10% of all courses will be computer based and by 2019, 50% of all courses will be online (Christensen & Horn, 2008). In Florida, school districts must provide full-time virtual instructional programs to students in kindergarten through Grade 12.

Kari Burgess-Watkins,
Technology Integration Specialist, Nassau County School District, 1201 Atlantic Avenue, Fernandina Beach, FL 32034.
Telephone: (904) 491-9941.
E-mail: burgesska@nassau.k12.fl.us

While the Nassau County School District has been using Internet-based courses for high school credit recovery purposes, the district did not have an established full-time virtual school program. During the 2006-2007 school year, Nassau County public high school students earned 201 one-half credits through the online credit recovery program offered by the district (Rodeffer, 2007). The number of one-half credits earned increased to 614 during the 2007-2008 school year (Rodeffer, 2008). Due to budget constraints, the district reformatted the credit recovery program for the 2008-2009 school year and students earned 235 one-half credits through the online program (Burgess-Watkins, 2009). In addition to the online credit recovery courses offered by the district, Nassau County public school students have been enrolling in online courses offered through the Florida Virtual School.

In the 2009-2010 school year, Nassau County School District opened the Nassau Virtual School, which offers free online courses for eligible elementary, middle, and high school students residing in Nassau County. Nassau Virtual School provides online learning for current public school students, hospital homebound students, home education students, and private school students.

The implementation of the full-time K-12 virtual instructional program has been a daunting task. Fortunately, other innovative K-12 Florida districts have been offering distance education programs for a few years and have proven instrumental in establishing the necessary framework for Nassau Virtual School. The Nassau Virtual School team met over the course of a year to determine the mission, goals, objectives, programs, courses, budgets, policies, procedures, job descriptions, teacher pay schedules, website development, advertising, and other administrative tasks.

MISSION STATEMENT

The mission of the Nassau Virtual School is to extend educational opportunities for growth to all students through a flexible online environment, and thereby foster the development of each student as an inspired life-long learner and problem-solver with the strength of character to serve as a productive member of society (Nassau County School District [NCSD], 2010).

GOALS AND OBJECTIVES

The goals of the Nassau Virtual School are to:

- meet the legislative requirements for K-12 students as established by Section 1002.45 of the Florida Statutes;
- provide public high school students with an online opportunity for credit recovery, grade forgiveness, and supplemental or acceleration coursework;
- provide all eligible hospital homebound students with the opportunity to take courses online;
- provide students in Grades 9-12 with an online opportunity to earn a high school diploma;
- provide online courses for Nassau County home education high school students; and

- Provide online courses for private high school students residing in Nassau County.

In order to meet the requirements of the legislation as well as fulfill other needs of students within Nassau County, Nassau County School District is using a multifaceted approach. Nassau County School District uses Florida Virtual School Full Time (FLVS FT) for students in Grades K-12, a franchise of the Florida Virtual School for students in Grades 6-12, EdOptions for students in Grades 6-12, and Florida Adult and Technical Distance Education Consortium (FATDEC) courses for adult education students.

FLVS FT FOR GRADES K-8

Florida Virtual School in partnership with Connections Academy created FLVS FT. By signing a contract with FLVS FT, Nassau County families and students have access to a high performing "A"-rated public virtual program (Connections Academy, 2011). The full-time, 180-day comprehensive program is offered to Nassau County kindergarten through 12th grade students. In order to qualify for the FLVS FT K-12 program, the student must reside in Nassau County School District's attendance area and meet one of the following criteria:

- the student has spent the prior school year in attendance at a public school in this state and was enrolled and reported by a public school district for funding during the preceding October and February for purposes of the Florida Education Finance Program surveys;
- the student is a dependent child of a member of the United States armed forces who was transferred within the last 12 months to this state from another state or from a foreign country pursuant to the parent's permanent change of station orders;

- the student was enrolled during the prior school year in a school district virtual instruction program under this section or a K-8 Virtual School Program under s.1002.415, Florida Statutes; and
- the student has a sibling who is currently enrolled in the school district virtual instruction program and that sibling was enrolled in such program at the end of the prior school year.

Through the FLVS FT program, students benefit from the flexibility of online courses, Sunshine State Standards curriculum, highly qualified Florida-certified teachers, regular communication, and personalized, instruction (Florida Virtual School Full Time, n.d.).

The majority of the FLVS FT K-8 curriculum is in print and supplemented through online content and resources. Once a student has applied and the district has verified eligibility, Connections Academy ships all of the required learning materials directly to the student's home.

FLVS FRANCHISE FOR GRADES 6-12

In order to provide FLVS courses to Nassau County students in Grades 6-12, Nassau Virtual School signed a franchise agreement with the FLVS. The franchise courses are taught by local Nassau County School District teachers. Nassau Virtual School teachers, students, and parents benefit from the expertise of the FLVS in terms of online instruction, instructional management, student management, support, and technology infrastructure. Teachers and students can login and work on their coursework any time and from any location with access to the Internet. In order to participate in the Nassau Virtual School franchise courses, the student must meet one of the following criteria:

- be enrolled in a Nassau County School District public school;

- be enrolled as a home education student with Nassau County School District; and
- be enrolled in a private school and whose legal guardian is a Nassau County, FL resident (NCSD, 2010).

HOME EDUCATION STUDENTS

High school home education students residing in Nassau County may retain home education status and utilize Nassau Virtual School courses to enhance their curriculum. Students have access to all offered courses and can take one or as many as six online courses per semester. The student's parent or guardian acts as guidance counselor to approve course selection (NCSD, 2010).

PRIVATE SCHOOL STUDENTS

Full-time private high school students residing in Nassau County can take one or as many as six online courses per semester with Nassau Virtual School. All private school students are required to meet with their guidance counselor in order to register for Nassau Virtual School courses.

HOSPITAL HOMEBOUND

High school hospital homebound students can take one or as many as six Nassau Virtual School courses with the approval of the hospital homebound facilitator and the guidance counselor from the student's home school. Course selection is determined by the student's guidance counselor (NCSD, 2010).

COENROLLED STUDENTS

Public high school students enrolled in a traditional Nassau County high school can take courses online with Nassau Virtual School as part of their schedule. A student's schedule may not exceed six courses between the schools. All public school students are required to receive approval from their guidance counselor in order to register for Nassau Virtual courses (NCSD, 2010).

FULL-TIME DIPLOMA-SEEKING STUDENTS

The full-time online program allows students to earn a regular high school diploma and complete their coursework online with Nassau County School District certified teachers. Students report to a campus for FCAT Testing and other assessments as necessary. Students are able to customize their education for accelerated learning or to accommodate their individual needs. In order to participate in the Nassau Virtual School diploma seeking program, a student should:

- have been promoted to the next grade the previous school year;
- have a 2.5 or higher grade point average;
- have scored at Level 3 or above on the FCAT Reading and Math during the previous school year; and
- meet all Nassau County Student Progression Plan Criteria (NCSD, 2010).

SELF-EVALUATION ONLINE LEARNING QUIZ

Online learning can provide opportunities for students to take courses any time and from anywhere; however, this style of learning may not be appropriate for every student (Florida Virtual School [FLVS], 2009). FLVS has developed a list of technical competencies, access, and learning style questions to help students determine if online learning is an option for meeting their educational needs.

In order to help a student determine if he or she will be successful learning in an online environment, he or she should carefully consider the FLVS "Is online learning for you?" questions (FLVS, 2009) prior to requesting Nassau Virtual School courses.

If the student can answer "YES" to ALL of the questions, online learning may be a viable option for his or her educational needs (FLVS, 2009). If the student answers "NO" to two or more, he or she will likely experience difficulty and should resolve these issues prior to attempting online coursework (FLVS, 2009).

TECHNICAL COMPETENCIES AND ACCESS

- Taking into consideration my personal, academic, work and extracurricular activities (sports, clubs, etc.), will I be able to devote as much or more time to my online class, as I do for my traditional studies?
- Am I comfortable using the Internet as a means of communication and research?
- Do I own or have access to a computer with Internet access and e-mail?
- Do I know or I am willing to learn how to copy, cut, and paste text/files between programs?
- Am I willing and able to learn and apply new software applications?

LEARNING STYLES

- Am I able to prioritize tasks, organize assignments and complete assigned work by the required date?
- Can I solve problems and work through difficulties independently?
- Are my writing, reading and communication skills above average?
- Do I prefer to work alone on assignments?
- Can I read and follow detailed instructions on my own without an instructor lecturing and giving verbal explanations? [Questions adapted from Florida Virtual School's Tips for Students signing up for FLVS classes (FLVS, 2009).

COURSES

Nassau Virtual School offers 42 middle and high school courses in the following subject areas: career education, critical thinking, English, Spanish, math, science, and social studies.

INSTRUCTION

The majority of the Nassau Virtual School policies are derived directly from the contract with FLVS. Nassau Virtual School teachers are required to speak via telephone with students and their parents at least once per month. In addition, the teachers and students interact regularly through e-mail, voice mail, and telephone. Students are encouraged to contact the teacher when there is any type of academic need. Teachers are required to respond to all e-mail and voicemail within 24 hours during the regular work week (Monday-Friday) and weekend communication (Saturday-Sunday) should be handled with integrity and professional judgment. All communication between the teacher, student, and parent is documented in the course management system. Unlike the traditional classroom where the student must move on with the rest of the class or physically attend their next class, in a virtual course, the student can call the teacher and work through the material until he or she is able to understand it (NCSD, 2010).

COURSEWORK

Students are expected to login to each course for active participation at least three times a week. All Nassau Virtual School courses have a pace chart. The pace chart outlines exactly what is expected to be submitted by the student on a weekly basis. Each student is required to submit a specific amount of coursework each week in order to maintain the appropriate pace. Teachers work with the student to modify the pace chart to reflect a traditional, extended or accelerated pace. Failure to maintain the required number of weekly submissions will result in warnings, grade penalties, and potential withdrawal from

the course. If a student will not be participating in a course due to travel or other commitment, the student must be on pace and notify the teacher in advance of the planned absence in order to discuss assignment completions and pacing (NCSD, 2010).

GRACE PERIOD

The grace period provides the student with an opportunity to "try out" the course while allowing the teacher to evaluate the student's performance. A student may drop a course without academic penalty by notifying the teacher before the 28th day in the course. If a student is not "on pace" with the coursework during the grace period, the teacher will contact the student and parent. If the student remains "off pace" by the end of the grace period, the student will be administratively dropped from the course without academic penalty. After the 28th day of the grace period, the student will earn a grade for the course regardless if the grade is passing or failing. Students must maintain pace in order to stay enrolled in the course (NCSD, 2010).

ASSESSMENTS

The teacher regularly conducts discussion-based assessments at certain points within the course with each student via telephone. During these assessments, the teacher discusses the student's coursework and the course content in order for the student to demonstrate mastery of the content while also verifying the authenticity of his or her work. Each student is required to take a final exam in all Nassau Virtual School courses. The final exam helps the teacher validate the student has demonstrated mastery of key course concepts and standards. The student is expected to take the exam as directed by the teacher. With the intention of maintaining the integrity of all Nassau Virtual School courses and grades, the teacher may choose to facilitate or require an oral or a face-to-face assessment at any point in the course (NCSD, 2010).

ACADEMIC INTEGRITY

In order to participate in Nassau Virtual School courses, the student must agree to the FLVS academic integrity policy. Academic integrity means:

- Your work on each assignment will be completely your own.
- Your collaboration with another classmate on any assignment will be pre-approved by your teacher.
- You will not practice plagiarism in any form.
- You will not allow others to copy your work.
- You will not misuse content from the Internet.
- You will not give any assistance to students scheduled to take the course in the future.
- Your parent or guardian will attest that you completed the work on your own (NCSD, 2010).

TEACHER RESPONSIBILITIES

As outlined in the Nassau Virtual School teacher's job description, teachers are expected to (NCSD, 2010):

- instruct assigned classes based on the curriculum established by Nassau Virtual School/Florida Virtual School;
- identify, select, create, and accommodate the needs of students with varying backgrounds, learning styles, and special needs;
- assist students in accomplishing course/program objectives;
- establish an environment that is conducive to learning and active participation in learning activities;

- establish relationships with students and parents through e-mail and monthly phone conferences;
- monitor student progress and encourage students to maintain pace established by the virtual school pace charts;
- participate in professional development and faculty meetings;
- utilize all required and recommended Nassau Virtual School computer applications.;
- maintain accurate and complete records in accordance with laws, rules, policies, and administrative regulations;
- regularly check the usage logs to verify that students are active in the course;
- provide timely feedback to students on their assignments and assessment tasks; and
- follow the policies stated in the memorandum of agreement as required by the Florida Virtual School Franchise Agreement.

In order to ensure each teacher effectively performs his or her assigned teaching responsibilities, virtual classroom walkthroughs are conducted based on a model from Broward Virtual School. During the observations, the teacher and program manager simultaneously view various portions of the course management system and discuss instructional practice, student progress, and student-teacher communication to make certain quality teaching and learning are taking place within the virtual classroom.

PARENTAL INVOLVEMENT

While the student is responsible for all of his or her own coursework, parental involvement is critical component to the student's success in online learning. A parent or guardian should consider the following questions in order to determine whether online learning is a viable solution for the parent or guardian and child. As a parent, are you willing to:

- Know and use your child's username and password to access their grade book, announcements, assignment feedback, etc?
- Make sure assignments, tests, and quizzes have been completed?
- Check weekly to see submitted assignments and grades?
- Help your child determine and stick to a schedule?
- Encourage your child to ask questions, call the teacher, or e-mail the teacher when he or she needs help?
- Provide the teacher with your e-mail address to receive monthly progress reports?
- Discuss problem areas with your child and communicate with the teacher and guidance counselor as often as needed?
- Make yourself available to discuss your child's progress with the teacher?
- Provide a quiet study space for your child with access to the Internet, telephone, and printer?
- Contact technical support as needed? [Questions adapted from Marion Virtual School's Making Virtual Learning Work —Tips for Parents (Marion County Public Schools, 2009)].

Nassau Virtual School offers students and parents a choice regarding their educational options. Together they must decide whether the student should attend a traditional brick and mortar school or opt to participate in a flexible educational model. Students take online courses for a variety of reasons, such as the opportunity to learn at their own pace, the ability to work and go to school, rigorous training schedule, or to makeup credits from academic setbacks. The Nassau Virtual School bridges a gap for those students whose needs are not being met in the traditional classroom. Since the legislative mandates regarding online learning are still new, Nassau Virtual School has the chance to be a part of the development process for K-12 online learning in the state of Florida. As Nassau County School District strives to implement online learning in the K-12 environment, Nassau Virtual School will continuously evolve and work with other districts to meet the diverse needs of Nassau County students as well as the requirements of the legislation and Florida Department of Education.

REFERENCES

Burgess-Watkins, K. (2009). *Credit recovery overview.* Fernandina Beach, FL: Nassau County School District.

Christensen, C. M., & Horn, M. B. (2008). How do we transform our schools? *Education Next, 8*(3), 13-19.

Connections Academy. (2011). *Florida Virtual School Full Time.* Retrieved from http://www.connectionsacademy.com/florida-school/free-online-public-school.aspx

Florida Virtual School. (2009). *Tips for students signing up for FLVS online classes.* Retrieved from http://www.flvs.net/Students/Pages/TipsforStudents.aspx

Florida Virtual School Full Time. (n.d.). *Florida Virtual School Full Time.* Retrieved from http://www.flvsft.com

Marion County Public Schools. (2009). *Tips for parents.* Retrieved from http://www.marion.k12.fl.us/schools/mvs/parents.cfm

Nassau County School District. (2010). *Nassau Virtual School Policy Manual.* Retrieved from http://www.nassau.k12.fl.us

Rodeffer, J. (2007). *Evaluation of NEFEC dropout prevention/credit recovery program.* Fernandina Beach, FL: Nassau County School District.

Rodeffer, J. (2008). *Evaluation of NEFEC dropout prevention/credit recovery program.* Fernandina Beach, FL: Nassau County School District.

Responding to Change
Online Education
at the College of Central Florida

Connie J. Tice

HISTORICAL PERSPECTIVE

In the mid 1950s when a group of community leaders and citizens began to envision a way to provide educational opportunities to three counties in Florida they had no idea what would happen in the decades to follow. In 1957 Central Florida Junior College was established to provide educational opportunities beyond high school to Marion, Citrus, and Levy counties. The following year Hampton Junior College opened and was one of the first Black 2-year colleges in the state. In 1966 the two colleges merged and in 1971

Connie J. Tice,
Senior Professor of Speech Communication,
College of Central Florida, 3800 S. Lecanto
Highway, Lecanto, FL 3446-9026.
Telephone: (352) 746-6721, ext. 6139.
E-mail: ticec@cf.edu

their name was changed to Central Florida Community College (CFCC). At this point in the history of the college all students attended classes on what is now known as the Ocala Campus; located in Ocala, Florida. Communication between students and the college was mostly accomplished via mail or students coming to the campus.

The college offered courses in Citrus County on a limited basis until 1984. To meet the continuing demands of the community for educational opportunities the Citrus County School Board partnered with the college and an educational complex was established in 1984; high school facilities were provided to accommodate the college classes. In 1996 a free-standing campus was opened—now called the Citrus Campus—and in 2009 a new building was opened to accommodate more classrooms and a new Learning and Conference Center.

To meet the growing needs in the Levy County area the Bronson Center was opened in 1987. In 1993 the Levy Center moved to a storefront in Chiefland, Florida where it is currently housed. In 2008 the college was able to procure a site for a permanent center in Levy County and when funds are available construction will begin (College of Central Florida, 2011).

In the fall of 2010 CFCC underwent another name change to the College of Central Florida (CCF). The name change came about because beginning in the spring of 2011 CCF began offering the community the opportunity to earn a bachelor of applied science in business and organizational management; in August 2011 a bachelor of science degree in early childhood education was also added to the curriculum.

RESPONDING TO CHANGE

According to Allen and Seaman (2008), "Over 3.9 million students were taking at least one online course during the fall 2007 term; a 12% increase over the number reported the previous year" (p. 1). Community colleges reported an increase of 11.3% in distance learning enrollment during this period; this increase accounted for the majority of the overall growth (Instructional Technology Council, 2008). As a result of this growth in distance learning on the community college campus, the institution has to look to new ways to engage both faculty and students in the learning process.

Community colleges and their faculty have been known for their ability to respond to both change and the needs of their students and the community; CCF is no exception. With the advent of the Internet and the introduction of personal technology that was more affordable the community college student began to expect and demand a different approach to education. To respond to this demand CCF not only brought more computer access in to the classroom they also developed courses that could be taught online.

EVOLUTION OF A PROGRAM

In the fall of 1997 a group of instructors, who Rogers (2003) would most likely label innovators, developed and taught the first 13 online courses for CCF. The instructors were self-taught in regard to course development for online learning and their e-learning platform was WebCT 4.1. As a response to the growing demand for online education the E-Learning Department was established in 2004; this depart-

ment now provides training for faculty and technical support to both faculty and students (J. Strigle, personal communication, November 16, 2010). According to CCF's *E-Learning Handbook* (2010-2011) e-learning at the college "involves any formal delivery method in which the majority of instruction takes place via the internet or other electronic means, such as video-conferencing, pod casting, educational software, etc." (p. 11).

The target population of the e-learning courses is primarily students who live within the tricounty area; Marion, Citrus, and Levy counties. Even though these students may not be geographically distant, e-learning courses may make the difference between completing a degree and dropping out of college. Geographically distant students are also accommodated and since the fall of 2002 CCF has been able to offer an Associate of Arts degree totally online.

The E-Learning Department continues to provide technical support; however, it has taken on the additional responsibilities of faculty training and the development of specific protocols for course development. To assist in the development of courses and training, a committee comprised of faculty from multiple disciplines serves as an advisory body for e-learning. In the early development of online courses, a faculty member presented the idea to the college curriculum committee and then the course was taught. It was not until 2010 that the *E-Learning Handbook* was published with definitions of online, hybrid, telecourses, and ITV courses and a protocol concerning the development of new courses (J. Strigle, personal communication, November 16, 2010).

The protocol involves: (a) decisions regarding the need for online courses are made within each department based on both departmental and college goals; (b) the faculty member completes an application, the deadline is one month after the start of each term; (c) the application is signed by the department chair and then submitted to the dean of learning resources; (d) the dean forwards the application electronically to the e-learning advisory board for discussion and approval; (e) when the faculty member is notified of approval he or she will sign up for a series of workshops that assist in the development of the course. This training involves technical training on the ANGEL LMS as needed, instructional design training, criteria for effective online courses, assistance with converting traditional class materials and activities into online format, utilization of learning object repositories, and software designed for the development of online courses (*E-Learning Handbook*, 2010-2011).

As the program grew it was necessary to define the differences between the different online learning courses. Online courses are defined as those courses distributed through the Internet, allowing flexibility in time and/or place (*E-Learning Handbook*, 2010-2011). Hybrid courses are defined as a combination of online and traditional face-to-face courses (*E-Learning Handbook*, 2010-2011). Telecourses are defined as those courses offered in videotape/DVD formats and these are checked out from the CCF library (*E-Learning Handbook*, 2010-2011). ITV courses are defined as interactive television courses allowing distribution of live classes through video conferencing equipment (*E-Learning Handbook*, 2010-2011). The growth of the E-Learning Department, in regard to the number of sections taught for both online and hybrid courses, is reflected in Table 1.

The types of courses being offered either online or using the hybrid format include: English, Spanish, algebra, calculus, statistics, speech, art history, several psychology courses, criminal justice, micro- and macroeconomics, wellness, environmental sciences, chemistry, and world civilization. It is anticipated that several courses using the hybrid format will be used for the two new bachelor degree programs (J. Strigle, personal communication, November 16, 2010).

In the 1950s, having a computer in a classroom or office was not considered. Standard procedure was for the professor to stand in front of a class, size determined by the number of desks, location determined by where the physical college was located, write instructions on a blackboard, and sometimes provide paper handouts. Now, a professor can sit at his or her desk, communicate with any number of students located in many different geographical areas, use virtual tours, and use creative

Table 1. E-learning Enrollment

Academic Year	Number of Online Sections	Online Enrollment	Number of Hybrid Sections	Hybrid Enrollment
1998-1999	54	712	0	0
1999-2000	71	1,065	0	0
2000-2001	65	1,094	0	0
2001-2002	78	1,373	0	0
2002-2003	82	1,724	0	0
2003-2004	103	2,460	3	54
2004-2005	135	3,120	10	213
2005-2006	173	3,812	20	251
2006-2007	206	4,451	32	509
2007-2008	240	5,288	54	841
2008-2009	299	6,886	83	1,509

programs to act as a catalyst for learning. Intermediate algebra and statistics is now being taught online using a program produced by Pearson called Course Compass; face-to-face students also use this program to practice math skills and ask questions of their professors via email.

FUTURE GOALS

The E-Learning Department has developed several goals in anticipation of an even higher demand for online education at the community college level. The E-Learning Department and the advisory committee have defined a number of goals for the next 5 years. Goals that impact the student are: increasing reliable and accessible technology support and developing courses that meet graduation requirements. Goals for faculty include: increasing reliable and accessible technology support and providing more training in regard to the development of, online, hybrid, and ITV courses. Beyond the environment of CCF the goals are to increase collaboration with other institutions, initiatives, and consortia involved with e-learning (J. Strigle, personal communication, November 16, 2010).

THE FUTURE

What will happen beyond the Internet and what is currently happening in online and face-to-face courses? According to the Horizon Report, 2009, we can expect an increase in the use of mobiles in the academic environment, the addition of cloud computing, geo-everything, the personal web, semantic-aware applications, and smart objects. This same report suggested that students are different, there is a need for both innovation and leadership in academia, institutions are pressured to prove students are learning, and higher education is expected to utilize technology.

REFERENCES

Allen, E., & Seaman, J. (2008). *Staying the course: Online education in the United States 2008.* Retrieved from http://www.sloan-c.org /publications/survey/pdf/staying_the_course .pdf

Central Florida Community College. (2010-2011). *E-learning handbook.* Retrieved from http://www.cf.edu/distance/ELhandbook .htm

College of Central Florida. (2011). Academic catalog. Retrieved from http://www.cf.edu/ smartcatalog/history.htm

Instructional Technology. (2008). *Instructional technology council 2008 distance education Survey results tracking the impact of e-learning at community colleges.* Retrieved from http:// www.itcnetwork.org/file.php?= 2FITCAnnualSurveyMarch2009Final.pdf

Johnson, L., Levine, A., & Smith R. (2009). *The 2009 horizon report.* Austin TX: The New Media Consortium.

Rogers, E. (2003). *Diffusion of innovations* (5th ed.). New York, NY: Free Press.

COMMUNITY COLLEGES AND THEIR FACULTY HAVE BEEN KNOWN FOR THEIR ABILITY TO RESPOND TO BOTH CHANGE AND THE NEEDS OF THEIR STUDENTS AND COMMUNITY.

A Closer Look at Distance Learning in the Kansas City, Missouri School District

Shelley Brown Cooper

INTRODUCTION

H ow, in a failing school district, does an administrative leadership team implement a district-wide distance learning program? Which district level management decisions were made? In short, how and why did Phase II of a transformation plan become a reality?

BACKGROUND OF KCMSD SCHOOL DISTRICT

It is necessary to gather a historical perspective of the large, urban, majority-

Shelley Brown Cooper,
Doctoral Student, Nova Southeastern
University, 4526 Francis Street,
Kansas City, Kansas 66103.
Telephone: (913) 710-3818.
E-mail: SC1317@nova.edu

minority Kansas City, Missouri School District (KCMSD) in order to understand the recent transformations that have taken place. Very few school districts have experienced as much turmoil, controversy, and bad press as this district. It has "shrunken from 22,000 students in 2008 to 17,000 students in 2011, and has had more than two dozen superintendents in the past four decades" (Sulzberger, 2011). It has held provisional accreditation since 2008 and lost state accreditation January 1, 2012 (About KCMSD website, 2011).

According to the *About KCMSD* website, the racial composition is now 63.3 African American, 25.4% Hispanic, and 8.6% Caucasian. It is considered a Title 1 district due to its 80.3% free and reduced lunch population (http://www.kcpublicschools.org). Discipline reports are reported to be above the state average. Discipline incident reports state wide are 2 incidents per 100 students. In the KCMSD, the rate is 8 incidents per 100 students. The dropout rate is 16. 9% for the district compared to 3% statewide. Composite ACT scores are 21 for Missouri students and 16.5 for students in the KCMSD (Missouri Comprehensive Data System, 2011).

The Missouri Comprehensive Data System (2011) reports discouraging statistics for the KCMSD because it failed to meet Missouri State Improvement Plan levels in both mathematics and communication arts for Grades 3-12 during the 2010-2011 school year (Missouri Department of Elementary and Secondary Education, 2011b). In addition, acceptable attendance levels and graduation rates were not attained in 2011. While most school districts' scores improved, the 2011 scores were lower than those reported in 2010 (Missouri Department of Elementary School Education, 2011b). Escalating Adequate Yearly Progress targets that are required under the federal No Child Left Behind law for student achievement will increase by 8 percentage points annually, on a pace to reach the federal goal of 100% proficiency by the year 2014 (Missouri Department of elementary and Secondary Education, 2011).

TRANSFORMATION PLAN

However, despite its numerous shortcomings and hardships, there was a plan. As a result of the district's drastic situation, John Covington, former superintendent of the KCMSD, has implemented a two-step transformation plan that has infused extensive technological advances into the school system during the 2009 through 2013 school years. Beginning with the 2011-2012 school year, virtual, online, and distance learning opportunities were created on the high school level. Digital portfolio assessment practices for all grade levels were to be used to promote student-centered learning. In addition, Covington incorporated student-centered and project-based learning in newly developed technology rich classroom environments (2009, p. 7).

KCMSD's mission and focus toward ensuring student readiness for the workforce has increased the district's emphasis on infusing technology in student learning, teacher preparation, administration and data management, resource distribution and technical support. The strategic planning leadership team was charged with implementing this new technology initiative throughout the district operating under demanding demographic constraints.

Covington's team developed the plan in an effort to revive a failing district and improve its chances of regaining its state accreditation. The plan is entitled The Transformation Plan: Phase I and Phase II. The transformation plan consists of five key initiatives to be executed from 2009 through 2013. It plans to create a system of student-centered learning; preparing college, career and workforce ready graduates; revolutionizing the district workforce, transforming the environment and cultivating communication (Covington, 2009).

Phase I of the transformation plan took place from 2009 through 2010 and focused on operational issues. Phase II, slotted to begin during the 2011 and 2012 school years, involves right-sizing the buildings and staff by cutting costs and unnecessary or antiquated programming. Covington uses the term "right-sizing the school district" instead of "down-sizing" to describe cutting the budget by more than $50 million to provide a balanced budget and saving the KCMSD from bankruptcy (p. 4). Over half of the district's 64 schools were closed and nearly 1,000 employees were eliminated. During Phase II of Covington's transformation plan, the district plans to "right-size" the school district and "implement a rigorous and relevant prekindergarten–12th grade system of student-centered teaching and learning" (Covington, 2009). One important tenet of this phase of the transformation plan involves building "technology rich classroom environments." As part of this technology initiative, massive changes were implemented during the 2011-2012 school year including a 3-year initiative:

> Equipping classrooms with interactive white boards, video projectors, classroom computers, audio systems, DVD players, and document cameras. Distance learning labs will be installed in each of the seven high schools and the Foreign Language Academy. In addition, a second lab will be added to each high school and

Carver Elementary School (Covington, 2009, p. 4).

Transformation Plan Phase II's five key initiatives are focused on producing more college, career and workforce ready graduates by providing additional technological learning opportunities. The plan specified implementing "virtual, online and distance learning" activities in order to provide KCMSD's students "access to a wide range of courses from advanced placement to fine arts to foreign language courses that they can access anytime, anywhere." Distance learning labs were specifically identified due to their ability to allow for virtual learning experiences, expand students' abilities to take college and dual-credit courses, and provide educational experiences not available in traditional classroom settings (Covington, 2009).

DISTANCE EDUCATION

The distance learning goals provided by the Missouri Department of Elementary and Secondary Education (2011a) dictate that "distance learning should enable students to achieve their educational goals by delivering academically sound courses and educational support services that are flexible, responsive and innovative. In addition, the distance learning courses should provide the same academic standards, criteria, quality, and content as traditional on-site programs" (p. 2). Also, the recent loss of accreditation by the KCMSD might possibly impact the implementation of the distance learning program within the district. Further study is needed to examine the implications resulting from the loss of accreditation on new curriculum efforts within a school district. In light of a possible state takeover, procedures are needed on how future planning will be conducted to proceed with the distance learning initiative within the KCMSD.

Distance education has a history spanning over 160 years. Simonson, Smaldino,

Albright, and Zvacek (2012), Moore (2007) and Rice (2006) trace the innovations in this educational method from correspondence, radio, television through present day video conferencing and Internet techniques.

Simonson et al. (2012), Moore (2007) and Smith (2009) describe the benefits of distance learning as the instructor and learner can be separated by time and space; instructor expertise can be utilized by many more students worldwide, regardless of either participant's location; collaborative activities can be explored via distance education and learning environments are no longer dictated by logistics. Simonson et al. (2012) also notes that distance education can "supplement existing curricula, promote course sharing among schools, and reach students who cannot (for physical reasons or incarceration) or do not (by choice) attend school in person" (p. 138). Harrison (2005) reports several reasons for the pursuit of distance learning in the K-12 school system, namely: the course is not available locally; to resolve timetable conflicts; to meet diploma requirements; for program enrichment; course required, and to improve grades (p. 15).

While it is difficult to estimate the scope of K-12 distance education, virtual schools have had a national impact for many years (Moore & Anderson, 2003). Virtual schools are present in Florida, Arkansas, Mississippi, Iowa, South Dakota, Kansas and many more (Simonson et al., 2012). Participation in K-12 distance education is more prevalent in rural areas due to lack of qualified instructors and potential low enrollment in more sparsely populated school districts.

The strategic planning conducted by the leadership team included a multitude of details: funding acquisition, facility design, construction, equipment purchases, staff training and development to curriculum design and evaluation. Leadership teams must seek funding for distance education programs. Increased use of the federally funded Star Schools Program has been cited as an example of supplemental distance learning with urban K-12 learners. However, some researchers claim that rural schools are more likely to achieve equity objectives through distance learning than high-minority and low-income schools (Tushnet & Fleming-McCormick, as cited in Moore & Anderson, 2003). Leadership teams in Iowa, Mississippi and Alabama sought Star Schools funding to assist in their distance education programs (Three Statewide Approaches to Distance Education, 2000).

Moore and Anderson (2003) reported that the federal government has seen educational technology and distance learning utilized as tools for use in education reform and school improvement efforts, such as group-based videoconference courses. These funds are geared more toward high-need school districts and low-income populations (p. 685). The KCMSD recounted unacceptable results in math, communication arts, and attendance and graduation rates. Its population consists of more than 80% eligible for free and/or reduced lunches. While distance learning technologies are far more commonly used for student enrichment in K-12 schools than for direct K-12 instruction, the superintendent's decision to implement distance learning opportunities throughout the district would provide additional avenues to address low test scores and declining graduation rates (Clark, 2003, as cited in Moore & Anderson, 2003).

After studying the literature, the KCMSD's strategic planning leadership team collaboratively suggested offering Advanced Placement courses within the distance learning labs at the six high schools (McBeth, 2011). The majority of courses taught via distance education in most high schools are Advanced Placement courses. The respective state boards of education mandate the requirements for Advanced Placement courses. English, U.S.

history, biology, chemistry, physics, calculus, and selected foreign languages were offered via distance learning at the majority of the high school's distance learning labs (Bral, 2007; Henly, 2009; McBeth, 2011; Sabatino, 2008; Smith, 2009; SREB, 2006).

Many of the decisions made by these areas with statewide distance learning programs provided guidance to the KCMSD's strategic planning leadership team. Specifically, South Dakota, Oklahoma, and Iowa began offering distance education in their schools. In 1996, South Dakota initiated the "Wiring the Schools Project" by wiring of all K-12 schools within the state allowing for high speed Internet and videoconferencing (p. 5). This initiative resulted in the Digital Dakota Network that linked every school building to a compressed video network. Oklahoma participated in the Star Schools Assistance program in 1988. It was selected to participate based on its status of being underfunded and disadvantaged (Martin, 2009). This early initiative equipped 35 schools with equipment necessary to participate in satellite-based programming: TVRO satellite C/Ku band antenna and receiver, television/monitor, videocassette recorder, TV/VCR cabinet and cordless telephone (Martin, 2009, p. 53). The purpose of this telecommunications project is to improve instruction at the elementary and secondary school levels, primarily in the areas of mathematics, science, and foreign languages (Martin, 2009, p. 51).

Berg (2002) posits five elements of distance education: physical separation; administration by an educational organization; frequent use of various media, including print, video, film, computer and audio; communication between student and teacher, synchronous or asynchronous; and administrative focus on the nontraditional learner (p. xvi).

Boschmann (1995) insisted that two fundamental steps take place when designing and building a distance learning lab: establish a design team and listen closely to the faculty and students. In addition, permanent and portable technologies need to be determined, along with distribution of electronics (p. 34). Designing a distance learning laboratory consists of three categories of design decision making.

> Environmental design is related to the project's architect. Technology design focuses on integrating audio, optical, video and computer technologies into one system. The third category, interface design, deals with ergonomics and human-technology systems. (p. 39)

When the distance learning labs were being built, the leadership team needed to utilize the expertise of the Facilities Management Department as the numerous design and construction issues were considered. Boschmann (1995) advise that four categories need to be considered when contemplating designing an electronic classroom: (1) when, where, and how people learn; (2) what and why they learn; (3) the evolving role of faculty; and (4) the future of the institution itself. The classroom must allow for interactive discussion, flexible model of student-teacher interaction. Access to information is an integral part of the design therefore, it must encourage learning that must be allowed to continue across time and place by expanding information resources and communication outside the classroom. The distance learning labs will allow for individuals to continue the learning process at different times, at different paces, and at different places, even when they happen to gather in the same place at the same time.

Three additional major categories of design must be considered when creating a distance learning facility: environment, technology, and interface. The environmental design project architect considers comfort factors, projection screens, lighting, writing boards, acoustics and audio systems, ergonomics, and ADA compliance (Americans with Disabilities Act). Technol-

ogy design focuses on integration of multimedia, audio, video, optical, and computer technologies into one workable system. The design team should also consider whether the equipment is user-operated, expandable, reliable, upgradable, capable of handling multiple platforms, maintenance-friendly, and secure. Interface design issues deal with ergonomics and human technology systems. In other words, can the equipment interact with humans and operate with other forms of technology. The human technology interface should be simple to operate and accessible to tech support 24/7 (Boschmann, 1995).

PLAYERS

The key players involved in the KCMSD's Strategic Planning Leadership Team are the superintendent, the executive director of instructional technology (technical), the director of secondary schools (curriculum), the manager of instructional technology (academic), the director of guidance and counseling (scheduling), and the director of facilities management (construction).

DEFINITION OF TERMS

Definitions of major concepts: distance learning, synchronous education, distance learning lab, distance learning facilitator, codecs, student-centered learning.

- Distance learning: Institution-based, formal education where the learning group is separated, and where interactive telecommunications systems are used to connect learners, resources, and instructors" (Simonson et al., 2012, p. 7).
- Synchronous education: live, two-way interaction in the educational process; occurring simultaneously and in real time. Teachers lecture, ask questions, and lead discussions. Learners listen, answer, and participate (Simonson et al., 2012).

- Distance learning lab: classroom providing instruction utilizing two-way, full motion video and two way live audio broadcasts to and from a remote location with a certified teacher acting as a facilitator (Moore & Anderson, 2003).
- Distance learning facilitator: certified teacher, trained as a distance learning instructor in a technology-enhanced, distance learning classroom
- CODECs: "A coder-decoder ... is used to convert analog signals, such as television, to digital form for for transmission and back again to the original analog form for viewing" (Schlosser & Simonson, 2010, p. 110).
- Student-centered learning: Students take ownership of their learning and show mastery through hands-on, project-based education (Covington, 2009).

BUILDING THE DLLs (COSTS/ EQUIPMENT + FACILITIES)

Each of the six KCMSD high schools located within the KCMSD contain distance learning labs with the following equipment: theater seating, CODEC, two interactive whiteboards, multiple monitors and microphones, document cameras, COWS (carts on wheels) with 33 laptops loaded with Microsoft Office, Rosetta Stone Spanish, and Rosetta Stone French. These schools are: East, Northeast, Southwest Early College Campus, Paseo Academy of Fine and Performing Arts, Lincoln College Preparatory Academy, and Central High Schools.

The Implementation Team's planning begins six months prior to the beginning of the next school year. Microsoft Project software that performs computerized Gantt charts assists the implementation team in designing, construction, ordering supplies and installation of equipment. The approximate cost of each distance learning lab is $160,000-$190,000 (Anstaett & Brenneman, 2011).

POLICIES AND PROCEDURES

Sabatino (2008) offers suggestions for classroom management techniques to be utilized when teaching K-12 students at a distance. Since videoconferencing and virtual environments offer the greatest potential for interactivity, classroom management is critical to optimum learning (Sabatino, 2008; Urban, 2006).

TRAINING FACILITATORS

New facilitators should be brought in and taught the Tandberg (videoconferencing) format. However, when facilitators are temporary, or if the Tandberg system needs to be revised, adjustments will be made accordingly. It is necessary that the full installation of the new system and the control boards are supervised to ensure they are installed correctly (Anstaett, 2011).

SCHEDULING

Six to 8 weeks prior to the beginning of school, the implementation team begins reevaluating and revising the distance learning lab facilitator training classes. Facilitators must be hired and trained on the job skills necessary to fulfill the facilitator's responsibilities. The teachers are assigned to labs and will complete training in ample time before schools. If necessary, training on the previous system might be necessary until the new system can be completely installed. Training documents should be developed to instruct teachers in running the document cameras, microphones, CODECS, computers, ENO interactive white boards and other equipment utilized in the distance learning labs (Anstaett, 2011; Brenneman, 2011).

Information technology trainers and the distance learning lab managers should work together in classrooms with facilitators and teachers to assist as they entered this new method of delivering education. Teacher reassignments and scheduling changes were made to accommodate the changes in curriculum and staffing. Additional construction and installation requests were made and are in the process of being completed. The labs are expected to be completely operational and identical in most design details. At that time, all teachers and facilitators will be provided additional and extensive training. The teachers have been the stable foundation for most of this (Anstaett, 2011; South Dakota Department of Distance Education, 2003).

TEACHERS

Several teachers are participating in the distance learning lab program by teaching the following subjects: Advanced Placement literature, Advanced Placement biology/chemistry/physics, French I and II, Spanish 3 and 4, calculus, and accounting.

SUCCESSES

All of the distance learning labs were open on time, according to the transformation plan. Students are able to take courses not offered by their local schools. Budget constraints were adhered to. Students can enjoy a state-of-the-art facility. Students can receive extrinsic motivation by learning in a separate setting from their peers.

CHALLENGES AND CONCERNS

Various distance learning lab hardware and equipment installation are not fully operational. Bell and assembly schedules periodically experience conflicts. There is concern that Advanced Placement courses will be discontinued and replaced with International Baccalaureate courses that are more holistic and very expensive. The state of Missouri pays for students to take the Advanced Placement examination to earn college credit. Some teachers would like to see a dual credit opportunity for students to get high school and college credit simultaneously. Communication between facilities needs to be better defined. More teacher and facilitator training is needed for troubleshooting equipment and software.

STATE TECHNOLOGY PLAN

The KCMSD's Technology Plan includes the installation of one additional distance learning lab in each of the district's six high schools by August 2012. One-to-one mobile/tablet devices are also planned to increase technical expertise within the student population.

FUTURE PLANS AND EXPECTATIONS

The distance learning labs will be used to initiate relationships with students in New York, England, France, and Spain. Neighborhood connections will commence as afternoon and evening programming is started in the distance learning labs. It is hoped that the increase in academic rigor will aid the KCMSD in raising its standardized test scores.

EVALUATION

An evaluation of the results of the combined efforts of the strategic planning leadership team and other departments will determine the success of the distance learning labs. Simonson et al. (2012) discussed the importance of evaluation as "part of the plans to move from traditional face-to-face instruction to distance education" (p. 348). In this work, Simonson (2012) describes an evaluation of distance education programs using five steps: reactions (Did they like it?); learning (Did they learn it?); transfer (Will they use it?); results (Will it matter?); and return on investment (p. 349). These evaluation steps will provide insight into the success of the new technological initiative.

The AEIOU Evaluation approach by Fortune and Keith (1992, as cited in Simonson et al., 2012), provided program evaluation specifically for distance education implementation projects. The five components of the AEIOU approach provide "formative information to the staff about the implementation their project and summative information about the value of the project and its activities (p. 353). Accountability (A) asks "Did the project planners do what they said they were going to do?" Effectiveness (E) asks "How well done was the project?" Impact queries "Did the project, course, or program make a difference?" Organizational Context (O) poses "What structures, policies, or events in the organization or environment helped or hindered the project in accomplishing its goals?" Unanticipated consequences (U) inquires "What changes or consequences of importance happened as a result of the projects that were not expected?" (p. 353).

These questions will provide insight into the processes, methods and decision-making activities utilized by the strategic planning leadership team while developing a distance learning program within the KCMSD.

REFERENCES

About KCMSD. (2011, January). Retrieved from http://www.kcpublicschools.org

Anstaett, D. (2011, September). Kansas City, Missouri School District Distance Learning meeting.

Berg, G. A. (2002). *Why distance learning? Higher education administrative practice.* Westport, CT: Greenwood.

Boschmann, E. (1995). *The electronic classroom: A handbook for education in the electronic environment.* Medford, NJ: Learned Information.

Bral, C. S. (2007). *An investigation of incorporating online courses in public high school curricula.* Available from ProQuest Dissertations and Theses database. Retrieved from http://ezproxylocal.library.nova.edu/login?url=http://search.proquest.com/docview/304844162?accountid=6579

Brenneman, T. (2011, September). Kansas City, Missouri School District Distance Learning meeting.

Clark, M. S. (2003). *Student support for academic success in a blended, video and web-based, distance education program: The distance learner's perspective.* Available from ProQuest Dissertations and Theses database. Retrieved from http://ezproxylocal.library.nova.edu/login?url=http://search.proquest.com/docview/305330802?accountid=6579

Covington, J. (2009). *Transformation phase II.* Retrieved from http://www2.kcmsd.net/pages/AboutKCMSD.aspx

Harrison, M. K., (2005). *Developing a model and evaluation tool for the laboratory component of K-12 senior science courses delivered by distributed learning methods.* Royal Roads University (Canada), AAT MR10813

Henley, B. F. (2009). *Developing eLearning: A case study of Tennessee High School.* Available from ProQuest Dissertations and Theses database. Retrieved from http://ezproxylocal.library.nova.edu/login?url=http://search.proquest.com/docview/304874653?accountid=6579

Martin, C. M. (2009). Oklahoma's Star Schools: Equipment use and benefits two years after grant's end. *The American Journal of Distance Education, 7*(3), 51-60.

McBeth, M. (2011, September). Kansas City, Missouri School District Distance Learning meeting.

Missouri Comprehensive Data System. (2011). Retrieved from http://mcds.dese.mo.gov

Missouri Department of Elementary and Secondary Education. (2011a). *Distance learning policies and procedures.* Retrieved from www.dese.mo.gov

Missouri Department of Elementary and Secondary Education. (2011b). *Student MAP Scores Continue Slow Climb, 45*(58).

Moore, M. G. (Ed.). (2007). *Handbook of distance education* (2nd ed.). Mahwah, NJ: Erlbaum.

Moore, M. G., & Anderson, W. G. (2003). *Handbook of distance education.* Mahwah, NJ: Erlbaum.

Rice, K. (2006). A comprehensive look at distance education in the K-12 context. *Journal of Research on Technology in Education, 38,* 425-448.

Sabatino, C. (2008). *Videoconferencing? Assessing its effectiveness as a teaching tool in the high school.* Available from ProQuest Dissertations and Theses database. Retrieved from http://ezproxylocal.library.nova.edu/login?url

=http://search.proquest.com/docview/ 304478924?accountid=6579

Schlosser, L. A., & Simonson, M. (2010). *Distance education: Definition and glossary of terms* (3rd ed.). Charlotte, NC: Information Age.

Simonson, M., Smaldino, S., Albright, M., & Zvacek, S. (2012).*Teaching and learning at a distance: Foundations of distance education* (5th ed.). Boston, MA: Allyn & Bacon.

Smith, S. G. (2009). *High school students' perceptions of distance learning.* Available from ProQuest Dissertations and Theses database. Retrieved from http://ezproxylocal.library .nova.edu/login?url=http://search.proquest .com/docview/305080539?accountid=6579

South Dakota Department of Distance Education. (2003). *Final report of the evaluation team of the South Dakota Alliance for Distance Education: South Dakota's Star Schools project (SDADE).* Retrieved from http://www2 .plymouth.ac.uk/distancelearning /finalreport.pdf

Star Schools Project (Producer). (2000). *Three statewide approaches to distance education.* [Video case study]. Available from www.schoolofed.nova.edu/cms/itde

Thomas, W. R. (2006). *Electronic delivery of high school courses: Status, trends and issues.* Atlanta, GA: Southern Regional Education Board Publications.

Tushnet, N. C., & Brzoska, K. (1994). Research in distance education. In B. Willis (Ed.), *Distance education: Strategies and tools* (pp. 41-66). Englewood Cliffs, NJ: Educational Technology.

Urban, L. L. (2006). *Developing a strategic plan for distance education at a multi-campus two-year technical college.* Available from ProQuest Dissertations and Theses database, Retrieved from http://ezproxylocal.library.nova.edu/ login?url=http://search.proquest.com/ docview/304909085?accountid=6579

Reaching Beyond the Conventional Classroom
NASA's Digital Learning Network

Damon Talley and Gamaliel "Dan" Cherry

THE DIGITAL LEARNING NETWORK

The National Aeronautics and Space Administration's (NASA) Digital Learning Network (DLN) connects K-16 students, educators, and families to NASA scientists, engineers, and education specialists through videoconferencing and webcasts. The DLN consists of all 10 NASA Centers across the country: Ames Research Center, Dryden Flight Research Center, Glenn Research Center, Goddard Space Flight Center, Jet Propulsion Laboratory, Johnson Space Center, Langley Research Center, Marshall Spaceflight Center, and Stennis Space Center. Each center has a unique and important role in NASA's mission.

Luckily one does not have to search across 10 different centers to find content of interest. The content catalog and webcast schedule can be found at: http://dln.nasa.gov/dln. Registration and scheduling of "events" or modules is free. Events in the catalog range from asteroids to robotics and users determine the date and time of the connection. Event descriptions include pre-/postactivities, a teacher lesson plan,

Damon Talley,
Digital Learning Network Coordinator,
Mail Code: OSU, NASA Kennedy Space
Center, FL 32899.
Telephone: (321) 867-1748.
E-mail: damon.b.talley@nasa.gov

Gamaliel "Dan" Cherry,
Human Resources Development Specialist,
NASA Langley Research Center, Mail Stop:
309, Hampton, VA 23668.
Telephone: (757) 864-6113.
E-mail: gamaliel.r.cherry@nasa.gov

and the corresponding national standards. DLN coordinators at each center facilitate scheduling, test connections, and presentation of events. DLN coordinators are highly trained in NASA content and bring diverse teaching backgrounds to the DLN.

The DLiNfo Channel section of the DLN website serves as a calendar of upcoming webcasts and provides the webcast stream. DLiNfo Channel webcasts can reach large audiences but still maintain interactivity through a chat room or questions submitted via e-mail. Webcasts include guest speakers, educational product showcases, and special events such as NASA launches.

AMERICA'S SPACEPORT:
JOHN F. KENNEDY SPACE CENTER

NASA's John F. Kennedy Space Center is the launch site for all U.S. human spaceflight and many of NASA's unpiloted vehi-cles. One of the most popular events on the DLN is an award-winning interactive virtual field trip to America's Spaceport. This author (Talley) grew up near Kennedy Space Center and is happy to share my excitement for it every single time I connect with students. Stunning aerospace imagery and enthusiasm is important in videoconferencing because "ultimately it is the photogenic nature of these displays, together with the affability and openendedness of the student presenter dialog, which determines the level of meaningful engagement" (Sumption, 2006, p. 931).

Participants in America's Spaceport explore the Vehicle Assembly Building (VAB), which was the largest building by volume at the time it was constructed. Originally designed to stack the Saturn V Moon Rocket in the vertical position, the VAB's high bay doors could accommodate the Statue of Liberty. The journey continues aboard the largest tracked vehicle in the

Figure 1. VAB.

Figure 2. Crawler.

entire world, the Crawler-Transporter. Capable of moving 12 million pounds worth of rocket and launcher, the Crawler gets 42 fpg (that's feet per gallon) and traverses the 4-mile journey to the launch pad in only 8 hours. Finally, students experience a Space Shuttle launch—sometimes live!

DLN "launchcasts" countdown launches live via a webstream on the DLiNfo Channel. Launchcasts usually begin streaming live at T-minus 60 minutes to launch and include content on: vehicle, payload, crew, and the mission. Participants can submit questions and get answers during the program live via e-mail. The prelaunch program includes special guests such as NASA engineers, scientists, program managers, and celebrity guests. Our biggest "get" was Neil deGrasse Tyson, director of the Hayden Planetarium in New York and host of *Nova scienceNOW.* Tyson braved a very hot day in May to help countdown the STS-125 Space Shuttle mission to service the Hubble Space Telescope.

INTEREST IN SCIENCE

NASA (2006) Category 2.4 regarding student involvement K-12, is to Engage: Provide K-12 students with authentic first-

Figure 3.   STS-125 launch.

Figure 4.   Talley with Neil deGrasse Tyson.

hand opportunities to participate in NASA mission activities, thus inspiring interest in STEM (Science, Technology, Engineering and Mathematics) disciplines. America's Spaceport transports students to NASA's Kennedy Space Center, providing just such an opportunity. Jarvis and Pell (2002) noted that after a visit to UK Challenger Learning Center "it is remarkable that a 2-to-3 hour experience should have been such a lasting positive experience for nearly a quarter of the children with regard to raising their career aspirations to become scientists" (p. 997).

Student feedback and teacher testimonials submitted via the online evaluation system evidence positive results in student interest in STEM after participating in NASA DLN sessions.

This author sees the evidence first hand every time I connect with a group of students on the DLN by watching the looks on their faces.

INTERPRETATIONS OF INQUIRY-BASED INSTRUCTION

Educators frequently have various interpretations of what inquiry learning is along with how they should practice inquiry-based instruction (Camins, 2001). The U.S. Department of Education has noted attention to inquiry-based science curricula since the late 1950s. Discussions of inquiry generally fall into two broad classes of inquiry: describing what scientists do professionally, and as a teaching and learning process. Evaluators from the National Research Council (1996) expressed this dichotomy in the following way:

> A scientific inquiry refers to the diverse ways in which scientists study the natural world and propose explanations based on the evidence derived from their work. Inquiry also refers to the activities of students in which they develop knowledge and understanding of scientific ideas, as well as an understanding of how scientists study the natural world. (p. 23)

Inquiry also refers to the actions of students in the classroom. Students should view themselves as scientists by recognizing science as a process, engaging in activities that reflect the work of scientists, designing investigations, revising knowledge, and understanding how scientists examine and make explanations about natural phenomena (NRC, 2000). Students are often encouraged to use prior knowledge to raise questions about the world around them and predict or formulate hypotheses about explanations and solutions to their questions. They are also asked to design and complete simple investigations, use observations to collect data, develop explanations based on collected data, consider alternative explanations, and communicate findings to other classmates (Biological Sciences Curriculum Study [BSCS], 1994; Layman, 1996; NRC, 1996). Applying an inquiry-based approach can pose challenges when presented with the constraints of a videoconferencing environment. However, using a learning cycle approach to instruction allows teachers to have flexibility when teaching science.

THE LEARNING CYCLE

The learning cycle approach to inquiry-based instruction is a widely used inquiry-based format for science instruction providing a structured way to implement inquiry in the classroom (Marek, 2008). This type of inquiry-based instructional methodology engages users in hands-on and minds-on activities throughout instruction providing learners with several opportunities to explore new concepts. Nuthall (1999) supported this approach, suggesting that elementary students need three or four experiences with a topic before they commit the information to long-term memory. These findings indicate that students should have the opportunity to use their prior knowledge and their experiences in an attempt to create new knowledge and understanding. Fur-

Table 1.   Summary of the BSCS 5E Instructional Model and Teacher Roles

Phase	Summary
Engagement	Prior learning is assessed and accessed to encourage problem solving, engagement, or the exploration of a new concept. Teacher role: facilitator, lecturer
Exploration	Activities in current topics are provided to encourage and facilitate conceptual change. Teacher role: facilitator
Explanation	Students' attention is focused on explaining their conceptual understanding of the new concept, process, or skill. Teacher role: facilitator, lecturer
Elaboration	Teachers challenge opinions and explanations to encourage a deeper understanding and cognitive engagement of the students. Teacher role: facilitator
Evaluation	Students evaluate their own understanding of their new abilities. Teacher role: facilitator

Note: Adapted from Bybee et al. (2006).

ther research suggested that student achievement, retention, and comprehension improve as a result of using the learning-cycle approach to instruction (Cavallo, 2005). One example of the learning cycle, the 5E model of instruction, draws from prior research in student learning.

5E-INSTRUCTIONAL MODEL

A more widely adopted learning cycle is the 5-E instructional model: engage, explore, explain, elaborate, evaluate (Bybee, 1997). This model was developed in the mid-1980s in part from the previous success of the Science Curriculum Improvement Study model by the Biological Science Curriculum Study and International Business Machines (1989). This model incorporates the three core learning-cycle phases of the Science Curriculum Improvement Study model as its core, but adds engagement and evaluation components to facilitate change.

PULLING IT ALL TOGETHER

Adjusting both content and presentation style to incorporate a 5E approach in a regular videoconferencing setting presents a few challenges. The instructor at the far end site is faced with the dilemma of how to adjust the 5E model on the fly. Originally, the 5E model was rooted in the science classrooms that depended on labs for instructional purposes, so some customization of the model is needed in order to achieve learning outcomes. The cyclical nature of the 5E instructional model allows instructors to build on what they have in a classroom, as opposed to trying to shoehorn an approach. For instance, Digital Learning Network presentations are developed to cover approximately 60 min of instructional time. The propensity for not completing a full learning cycle approach in a 50-60 minute block of instruction is very high. Thus, DLN presenters rely on teachers for pre- and postactivities that will make the experience more meaningful for the students when using a 5E approach. Despite evidence that points to using an inquiry-based approach to teach science, the amount of research examining instructional strategies used via videoconferencing suggests room for a closer look.

REFERENCES

Biological Sciences Curriculum Study. (1994). *Middle school science & technology.* Dubuque, IA: Kendall/Hunt.

Biological Sciences Curriculum Study & IBM (1989). *New designs for elementary science and health: A cooperative project between Biological Sciences Curriculum Study (BSCS) and International Business Machines (IBM).* Dubuque, IA: Kendall/Hunt.

Bybee, R. W. (1997). *Achieving scientific literacy.* Portsmouth, NH: Heinemann.

Bybee, R. W., et al., (2006) *The BSCS 5E Instructional Model: Origins, Effectiveness, and Application.* Colorado Springs, CO: Biological Sciences Curriculum Study and National Institutes of Health.

Camins, A. (2001) Dimensions of inquiry. *Full Option Science System Newsletter, 18,* 8–13.

Cavallo, A. 2005. Cycling through plants. Science *and Children, 42*(7), 22-27.

Jarvis, T., & Pell, A. (2005). Factors influencing elementary school children's attitudes toward science before, during, and after a visit to the UK National Space Centre. *Journal of Research in Science Teaching, 42* (1), 53-83.

National Aeronautics and Space Administration. *NASA Education Strategic Documents* Retrieved from http://insidenasa.nasa.gov/portal/site/insidenasa/menu-item.448b8e4ce1c84d12b649cc1036793ea0/

National Research Council. (1996). *National science education standards.* Washington, DC: National Academy Press.

National Research Council. (2000). *How people learn: Brain, mind, experience, and school* (expanded ed.). Washington, DC: National Academy Press.

Layman, J. (1996). *Inquiry and learning: Realizing the science standards in the classroom.* New York, NY: College Entrance Examination Board.

Marek, A. E. (2008). Why the learning cycle? *Journal of Elementary Education, 20*(3), 63-69.

Nuthall, G. (1999). The way students learn: Acquiring knowledge from an integrated science and social studies unit. *Elementary School Journal, 99,* 303–341.

Sumption, K. (2006). Beyond museum walls: An Exploration of the origins and features of web-based, museum education outreach. In J. Weiss et al. (Eds.), *International handbook of virtual learning environments* (pp. 915-937). The Netherlands: Springer.

"DESPITE EVIDENCE THAT POINT TO USING AN INQUIRY-BASED APPROACH TO TEACH SCIENCE, THE AMOUNT OF RESEARCH EXAMINING INSTRUCTIONAL STRATEGIES USED VIA VIDEO-CONFERENCING SUGGESTS ROOM FOR A CLOSER LOOK."

The Virtual Campus at the International Academy of Design & Technology-Online

Andrea Vassar

INTRODUCTION

The International Academy of Design and Technology (IADT) is a for-profit, 4-year art and design career college. It has traditional "brick and mortar" campuses in 10 cities in the United States. IADT is owned and operated by its parent company, the Career Education Corporation (CEC). In 2005, CEC began to discuss the initiative to expand IADT into

Andrea Vassar,
International Academy of Design & Technology, 5104 Eisenhower Blvd.,
Tampa, FL 33634.
Telephone: (813) 889-3406.
E-mail: avassar@academy.edu

the field of distance education with the addition of a new branch campus—the International Academy of Design and Technology-Online (IADT-Online). Leaders at both CEC and IADT envisioned a virtual college that could serve as a self-contained branch campus, as well as offer distance education opportunities to the current traditional IADT students in a hybrid format. IADT-Online offers prospective students a way to earn a career-focused, creatively driven degree.

> IADT Online offers the opportunity to earn a degree tailored to your dreams, imaginative ideas and creatively motivated professional goals. When innovative technology hooks up with the power of a broadband Internet connection, amazing things become possible for motivated students who have the talent to think visually and communicate graphically. (IADT, 2009b)

The cornerstone of the IADT-Online virtual college is the proprietary learning management system (LMS), the Virtual Campus (VC). The VC was developed by a team of information technology specialists, instructional designers, and software developers at CEC. After conducting research of currently available LMSs, the team determined that an entirely new LMS, rather than an existing proprietary system, was the best solution for IADT-Online for two reasons: the ability to have control over the look and feel of the interface so that it could match the existing IADT brand identity; and to integrate with the college database system, CampusVue, already in use by all of the IADT branch campuses.

The Virtual Campus was launched along with newly developed online general education and graphic design courses in July of 2007. This has since been expanded and students can now pursue degree programs in the following areas: graphic design, web design, web development, fashion merchandising, advertising and design, game production, and digital media production (IADT, 2009a). In the last two years the VC has grown and evolved with these new programs into a very successful LMS; upgrades and new features are continually being added to improve the quality of interaction for both students and instructors.

Today, the IADT-Online VC provides quality educational experiences to over 1,400 online college students and approximately 900 hybrid students at the traditional campuses (Carlson, 2009). It is a vibrant learning community. As frequently debated in the field of distance education regarding virtual learning environments, it is a place that is far from "virtual," where actual interactive, engaging, and innovative learning in happening in real time (Simonson, Smaldino, Albright, and Zvacek, 2009).

KEY FEATURES OF THE VIRTUAL CAMPUS

The Virtual Campus is a fully functioning online college campus. It has many of the key features that students expect to have access to on a traditional campus. There are some features that are only available through the technology of the online environment and are currently unavailable to traditional students. These features include: 24/7 technical support, online student services, and instant messaging with all contacts, classmates, and instructors. An example of the VC interface can be seen in Figure 1.

The VC can be accessed by any computer platform through a standard Internet connection. Certain aspects of the VC can also be accessed through mobile technology. The VC uses MobiClass, a mobile software program that supports a long list of mobile devices. MobiClass allows students to stay current with their courses by allowing them to download course podcasts, download course videos, view class assignments, access school e-mail, check their grades, and access faculty contact information (IADT, 2009c).

Many best distance education practices are an integral part of the VC. Both synchronous and asynchronous learning are supported and encouraged through its design and technological features. The VC is divided into five distinct areas, each one designed to assist the students in their learning: the classroom, online library, learning center, virtual commons, and technical support.

THE CLASSROOM

The virtual classroom is the place where all essential learning activities occur both in real-time and on-demand. Online students can access important information that they need in order to successfully complete each course. Figure 2 shows an example of an online course in the VC. The students can access the course overview which includes the syllabus and the list of assignments for the course. The course work section of the virtual classroom includes the discussion board feature. The discussion board assignments are mandatory for all online students for every course to ensure quality interaction with the course content. The course work feature includes a course gallery where the art and design students can post their class proj-

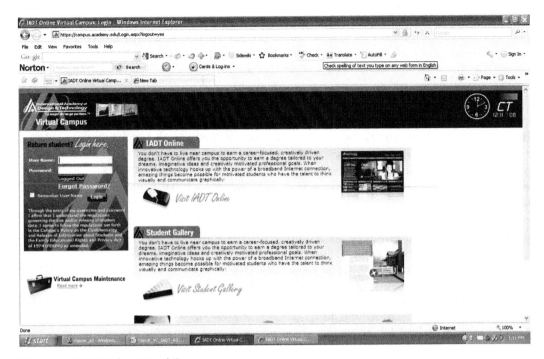

Figure 1. IADT-Online Virtual Campus.

Figure 2. IADT-Online classroom.

ects for critique by both instructors and peers. This is also the section where students submit assignments and receive communication from their instructors regarding their grades.

The most dynamic feature of the virtual classroom is the interactive learning section. This section has three main areas: course materials, small group discussions, and live chat. The course materials are Flash-based, animated, and interactive materials and provide additional course content that supports the reading assignments, individual and group projects, and discussion boards. An example of interactive material is seen in Figure 3. The small group discussion feature is a vehicle for instructors to organize students into groups for the purposes of collaborative learning assignments and projects.

The live chat feature is the cornerstone of the virtual classroom. All courses are required to provide two live chat sessions per week on pertinent course topics such as software demonstrations, lectures, and project critiques. Live chats are primarily delivered synchronously, but are recorded for students to use asynchronously. Figure 4 shows a recorded live chat session that can be viewed by students at their convenience. The live chat feature is also used for all additional synchronous academic events including tutoring, academic advising, meetings, and seminars.

Adobe Acrobat Connect Pro is the software that is used to support the live chat feature. It is an effective, robust tool that can be used for eLearning due to its design and capabilities. Adobe promotes Adobe Acrobat Connect Pro for specific online classroom use:

> Technology should make eLearning a rich, interactive experience—not a slow, cumbersome ordeal. That's why Acrobat Connect Pro offers a captivating interface and interactive tools to help participants learn and retain the material that you teach in virtual classes and self-paced

Figure 3. Flash-based interactive learning material.

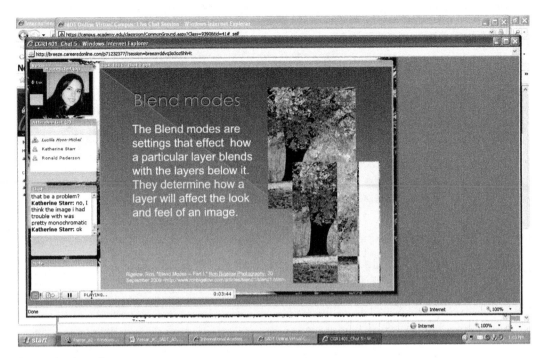

Figure 4. Live chat session.

courses—and enjoy doing it. You can quickly design compelling courses with templates and a library of content, teach more effectively with instructor management tools, and track learner progress to make sure your eLearning is actually achieving its goals. (Adobe, 2008, p. 2)

The flexibility and interactivity are the elements that make the IADT-Online VC classroom a successful learning environment. Students are able to learn at convenient times and to collaborate with their instructors and classmates to complete career-focused, problem-based learning tasks.

ONLINE LIBRARY

The VC online library, or eBrary, is a full-service online media center as seen in Figure 5. The IADT-Online VC library is linked to the CEC-owned company-wide online library the CECbrary. The CECbrary is used by all colleges and universities in the CEC system of school and therefore can provide extensive media resources to all its schools. Online students have instant access to these electronic library resources.

The eBrary provides student access to eBooks through NetLibrary, PsycBOOKS, and Safari Tech Books. The eBrary also subscribes to an extensive list of online library databases featuring journals and periodicals including the new resource, EBSCOhost Mobile, for learners who access course content via mobile technology. Additionally, the eBrary has web learning resources that are listed by subject. This is a list of about 2000 webpages selected by librarians, students and instructors as being high quality information sources on the topics discussed in the IADT-Online general education and design courses (IADT, 2009b).

There is always a qualified, professional online librarian available to assist students with research questions at flexible times. This assistance is provided either through specific live chat times, the instant messag-

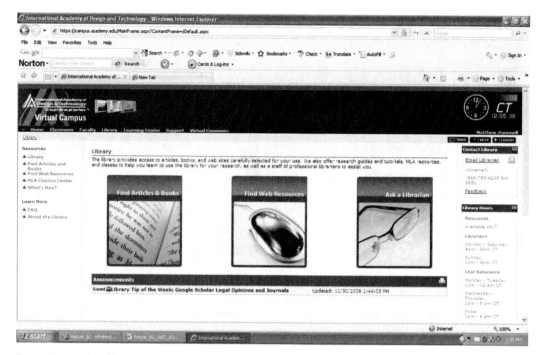

Figure 5.   Online library.

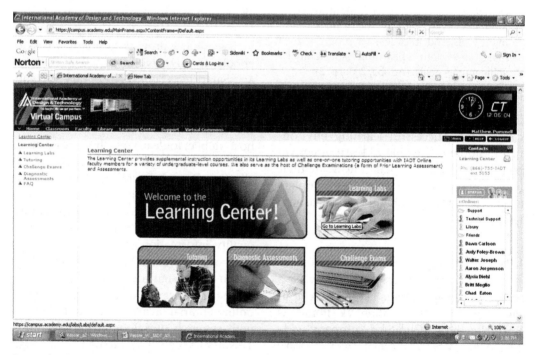

Figure 6.   Learning Center.

ing feature, e-mail, or phone. There is also the MLA Citation Center to assist with the formatting and citation of sources in research-based papers and assignments.

LEARNING CENTER

The Learning Center (LC) feature of the VC provides an additional level of in-depth educational support to online students. The LC is shown in Figure 6 and encompasses learning labs, tutoring, diagnostic assessments, and challenge exams. Learning labs are a unique student-centered feature of the VC. Learning labs are geared toward students' areas of interest. Learning labs are available in two forms—generic interactive Flash-based tutorials (as seen in Figure 7) or specially recorded Adobe Acrobat Connect Pro live chats conducted by instructor on pertinent and/or specialized design topics.

Students attend live tutoring sessions in the LC in a variety of subject areas including college-level mathematics and English composition. Tutoring sessions are also offered in core concentration subject areas. Tutoring sessions are scheduled by individual instructors and conducted through the live chat feature.

The diagnostic assessments and challenge exams in the LC are designed to assist students in the preparation for life-credit test-out examinations. Students who possess certain prerequisite skills, educational experience, or life experience can qualify to take an examination and earn college equivalency credit for those skills and experience. The LC gives them a way to prepare themselves for the test-out process.

VIRTUAL COMMONS

The Virtual Commons is an online community that allows IADT-Online students to participate in social networking opportunities with other students and instructors. The Virtual Commons also has the instant messaging feature that is integrated

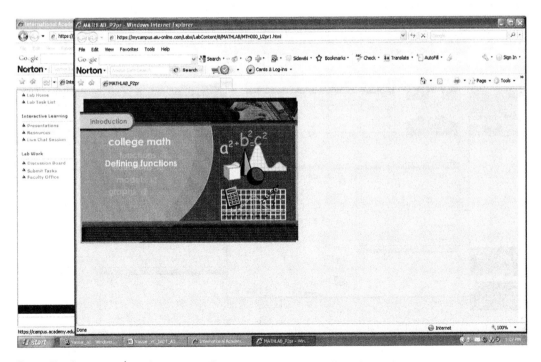

Figure 7. Interactive learning presentation.

Figure 8. Virtual Commons.

Figure 9. Profile listing in the Virtual Commons.

into every "place" a student visits in the VC. This feature can be seen in Figure 8. Like all social networking websites, the Virtual Commons allows its users to create profiles (Figure 9) and become "friends" with other members of the university community. These friends become part of a student's social network.

Like traditional students, online students want to get involved in campus life. This can be challenging in a virtual learning environment. The Virtual Commons in the IADT-Online VC provides students with student club opportunities. Virtual student clubs have faculty moderators, members, and hold virtual club meetings using the same live chat feature that is used in course delivery. These clubs are academic in nature and give the students a chance to participate in book and movie reviews, get career advice, join interactive discussion boards, and attend dynamic presentations (IADT, 2009b). A sample of these clubs is listed here: Graphic Design Club, Military Students Club, Study-Buddy Club, The Fashion Forward Club, and The Freelancer's Society.

During each term, the student clubs in the Virtual Commons host an event. An event is a live chat session in which guest speakers discuss topics related to the subject area of the club. The guest speakers have a wide knowledge base of the club's subject matter and provide valuable information to students on this topic. Topics for events originate from club members and the faculty moderator. Events typically last one hour and provide time for a question and answer period.

TECHNICAL SUPPORT

A feature that is always present but very much working in the background is the 24/7 technical support feature. This is where students go to get technical assistance, important software downloads, and the ability to check a computer for the required Internet browser plug-ins. The technical support area also includes contact information for important functional departments of the online university such as financial aid, student accounts, student services, and the registrar.

Technical support runs on a ticket system as shown in Figure 10. If a student has a technical issue, he or she submits a ticket and a professional information technology specialists work on its resolution, contacting the student when the ticket is closed. Students can also contact technical support from the instant messaging screen, by e-mail, or by phone. Because technology is a part of every experience in the VC, technical support keeps things running smoothly so that students can focus on the important task at hand—learning.

ADVANTAGES AND LIMITATIONS OF THE VIRTUAL CAMPUS

According to Simonson et al. (2009), there are many advantages, as well as limitations, of online learning as compared to conventional teaching. Some of these advantages are: the fact that students can participate from a variety of locations; access asynchronous course components 24 hours a day at their convenience; work at an independent pace; learning materials are available across the Internet and work on multiple platforms; the Internet can provide a student-centered learning environment; and online courses provide a variety of active learning experiences that allow for different learning styles.

There are also limitations of online course delivery models, including: potential students do not have the access to the technology; well-designed online courses require many labor-intensive resources; courses that were teacher-centered are not sufficiently adjusted and adapted to the learner-centered model; instructor-student communication and feedback may be significantly delayed and can affect the quality of learning; bandwidth limitations impact the use of advanced technologies;

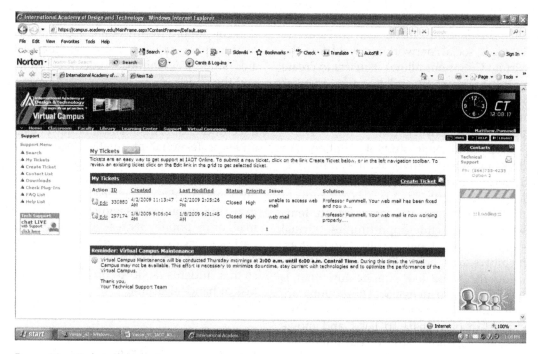

Figure 10. Technical support.

and the technical support infrastructure may be minimal.

When compared to these lists of advantages and limitations, the IADT-Online Virtual Campus measure up very well. It is a vibrant learning environment with very few limitations. The advantages of the VC are its flexible delivery model, student-centered learning, interactive experiences, and creative community. The two biggest limitations of the VC are the significant amounts of bandwidth space required to deliver the industry-current technologies and the time and resources it takes to produce the quality interactive learning experiences (Pummel, 2009).

FLEXIBLE DELIVERY MODEL

The VC emphasizes the flexible delivery model by providing many types of learning in multiple formats. Students can participate in both synchronous and asynchronous learning. They can access course materials from anywhere, at any-

time via the Internet, as well as through advanced mobile technology applications and devices. Students learn independently and have control over when, where, and how they learn course content.

STUDENT-CENTERED LEARNING

The primary focus of the VC is on the student. This is evidenced by the many in-depth support services available to students, from the extensive online library resources and customized web resources to the personal tutorials, interactive learning labs, and student-centered extracurricular clubs. The VC at IADT-Online is all about the student and the students' learning experiences are designed to provide them with quality career-focused education.

INTERACTIVE EXPERIENCES

Every "place" in the VC is interactive—from the classrooms to the technical support center. Instant messaging is a feature throughout the campus. Each classroom has a library of course-related interactive materials. The Learning Center and the Virtual Commons also provide students with interactive experiences. The live chat, the foundation of the VC, is completely interactive allowing the students and instructors to communicate in real-time.

INDUSTRY-CURRENT TECHNOLOGY

CEC and the IADT family of schools have invested many resources on the technology behind the Virtual Campus. The VC is industry-current and provides many applications of advanced technologies including multimedia, graphic, and mobile delivery options. The students participate in the classrooms using the latest Internet meeting software, Adobe Acrobat Connect Pro. Additionally, the students at IADT-Online pursue art and design degrees that require them to use the newest graphic, web, and production software—Adobe Creative Suite 4 Master Collection. Every student and instructor is provided with this software so that they can effectively learn and use these tools in the virtual classroom.

CREATIVE COMMUNITY

The Virtual Commons is a unique feature of the VC allowing students to collaborate with mentors and peers through a common social networking community. This experience greatly enhances every online student's learning experience through the networking opportunities associated with the student-centered clubs and events. This creative community effectively mirrors and simulates the networking that occurs so often in the professional design community. This gives students a real-world experience that transfers to their potential careers in design and technology.

BANDWIDTH LIMITATIONS

The greatest limitation for the VC is the advanced technology that it utilizes and relies on for course delivery. Bandwidth limitations are a serious concern for the CEC and IADT instructional designers and developers. They are tasked with the creation of interactive multimedia and video content that must be effective when delivered via the Internet. Similarly, the same bandwidth issues that affect content development also have an impact on the live chat feature and content delivery. Although video is enabled in the live chat application, many instructors choose not to use this option because it "bogs down" and "lags" during the class causing the flow of course content delivery to be interrupted. In response to this issue, many instructors choose to deliver the chats only using the audio features.

COURSE DEVELOPMENT

An additional limitation to the VC is the amount of time, funding, resources, and personnel involved in the creation of original content and its continual updating. IADT-Online is part of the larger corporation, CEC, and must rely on budgetary and resource limitations from this level of administration. This significantly slows the natural cycle of curriculum development and causes great frustration for those at the local administration level. The VC is proprietary and the program chairs and instructors have very little control over quickly changing course content to meet the ever changing students' needs (Pummel, 2009).

SUMMARY

The IADT-Online Virtual Campus is an exemplary distance education application. It is obvious that attention to best practices of distance education were considered by the CEC and IADT instructional designers and software developers during the creation of the VC. This virtual career college has a long list of advantages when compared to the relativity few limitations. The highlights of the VC are its interactive, student-centered, flexible features; the utilization of advanced instructional and web-based communication technologies; and the truly unique creative social networking community of the Virtual Commons. In the words of an IADT-Online graphic design instructor, Glen Perotte (2009), the Virtual Campus is "an exciting, interactive experience for the students."

REFERENCES

Adobe. (2008). *Adobe Acrobat Connect Pro: High-impact web conferencing and eLearning that everyone can access.* San Jose, CA: Adobe Systems Incorporated.

Carlson, D. (2009). *Current IADT-Online enrollment figures* (A. Vassar, Ed.). Tampa, FL: International Academy of Design and Technology.

International Academy of Design and Technology. (2009a). *IADT Online.* Retrieved from http://online.academy.edu/

International Academy of Design and Technology. (2009b). *IADT Online Virtual Campus.* Retrieved from https://campus.academy.edu/login.aspx?ReturnUrl=%2fdefault.aspx

International Academy of Design and Technology. (2009c). *IADTmobile.com.* Retrieved from http://online.academy.edu/iadtmobile/?url20=%2Fiadtmobile%2F

Perotte, G. (2009). *Benefits of the live chat feature* (A. Vassar, Ed.). Tampa, FL: International Academy of Design and Technology.

Pummel, M. (2009). *Advantages and limitations of the Virtual Campus* (A. Vassar, Ed.). Tampa, FL: International Academy of Design and Technology.

Simonson, M., Smaldino, S., Albright, M., and Zvacek, S. (2009). *Teaching and learning at a distance* (4th ed.). Boston, MA: Allyn & Bacon.

IN THE WORDS OF AN IADT-ONLINE GRAPHIC DESIGN INSTRUCTOR, THE VIRTUAL CAMPUS IS AN EXCITING, INTERACTIVE EXPERIENCE FOR THE STUDENTS.

U.S. Army and U.S. Navy Staff Officer Distance Education Programs

Lawrence L. Gruszecki

In a recent copy of *Army*, the magazine of the Association of the United States Army, Lieutenant General (Retired) James M. Dubik paints a grim picture of the education needs of Army's officers. Dubik warns that, "The current leader-to-led ratio is too low for what the Army is being asked to do now and in the future" (Dubik, 2010, p. 22).

America's continual and increasing involvement in areas such as Iraq, Afghanistan, and Kuwait is creating a demand for a particular type of officer, the staff officer.

Lawrence L. Gruszecki,
Science Teacher, E. T. Booth Middle School,
Woodstock, GA 30189.
Telephone: (770) 926-5707.
E-mail: lawrence.gruszecki@cherokee.k12.ga.us

Within these areas of operation, America's military forces are molded into "joint forces" to meet combat, intelligence, logistics, and civil affairs requirements in these countries. Additionally, U.S. military forces are engaged with the forces of other countries creating multinational headquarters. Even more demand is created by reorganizing large units into numerous smaller units. These units are represented by the brigade combat team, which consists of approximately 4,000 personnel (Brigade, n.d.).

Dubik notes that the leader-to-led ratio in the Army alone has steadily risen over the past 20 years. The interaction of America's four military branches, interaction of their forces with the military of other countries, and a greater quantity of smaller units has created a need for more officers. He advises that well educated and experienced leaders are presently required. To meet these needs, Dubik further identifies the need for these officers to attend the necessary military schools to be prepared to perform as leaders and staff officers.

Staff officers plan and control military operations as well as provide administrative, intelligence, and logistic support. An historical statistic from Desert Storm suggests that the staff officers of the United States military can be quite effective. Realizing that political issues and operational concerns are not exactly parallel, the comparison is nevertheless provocative. From

1963 to 1964, the U.S. military transported only 184,000 personnel to Vietnam. As a contrast, in preparation for Desert Storm, 184,000 personnel were moved into Saudi Arabia in less than 90 days (Swain, 1994).

One may find staff officers of many different ranks ranging from lieutenant to colonel. The level of staff officer of particular concern is at the O-4 field grade rank. In the Army, the O-4 field grade officers are majors and the Navy's O-4 field grade is lieutenant commander. These officers are also referred to as middle grade officers.

The examination of the Army and Navy officer education program for these officers presents an interesting contrast based on their operations. As is seen in various media, Army operations are conducted on and above land and the Navy's operations that are principally conducted on the seas and oceans of the world. Regardless of the geographic location, the work of field grade staff officers is an integral component.

The Army's field grade staff officer education program is the Command and General Staff College and is located at Fort Leavenworth, Kansas. The Navy's field grade officer program is the College of Naval Command and Staff and is taught at the Naval War College located in Newport, Rhode Island.

The Joint Chiefs of Staff's Office of Professional Military Education Programs determines the curriculum of both colleges, as well as the Marine and Air Force colleges. The Joint Chiefs of Staff prescribe policies, guidelines, and procedures, which are followed by each service. As the college of each branch of service teaches a common curriculum, the graduates of the Joint Military Education Program Phase I are imbued with the same knowledge.

The Joint Military Professional Education curriculum is required by the Goldwater-Nichols Defense Reorganization Act of 1986 and established by the Skelton Committee on Armed Services in 1989. The Goldwater-Nichols legislation stressed the interoperability of the services. The completion of the Command and General Staff College or the College of Naval Command grants an officer a Joint Military Professional Education Phase I diploma. (Joint Professional Military Education, n.d.).

Both colleges strictly follow the Joint Military Education Program curriculum and undergo accreditation reviews by the Joint Chiefs of Staff. Additionally, each college presents the curriculum from their service's point of view. Regardless of approach, both colleges educate and train officers to be adaptive leaders, capable of critical thinking, and prepared to plan and conduct operations within their service, other services, governmental agencies, and multinational environments (J. Hickey, personal communication, July 20, 2010; T. Kallman, personal communication, July 26, 2010).

Approximately 950 active officers are chosen per year to attend the resident courses at Fort Leavenworth or the Naval War College. However, many more field grade officers compose the ranks of the Army and Navy. As Dubik indicates, officers should be afforded the education that will allow them to be effective staff officers in many different types of assignments.

To reach all field grade officers, both colleges project a demanding and vibrant non-resident distance education program to the balance of the Army and Navy personnel. Active, Reserve, and National Guard officers as well as officers of sister branches and senior Federal employees can earn the Joint Military Education Program Phase I diploma through these distance education programs. As an example, the Command and General Staff College extends their program to approximately 6,000 officers each year who are at duty locations around the world (Command and General Staff School Mission, 2010).

The Command and General Staff College organizes the Joint Military Education Program Phase I curriculum into the Intermediate Level Education Core and the

Advanced Operations and Warfighting Course. The Intermediate Level Education Core course is composed of six components, which account for approximately 300 hours of classroom instruction with a focus on the spectrum of operations which the Army currently accomplishes along with warfighting. Instruction begins with the foundations component. Topics range from creative thinking and problem solving to topics as international security environment, leader development, operational law, and civil-military relations. The strategic environment component follows and addresses topics as strategic concepts, national security, national strategies, strategic communications, and strategic logistics. The doctrine component provides instruction in Joint Operations with operational design, operational art, and battle command. Joint operations instruction continues with Joint Functions component, which studies topics as the command and control of forces from sister services when they operate together. The planning component specializes in the understanding of the joint operations planning process and its application.

The Command and General Staff Advanced Operations Course is adapted to the officer's functional area as Infantry or Communications. The instruction is divided into components over a period of four months (Command and General Staff School Mission, July 2010).

The College of Naval Command and Staff Joint Military Education Program Phase I curriculum is organized into three core courses. Instruction begins with the National Security and Decision Making course. Instruction provides an insight into command and staff decision-making. Topics include political science, leadership, psychology, management, anthropology, and other related disciplines. Strategy and War is the next course. It is an analytical study of war, which focuses on the methods to achieve global and multi-national interactions, strategic and political inter-

ests, and goals. The Joint Military Operations course addresses the Joint Operational Planning Process to plan the employment of U.S. military forces across the range of joint and combined military operations, prepare military officers to participate in joint operational planning and to advise senior commanders (Academics, n.d.).

The Army and Navy nonresident Joint Military Education Programs provide face-to-face classes, online, and compact disk instructional formats. They represent a tremendous effort to provide high quality instruction to officers across the United States as well locations around the world. The Army and Navy nonresident programs also fulfill Dubik's concern for developing and maintaining well-educated officers.

The Total Army School System is the overarching administrative organization for the Army. The Total Army School System prescribes and supports all levels of education for recruits to general officers provided by the Army (Army Regulation 350-18, 2007). The Command and General Staff College is included in the Total Army School System.

The Army projects face-to-face instruction to nonresident students in six regions of the United States. A training division serves each region. A seventh training division provides support to personnel in Germany, Japan, Korea, and Puerto Rico. The administrative personnel and instructors of the divisions include active and reserve military and Federal civilian employees.

A professional development brigade is assigned to each division. A battalion in each brigade is dedicated to the Command and General Staff College instruction. The Command and General Staff College at Fort Leavenworth is responsible for the curriculum taught by the instructors. The Command and General Staff College is also responsible for the training and certification of the instructors in the battalion who teach the Joint Military Education Program curriculum.

The face-to-face program taught by the battalions consists of three phases. The instruction may take place during active duty for training or inactive duty for training formats. Instruction is based on a ratio of one instructor to eight students. Additionally, a portion of the instruction is completed online. Students are required to comply with a strict attendance policy.

An 18-month web-based nonresident course is also offered to students. Much support is provided to the students throughout their instruction. As an example, students are assigned a counselor during their enrollment. Students interact with each other as they participate through Blackboard and SharePoint asynchronously. While students and their counselor or an instructor may meet synchronously in a chat room, instruction is asynchronous due to the many time zones in which the students reside. Weekly assignments, threaded discussions, and instruction through Blackboard are enriched with Flash files of video instruction. Notably, the distance education staff is attempting to expand this type of instruction with Adobe Flash Mobile so the instruction may be seen on Android type cell phones and soon on iPhones.

The third format is designed for officers who are assigned to remote locations and do not have access to the Internet. These officers are provided the program courseware on compact disks. The compact disks include activities and instruction of the web-based format. (CGSC Circular 350-3 dated 1 December 2005; T. Kallman, personal communication, July 26, 2010; D. Ward, personal communication, July 26, July 28, and August 2, 2010).

The Fleet Seminar Program of the Navy provides similar coverage across the United States. The program is administered by the Naval War College's College of Distance Education. The program is offered at 20 locations in and around the

United States. Norfolk, Virginia, Jacksonville, Florida, New Orleans, Louisiana, San Diego, California, and Everett, Washington represent locations along the east, south, and west coasts of the United States. Inland locations include Great Lakes, Illinois, Millington, Tennessee, and Fort Worth, Texas. The Fleet Seminar Program is also offered at Pearl Harbor, Hawaii.

Each Fleet Seminar location offers one to all three of the Navy's core courses. Students enroll each year for a particular course. Courses begin in September and meet 34 weeks for 3 hours until the following May.

One unique location offering the Fleet Seminar Program is the Naval Post Graduate School at Monterey, California. The Naval War College at Monterey offers the three core courses in a class format. To attain their Joint Military Education Program diploma, students complete four courses (Naval War College Monterey, n.d.).

The Web-Enabled Program is available to officers who have Internet connectivity. When students are enrolled they are assigned to online cohort groups. Students are also assigned a Naval War College faculty member who assists the student as a tutor.

Interaction among students and their advisors is typically asynchronous. Synchronous interaction is inhibited due to the numerous time zones in which the students reside. Academic requirements include readings, an active requirement each week, threaded discussions online, and responses.

The Web-Enabled Program is designed to be completed in about 18-24 months. The Naval War College recognizes that student success is predicated on the amount of time dedicated to coursework. As a result, when students enroll they accept a commitment to dedicate a minimum of two study periods of 3 or more hours each week.

Officers of all services may apply to the Fleet Seminar Program and Web-Enabled Program. Eligibility is extended to all senior lieutenant to captain sea service officers who are active and reserve, and defense-related civilians. Army and Air Force officers majors and above are also eligible.

The Naval War College also extends the Joint Military Education Program instruction to officers who cannot attend the Fleet Seminar Program or do not have Internet access. The CD-ROM program is composed of video lectures by Naval War College professors and audio presentations, student activities, and self-assessment exercises to broaden and emphasize the content. The program is designed for officers on sea duty or assigned to remote or isolated locations. The student is expected to complete the CD-ROM program in 18 months (Naval War College Provides JPME I to the Fleet, 2004).

The distance education staff of each college is composed of experts in instructional design and distance education. Each staff possesses the expertise to create their own courseware. Both colleges follow a similar distance education course instructional design process.

A central concern in the course design is to maintain their accreditation by the Joint Chiefs of Staff. To do so, instruction adapted for distance delivery is based on the essential content that is presented in the classroom. To ensure alignment of the classroom format and distance education format the colleges follow a rigid development process. As an example, the Command and Staff College distance education developers form a working group for each course.

A unique quality control element of course development is the inclusion of the author of the resident course in the process. The resident author is a member of the distance education course development group. To ensure equivalency of the resident and distance education courses, the resident author takes ownership of the content. With the essential content is identified, the distance education staff selects or develops appropriate media to deliver the instruction. While the Dick, Carey, and Carey (2005) model of instructional design is not specifically used, the distance education course developers in the staffs at each college speak in those terms and elements of the design process are used (D. McGill, personal communication, July 28, and August 5, 2010; D. Ward, personal communication, July 26, 28, and August 2, 2010).

Both colleges recognize that the quality of the instructors is a critical component of the nonresident education process. Distance education instructors for the web-based programs are typically retired military and are specifically trained to facilitate the online courses (J. Hickey, personal communication, July 20, 2010; T. Kallman, personal communication, July 26, 2010).

A significant indicator of the course design success is the end-of-course assessment. As an example, assessment is highly regarded by the Naval War College distance education department. Student cannot continue on to the next instruction until they have submitted their assessment of the completed course. Data from the required assessments is anonymous and reviewed by the distance education faculty (J. Hickey, personal communication, July 20, 2010).

The administration and support of online students in the Army's Web-Based course or the Navy's Web-Enabled Program is similar to online schools in the public sector. The descriptions of the Command and General Staff College and Naval War College online programs indicate a significant connection to each student as well as support. Students who enroll in these programs realize that their continued career progression is dependent on the successful completion of the Joint Military Education Program Phase I instruction. As a result, they are quite motivated (J. Hickey, personal communication, July 20, 2010).

The descriptions of the programs suggest a student-centered support paradigm. The student is surrounded by components that support their academic success. Students may converse with instructors and other students through the threaded discussions on Blackboard. Chat rooms are available for students to converse with counselors and instructors. Students may contact their instructors and counselors by telephone and e-mail. Students of both services have full online access to their college's libraries. Counselors play a key role, as students must be aware of the requirements placed upon them to graduate and that they must complete the requirements within a specific amount of time (T. Kallman, personal communication, July 26, 2010).

From an overall perspective, America's military has two general components. One component is referred to as the generating force and the other is the operating force. The active and reserve faculty members and resident students of each college are part of the generating force. As Dubik (2010) indicates, fewer military personnel are being assigned to the generating force, which suggests that each college has a reduced faculty. It appears that the web-based programs serve as an educational multiplier by being able continue high-level support and expert instruction to officers in operational duty assignments.

The online distance education program of today's military, particularly the Army and Navy, appear to be as contemporary as leading online schools. Both colleges are adapting current technology to virtually place the online line student in the resident classrooms. One example is the use of MilBook, which is the Department of Defense's combined version of Facebook, Twitter, YouTube, and Wiki (D. Ward, personal communication, July 26, 28, August 2, 2010).

Just over a decade ago, the Joint Military Education Program for the Command and General Staff College distance education program was the exchange of printed course materials between an instructor at the college and the student (T. Kallman, personal communication, July 26, 2010). This relationship is almost reminiscent of the late 1880s University of Wisconsin correspondence course for farmers (Simonson, Smaldino, Albright, & Zvacek, 2009).

Since those days, the distance education departments at both colleges have become as current as any online university. As an example, distance education experts of the Naval War College attend the University of Wisconsin's yearly Conference on Distance Teaching and Learning. This year, distance education faculty of the Naval War College presented a workshop on "Best Practices in Military Distance Learning" (D. McGill, personal communication, July 28 and August 5, 2010).

During the Sister Service College conference in January of 2010, Lieutenant General Caldwell, the commandant of the Command and General Staff College, aptly described the education mission of the all the services Joint Military Education Programs. He noted that all the colleges are composed of world-class faculties that develop, administer, and teach. The courses at the colleges are designed to create adaptive leaders with command, control, and support skills to succeed in complex missions during operations (Caldwell, 2009). The students of these colleges, resident and nonresident, receive common instruction specified by the Joints Chief Staff. They compose the core of a formidable force, as they are equally capable to be staff officers and leaders in their respective assignments.

The distance education faculties of the Command and General Staff College and of the Naval War College are answering Dubik's (2010) call for more leaders and staff officers. The nonresident programs of these colleges are a dynamic part of meeting the need for well educated officers.

REFERENCES

Ausiello, D. (2004, April). Naval War College provides JPME I to the fleet. *Navy.mil Official Website of the United States Navy.* Retrieved from http://www.navy.mil/search/display .asp?story_id=12523

Army Regulation 350-18. (2007). *The Army school system.* Retrieved from http://www.tradoc .army.mil/tpubs/regs/r350-18.htm

Brigade. (n.d). *Brigade unit of action.* Retrieved from http://www.globalsecurity.org/military/ agency/army/bua.htm

Caldwell, W. (2010, January.) *5 questions for the Command and General Staff College commandant.* Retrieved from http://www.army.mil/- news/2009/01/22/15992-5-questions-for-the- command-and-general-staff-college-com- mandant/

Command and General Staff School Mission. (2010, July). *Command and General Staff School (CGSS) mission* [PowerPoint presentation]. Fort Leavenworth, KS: Command and General Staff College.

Dick, W., Carey, L., & Carey, J. (2005). *The systematic design of instruction* (6th Ed.) New York, NY: Addison-Wesley.

Dubik, J. M. (2010, August). Studying the future security environment. *Army, 60*(8), 22-24.

Office of the Joints Chief of Staff. (n.d.). *Joint professional military education (JPME)* Retrieved from http://www.mcu.usmc.mil/ MilitaryEducation/JPMEInfo.pdf

Naval War College. (n.d.). *Academics.* Retrieved from http://www.usnwc.edu/Academics .aspx

Naval War College Monterey. (n.d.). *Naval War College at Monterey.* Retrieved from http:// www.nps.edu/Academics/Programs/NWC/

Simonson, M., Smaldino, S., Albright, M., & Zvacek. S. (2009). *Teaching and learning at a distance: Foundations of distance education* (4th ed.) Boston, MA: Pearson.

Swain, R. (1994). *"The lucky war" Third Army in Desert Storm.* Retrieved from http:// www.cgsc.edu/carl/resources/csi/swain/ swain.asp

U.S. Army Command and General Staff College. (n.d.). *CGSC Circular 350-3 dated 1 December 2005.* Retrieved from http:// www.cgsc.edu/repository/dde_7_ catalogAppC.pdf

"THE ONLINE DISTANCE EDUCATION PROGRAM OF TODAY'S MILITARY, PARTICULARLY THE ARMY AND NAVY, APPEAR TO BE AS CONTEMPORARY AS LEADING ONLINE SCHOOLS."

MOOC Madness

Michael Simonson

"Though this be madness, yet there is method in't"

—Hamlet, Act II, Scene ii, line 211, Shakespeare

Massive open online courses, or MOOCs, pronounced interestingly enough as mooooks as in cow sounds, are the "talk of the town." The October 5, 2012 Section B of *The Chronicle of Higher Education* dedicated its entire issue to the topic of MOOCs. The *New York Times* has written about MOOCs, and even South Florida's own *Sun Sentinel* has opined on the topic of MOOCS.

Michael Simonson, Editor, *Distance Learning*, and Program Professor, Programs in Instructional Technology and Distance Education, Fischler School of Education, Nova Southeastern University, 1750 NE 167 St., North Miami Beach, FL 33162. Telephone: (954) 262-8563. E-mail: simsmich@nsu.nova.edu

Just what are MOOCs and what do they offer to the field of distance education? Simply, the name tells it all. MOOC courses are massive, often with enrollments in the tens of thousands. Next, they are open, meaning open access courseware is used to deliver the course, and enrollment is open to anyone who is interested. Next, MOOCs are online, fully online and asynchronous. And last, they are courses, often a digitized version of a traditional lecture class with sessions recorded in video, audio, and posted online.

But, are MOOCs distance education, as many think? First, one needs to define distance education. *Distance Learning* journal has regularly applied this definition: "Institutionally-based formal education, where the learning group is separated, and where interactive communications technologies are used to connect the instructor, learners and resources" (Simonson, Smaldino, Albright, & Zvacek, 2012).

At first glance this definition does seem to include MOOCs as they are most often configured. MOOCs are institutionally-based; at least originally they were. The great universities of the United States, such as the Massachusetts Institute of Technology, and Stanford, offer MOOCs. Interestingly, many of the instigators of MOOCs initiatives have left their universities to offer massive online courses via private corporations.

Next, it is obvious that the learning group is separated; at least the learners and resources are geographically separated. But what about the instructors? Certainly MOOC designers and the talent featured in the videos can be considered instructors, but are these individuals actually involved in the use of the MOOC or are they "just talent?" Instructor involvement in the teaching and learning process is unclear.

Most definitely, communications technologies are used to deliver content and make the content available to learners; most often content is digitized content via the Web. Often, class presentations are video recorded, documents are digitized, and self-test quizzes and exams are written and programmed, often with self-scoring. Great stuff, but ...?

So, are MOOCs distance education? A closer examination of the definition of distance education may be helpful. Distance education consists of distance teaching AND distance learning—two components of the education process. Do MOOCs provide both teaching and learning? Some say no, since the instructional aspects of MOOCs are programmed and offered but only as a prepackaged self-study system.

MOOCs are usually loaded with outstanding content, and well-delivered presentations, but those who would claim that MOOCs are the future of higher education need only review the instructional films and instructional video phenomena of the 1960s and 1970s. Excellent self-study, but not education.

And finally, there is much to be learned from the study of MOOCs. As Shakespeare wrote in Hamlet, "there is method in't."

REFERENCES

Shakespeare, W. *Hamlet*, Act II, Scene ii, line 211

Simonson, M., Smaldino, S., Albright, M., & Zvacek, S. (2012). *Teaching and learning at a distance: Foundations of distance Education* (5th ed.). Boston, MA: Pearson.

Part III
International Applications
of Distance Education

The University of the West Indies Open Campus

A Beacon for Distance Education in the Caribbean

Beverly S. Crooks-Johnson

INTRODUCTION

The University of the West Indies (UWI) evolved over the past 60 years in response to the demand for higher education in the Caribbean region. Over the years UWI has provided quality educational opportunities and has been producing thousands of intellectuals, and many of renown. Although the institution continued to experience recognition and growth, there were still numerous

Beverly S. Crooks-Johnson,
Head of Computer Department,
Mico University College, 1A Marescaux Road,
Kingston 10, Jamaica W.I.
Telephone: (876) 929-5260.
E-mail: bcrjohnson99@gmail.com

individuals, particularly from noncampus countries who faced challenges in accessing higher education. UWI Open Campus' development was a means of reengineering UWI's educational infrastructure to resolve the problem of tertiary education access in the Caribbean.

This article gives a brief overview of UWI's beginnings, looks at the institution's present status, and briefly traces of the genesis of distance education at UWI to the materialization of its fourth campus, the Open Campus (UWIOC). Discussion of UWIOC pursues with a look at the program offerings, telecommunications infrastructure, enrollment, and the necessity for quality assurance. Despite increasing competitiveness and other challenges UWI, and by extension UWIOC, has maintained the position of being the institution of first choice for higher education in the Caribbean.

HISTORICAL OVERVIEW: UWI's HUMBLE BEGINNINGS

The University of the West Indies (formerly the University College of the West Indies) evolved from the positive response of the West Indian people to dispossession, resulting from years of colonial rule that marked their history. The first office of the University College of the West Indies (UCWI) was opened at 62 Lady Musgrave

Road, Kingston, Jamaica on February 1, 1947. The institution was relocated to Mona, Kingston on the Gibraltar Camp. The Mona campus was officially opened on October 3, 1948, with an enrollment of 33 students, comprising 10 females and 23 males. By 1950 there were 304 residential students enrolled. It was the UCWI that provided necessary skilled manpower, expertise, and knowledge about the West Indian cultures and economic systems, and stood as an emblem of regional unity. It was quite befitting, therefore, when R. M. Homer, the principal of Queen's Royal College in Trinidad, recommended UWI's Latin Motto, which appears on its armorial bearings: "Oriens Ex Occidente Lux," meaning "Light Rising From the West" (UWI: Time Capsule: Past, 2008).

In 1960, UCWI's second campus, in St. Augustine, Trinidad came into existence. By April 1962 the royal charter was passed conferring on the UCWI degree-granting status, and declaring the intuition as the University of the West Indies. The third UWI campus, Cave Hill, Barbados was established in 1967. The then vision of Sir Phillip Sherlock, UWI's founding father and first vice chancellor, well articulated that of the mandate institution, which was to: (1) multiply opportunities for vertical mobility; (2) provide the society with a corpus of knowledge based on research; and (3) broaden the intellectual base that universal suffrage and political independence demanded (UWI: Time Capsule: Past, 2008).

UWI AT PRESENT

The UWI has grown into a landmark regional institution, providing higher education in 16 Caribbean countries. Table 1 below shows UWI's three campus countries and all the other participating countries in the region. Figure 1 serves as an indicator of the size and locations of UWIOC's 16 participating countries.

Since its inception UWI has experienced considerable changes which "have helped reposition some of the University's original configurations and traditional directions" (UWI: Present, 2008, para. 1). Currently UWI offers over 800 accredited programs to over 45,877 students, through its nine faculties, three physical campuses, and 12 centers within the English speaking Caribbean.

DISTANCE EDUCATION: NO NEW PHENOMENON AT UWI

According to Thomas and Soares (2009), UWI has traditionally been governed by campus-based education, with the three campuses in Jamaica, Barbados, and Trinidad and Tobago, giving campus countries the competitive edge in attracting scholars at the tertiary level. Furthermore, statistics reveal that tertiary education is not sufficiently developed within the Organization of Eastern Caribbean States (OECS) and that the number of persons accessing higher education within the region represents only 3-7% of the population. This highlights the need for the expansion of increased learning opportunities for OECS nationals, and to stem increasing practice where students have to migrate to further their studies. It is against this background that UWI developed distance education (DE) initiatives to help level the playing field and facilitate increased access to ter-

Table 1.   UWI's Three Main Campuses and 12 Participating Countries

UWI Campus Countries	Participating Countries
Barbados	Angulla, Antigua and Barbuda, Bahamas, Belize, Bermuda
Jamaica	British Virgin Islands, Cayman Islands, Dominica, Grenada, Montserrat
Trinidad and Tobago	St. Kitts and Nevis, St. Lucia, St. Vincent, Turks and Caicos

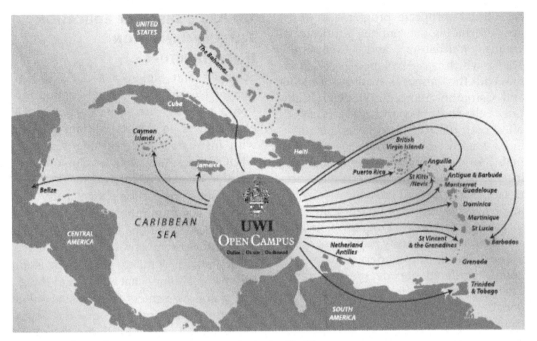

Figure 1. Open Campus participating countries in the Caribbean.

tiary education by noncampus countries of the OECS (OECS, 2013). This propelled UWI's bifocal approach to instructional delivery, as the "bifocal approach meant firstly, widening student access, and secondly, responding to the needs of those students in the noncampus countries who could not afford to move to a campus country" (OECS, 2001, p. 6).

UWI started offering distance learning programs from as early as 1958, through radio broadcasts on its Radio Education Unit on the Jamaica campus (Thomas & Soares, 2009). The Radio Education Unit produced radio programs, which were aired in schools and teacher training colleges in Jamaica and throughout the Caribbean. Instructional recordings were also distributed to different radio stations in the region. In late 1970 UWI introduced a new DE project, the Challenge Examination Scheme, which in 1983 was incorporated into the University Distance Teaching Experiment. University Distance Teaching Experiment later transitioned into the Uni-

versity Distance Education Centre, in 1996 creating a dual mode operation for the institution. It was from this vantage point that UWI started to realize usefulness of a telecommunications network for educational outreach in the Anglophone Caribbean (Thomas & Soares, 2009).

THE EMERGENCE OF THE UWIOC

UWI's newest campus, the Open Campus (OC) was officially opened in Antigua and Barbuda in June 2008, after obtaining the approval of the Council of The University of the West Indies in April 2007. The OC is a merger of the former offices which held responsibility for DE and continuing studies: the Office of the Board for Non-Campus Countries and Distance Education, the School of Continuing Studies, the UWI Distance Education Centre, and the Tertiary Level Institutions Unit (About UWI Open Campus, 2004-2013).

In the first year of operation the OC developed its first set of programs, which constituted certificate programs in three areas including an online certificate in Online Journalism and Community Media, which was developed in collaboration with the Caribbean Institute of Media and Communications (UWI Open Campus: Self Study Report, 2012). Today it offers over 800 accredited programs utilizing a variety of methodologies and formats for delivery. Delivery methods include blended learning modalities, face-to-face, online, and distance learning involving the distribution of print and software materials. Programs include courses for preuniversity education, certificate, diploma, and undergraduate programs, postgraduate degree programs, extension courses, technical and vocational, and other continuing studies courses. The institution uses this multimode teaching and learning approach for both physical and virtual instructional locations at its 42 sites in 16 English-speaking Caribbean countries.

The fourth campus therefore emerged as a solution to the issue of regional human resource development and aimed at: (1) creating a student–centered learning environment; (2) establishing a viable and sustainable financing mechanism; (3) designing and implement an administrative and organizational structure; (4) formulating policy for managing, developing, and implementing open and flexible learning; and (5) establishing policy for managing/building interinstitutional relationships/partnerships (Thomas & Soares, 2009). UWIOC is thereby guided by the following principles:

> The Open Campus of the University of the West Indies is based on the idea that the high-quality university education, research and services available at our institution should be open and available to all people who wish to reach their full potential inside and outside of the Caribbean region. (About UWI Open Campus, 2004-2013)

UWIOC's Distance Education Telecommunication Infrastructure

Schlosser and Simonson's (2006) definition of DE signifies that telecommunications systems are critical to a DE environment to connect distant learners with instructors and learning resources. UWIOC uses the Moodle Open Source learning management system (LMS) in dual mode instructions for faculty and students communication within and outside of class schedules. The learning management system provides interactive, collaborative features like discussion forums, real-time chat tools and blogs, and course assessment features like online quiz and exam, and drop box for assignments. In recent times campus classrooms have been upgraded with multimedia technological access and lectures for many programs, and are streamed over broadband. UWIOC uses Elluminate and BigblueButton applications for live online courses and to facilitate communication for both educational and administrative purposes. In addition, web conferences are used for asynchronous sessions (OAS, n.d.).

The Computer and Technical Services division of the Open Campus has responsibility to manage all the technical and technological requirements of UWIOC throughout the Caribbean. UWIOC recently upgraded student portals to an integrated portal (my.uwi.edu), which allows for single sign-on access to several applications like the Moodle LMS, e-mail, and library resources, among others. Recent upgrades now enable mobile access to the portals. At present web-based polling allowing students to respond to interactive polling questions is being pilot tested (OAS, n.d.; UWI Open Campus: Computer & Technical Services, 2004-2013).

UWIOC's Programs and Student Enrollment

The Marketing and Communications units in the territories have been instrumental in UWIOC's policies and initiatives development, which help to control the University's image and identity. Program development emerges from researches conducted by Marketing and Communications to determine the relevance and viability of courses offered. UWIOC offers several graduate, undergraduate, continuing, and professional education programs in response to students' needs and contribution to workforce and regional development. Student enrollment has gradual increased over time. Undergraduate intake, for example, grew by 6% during the first 4 years, and new postgraduate programs attracted over 600 students in the first semester of the OC operation. Table 2 gives a summary of the total enrollment for online/blended program for the 2011-2012 school year. The bachelor of science, bachelor of education, and associate degree programs had enrollments of 3,817, 1,154 and 733 respectively, with the master of education registering over 200 students. The statistics in Table 3 gives the breakdown of student enrollment UWIOC's over the first 4-year period. The data reveals that campus countries' enrollments are comparatively much larger than that of the noncampus (UWI-12) countries combined.

The Organization for Economic Cooperation and Development's report (2011) highlights the changing criteria by which

Table 2. Total Enrollment for Online/Blended Programs 2011-2012

Program	Total Enrollment
Associate degree	733
Bachelor of education	1,154
Bachelor of science	3,817
Certificate	183
Diploma	68
Postgraduate diploma	45
Master of education	226
Specially admitted	111
Transient programs	162
Grand total	6,499

Table 3. Enrollment in Open Campus Continuing Education Programs 2008–2012

Countries	2007/2008	2008/2009	2009/2010	2010/2011	2011/2012
Total UWI-12 countries	984	1,283	1,864	2,004	3,873
Barbados	850	789	660	809	919
Jamaica	3,636	3,900	5,331	4,974	4,877
Trinidad and Tobago	12,349	14,972	11,800	11,369	8,179
Total campus countries	16,835	19,661	17,791	17,152	13,975
Grand total	17,819	20,944	19,655	19,156	17,848

educational success is judged. The report stipulates that the aim of educational delivery is no longer to provide fundamental education for all, but to "increase the demand for people who are capable of doing knowledge work," persons who are able to function effectively in today's global community and "compete for jobs not just locally but internationally" (p. 15). The OC responded to increased demanded for workforce development programs by taking on the commitment to develop training programs at the local level in partnerships with local, regional, and international entities (UWI Strategic Plan, 2012 -2017).

UWIOC AND QUALITY ASSURANCE

The UWIOC management teams with delegated responsibility periodically assess the institutions' performance against the aims and objectives of its Strategic Plan. Consistent with the institution's goal to sustain quality, institutionwide surveys were conducted, particularly toward the period of accreditation. Representative student samples, all members of staff and stakeholders were surveyed and the analyzed results returned favorable findings. UWIOC's response as documented in the Self Study is instructive: "We were humbled by the magnitude of best practices we unearthed within our Campus and motivated to correct the ills that still plague us" (UWI Open Campus, Self Study Report, 2012, p. 221). Over the first 4-year period there were improvements made to the curriculum, including pedagogical reform and as the introduction of various new and cutting-edge programs. External review of the campus Quality Assurance Unit resulted in recommendations for the continued development of the quality assurance function at the UWI (UWI Strategic Plan, 2012-2017).

Morabito (1997), in addressing the increasing demand for distance learning opportunities through online institutions,

speaks to the importance of accreditation for online programs, a process which strengthens the institution's reputation and also "serves as a sign of quality and legitimacy" (p. 22). UWIOC stood the test for quality assurance and was accredited for a 6-year period by the Barbados Accreditation Council in July 2013. The declaration of the Barbados Accreditation Council report speaks volumes for the institution's operations:

> The commitment to quality was clear from all of those the team met, from the design and delivery teams in APAD to the online and face-to-face tutors. There are effective systems of monitoring and review of programs and appropriate international benchmarking of standards. The Quality Assurance Unit provides an appropriate and high quality service to the Open Campus. (UWI Open Campus: Institutional Accreditation, 2004-2013)

Achieving and maintaining quality is not just an institutional exercise. Parents, students, teachers, and educational stakeholders seek to determine the extent to which educational institutions prepare students for life.

While many countries monitor and make comparative assessments of student learning outcomes, the yardstick for determining academic results "is no longer [seen as] improvement against national educational standards, but also improvement against the most successful education systems worldwide" (Organization for Economic Co-operation and Development, 2011, p. 19). Internationally UWI was ranked by Webometric, in January 2011, as one of the world's five top ranking organizations at 705 out of 12,000 universities worldwide. The Webometric ranking places UWI in the top 6% worldwide, at number two in Caribbean, behind the University of Puerto Rico and first place in the English speaking Caribbean (UWI Office of Planning and Development, 2011).

Today, UWI is still seen as the undeniably "the only truly regional higher educational institution in the Caribbean in concept, scope and reach" (Tewarie, 2009, p. 6). However, the author cautions that with the emergence of other local and competing universities, like University of Technology and Northern Caribbean University in Jamaica, the University of Guyana, and the University of Trinidad and Tobago, UWI cannot be complacent but will have to consistently aim at attaining world ranking criteria to maintain its competitive edge in the region while competing with other international universities.

Consistent with the university's mission of promoting economic, social, political, and cultural development of the West Indian society, the guiding principles of UWIOC is the long arm which is extending the institution's reach to "provide high-quality university education, research and services available ... [and to] be open and available to all people who wish to reach their full potential inside and outside of the Caribbean region" (UWI Open Campus, Self Study Report, 2012, p. iii). Consistent with UWI's motto, UWIOC's reputation and modes of operation provide a sound platform from which the intuition can shine its educational torch to brightly illuminate within and well beyond the boundaries of the Caribbean region.

REFERENCES

Morabito, M. G. (1997). The importance of accreditation and infrastructure for online schools. *Distance Learning Magazine, 5*(3). Retrieved from http://www.usdla.org/ assets/ pdf _files/DL_5-3.pdf

OAS. (n.d.). ICT Initiatives and innovation at UWI. Retrieved from http:// www.oas.org/ en/scholarships/virtualeduca/PP/UWI.pdf

Organization for Economic Co-operation and Development. (2011). *Lessons from PISA for the United States. Strong performers and successful reformers in education.* Retrieved from http://dx.doi.org/10.1787/9789264096660-en

Organization of Eastern Caribbean States. (2013). Reforming tertiary, adult and continuing education. Retrieved from http://www.oecs.org/education-reform-initiatives/589-reforming-tertiary-adult-and-continuing-education

Organization of Eastern Caribbean States. (2001). Education reform unit strategic plan 2001-2010. (2001). Retrieved from http://www.oecs.org/publications/doc_download/177-oeru-strategic-plan

Schlosser, L. A., & Simonson, M. (2006). *Distance education: Definition and glossary of terms* (2nd ed.). Retrieved from http://www.schoolofed.nova.edu/bpol/pdf/distancelearning_def.pdf

Tewarie, B. (2009, July). *The regional university model: Does it still stand? A perspective from the University of the West Indies.* Presented at the Policy Forum on Tertiary Education in Small States, International Institute for Educational Planning, Paris, France.

Thomas, M. L., & Soares, J. (2009). Increasing public access to university qualifications: Evolution of the University of the West Indies Open Campus. *International Review of Research in Open and Distance Learning, 10*(2).

University of the West Indies. (2004-2013). Open Campus: About UWI Open Campus. Retrieved from http://www.open.uwi.edu/about/welcome-uwi-open-campus

University of the West Indies. (2004-2013). Open Campus: Computer & Technical Services. Retrieved December 2013, from http://www.open.uwi.edu/academics/computer-technical-services

University of the West Indies. (2004-2013). Open Campus: Institutional accreditation. Retrieved from http://www.open.uwi.edu/accreditation

University of the West Indies. (2008). Time capsule: Past. Retrieved from http://www2.sta.uwi.edu/uwi60/evolve/timecapsule.asp

University of the West Indies. (2008). UWI: Present. Retrieved from http://www2.sta.uwi.edu/uwi60/evolve/present.asp

University of the West Indies, Open Campus. (2012). Self study report for institutional accreditation. Retrieved from http://www.open.uwi.edu/sites/default/files/UWI_Open_Campus_Institutional_Accreditation_Self_Study_Report_2012.pdf

The University of the West Indies, Office of Planning and Development. (2011, February 04). A review of world university ranking Methodologies: What UWI must do to improve its ranking in Latin America and the world. Retrieved from http://www.uwi.edu/planningoffice/ default.aspx

Online Education in the Bahamas
What Is its Position?

Kendra Spencer

W e live in a world where technology seems to be taking over. However, in spite of the growing trend of technology in our daily lives, there are many countries that have not reached this point as yet. I live in one of those countries. A country where one is unable to perform a self-cash out at the grocery store, a country where our local network has just migrated to high-definition television, a country where the majority of our schools are not computerized. Yes, there are many adult learners who are involved in online education through

Kendra Spencer,
Educator, Nassau, N.P. Bahamas.
E-mail: kendispend@gmail.com

schools such as Nova Southeastern University, the University of Phoenix, and Walden University. However, when it comes to the K-12 sector as well as our local colleges, online classes are practically at a level of nonexistence. Hence, the focus on online education in the Bahamas: what is its position?

In approaching the topic, I imagined having such a program being implemented in the educational system in my country. Hence my aim to gather the views of others as it relates to this subject. Therefore through voluntary acceptance to participate in this project, I interviewed instructors from local colleges. I found that their responses were common and their concerns the same.

The first instructor, Ron Clarke, serves as acting head of a math department at a technical college. He stated that technology in the classroom in the Bahamas is in dire need of advancement. While teachers use technology such as smart boards, and various computer forms, the students do not have immediate access to computer technology in the classroom. As it relates to the question comparing the prevalence of computer technology in the Bahamian education system to other countries, Clarke added that we actually have to get to that stage of technology prevalence in the classroom, and make it available to our students. He also mentioned that in spite of the fear of older teachers to embrace the technology phenomenon, younger teachers are ready to take on this route of teaching, but more training is needed.

Clarke stated that he uses the ENO Board as a form of technology into his lessons, along with the Skills Tutor Educational Software, which allows students to log in online and complete assignments and quizzes as well as tutorials that are made available for practice and skill building. Nonetheless, he summed up the interview by saying that we need more persons who will do research and produce documents to say that this mode of teaching and learning is the way forward.

The second educator I interviewed is an adjunct instructor at one of the local colleges. This well-versed young man, Alonzo Smith, shared his views about distance education and online learning in the Bahamas by stating that this mode of instruction and learning has global advantages and that it is certainly the wave of the future, especially with the advances in technology and the busy lives of many. He said that it is something that really needs to be tapped into since there are also many individuals who are not able to attend a traditional campus for many reasons. Smith added that he does not see online learning being integrated into K-12 classrooms in the Bahamas in the very near future, but rather as a long-term goal. The reason being, he added, is that the government, who is responsible for this implementation is not prepared for this move financially, and probably do not see it as an area of importance, since they are presently focusing on other areas of education, such as national exams and improving the national average. Conversely, he added that it would be advantageous to all students in the K-12 age groups because most of these students spend a lot of time online in their spare time, and since it is something that they enjoy doing, they are more likely to respond to this method of learning in a positive way.

In response to his school's move toward online learning, Smith stated that attempts were made and; introductory courses were offered, though not on a large scale. Sadly, there was a disconnect and tension arose since a lot of the instructors were not prepared to put in the overtime with teaching online, as they were still required to teach the regular load of traditional sessions. In addition, he added that many were trying to feel their way through the online instructional process. Moreover, Smith noted that more training is needed because most teachers do not know how to attack such a task. However, he said that his school is looking into revisiting this area, and that they are simply trying to find out what needs to be done to make it a reality. Nonetheless, he continued to say that, like the government system and the K-12 classrooms, his school is also "just not there as yet."

The responses from both Bahamian educators focused on some barriers to distance education. These barriers included increased time commitment, lack of money to implement the programs, organizational resistance to change, and definitely a lack of shared vision. Berge and Muilenberg (2000) asserted that the shortage of technology-enhanced classrooms, labs, or infrastructures can be grouped among the greatest setbacks in education. Therefore, there needs to be more discussions about how educational institutions can keep current with changing trends in technology.

The Nassau Guardian published an article that described the views of the leader of the Free National Movement, the opposition party of the Bahamas government, as it relates to technological proficiency in a new Bahamas. The leader, Hubert Minnis, stated that competency in science and technology is crucial to effectively manage a nation. He also mentioned the importance of recognizing that becoming technologically ready means more than paying bills online or accessing Bahamian law on one's computer or smartphone. In addition, he noted that the country needs to replace its archaic relics and become more tech savvy. Minnis described tech savvy in the new Bahamas as having the appropriate government services and assistance online; having accessible computerized education for all; access to the proper medical and healthcare innovations on virtual platforms, and expanded opportunities in financial services (Minnis, 2013).

The words that really grasped my attention were "having accessible computerized education for all." I was happy to know that someone in the governmental hierarchy, in spite of being the opposition, recognized the importance of moving beyond where we are today. Minnis shared his view that the Ministry of Education, which is where our greatest expenditure exists, has not risen to the occasion to embrace science and technology. He stated that in a "New Bahamas," he recognizes that marrying the two will mean more than a few whiteboards and computers, but additional teacher training will be required to better equip teachers with the skills to use the new and emerging technology as teaching tools. This, he added, means equipping every classroom, from prekindergarten to college with the necessary technology to produce students equipped for the 21st century. Moreover, he announced that this also means making distance education accessible through the use of technology and media services (Minnis, 2013).

As I began to bring it all together, I reflected on Clarke's statement that the need for more research about distance education and online learning as it relates to the Bahamas is a necessity. While this is essential, we can look at the research of many of the pioneers of distance education and online learning and use these frameworks to build our own system. Of course cultural adjustments will have to be made, but lots of work has already been done; the information is out there, so we just need to collect the data and scrutinize the reported success. Simonson, Smaldino, Albright, and Zvacek (2012), stated that the distance

education research agenda has also evolved, and that researchers are no longer focusing only on achievement, but are now examining learner attributes and perceptions as well as interaction patterns and how these contribute to the overall learning environment.

There is a lot of ground work that has to be set before distance education and online learning can be implemented or become a norm in the Bahamas. The high school graduation rate in the Bahamas has decreased, in part due to students not attaining the required minimum grade point average of 2.0. In addition, the Ministry of Education also face challenges with recruiting and retaining highly qualified teachers in specialized subject areas to ensure that "no child is left behind." Concomitantly, the national grade point average as it relates to the national exam, BGCSEs, is a D (Massey, 2009), but many schools do not have the funding needed for technology upgrades and, in most cases, the actual implementation.

As I researched the implementation of successful distance education programs, I was drawn to the steps taken by the state of Alabama. Stancil (2011) mentioned that, based on the deficiencies listed, members assigned to a task force on distance education that was led by the governor formulated a list of objectives to guide their vision. They also created a strategic plan about how and when to implement this initiative.

Stancil (2011) noted Meredith and Newton's three strands of intervention that must unite to ensure the success of an e-learning intervention. These include learner capability, technology and teacher pedagogy. Of course, one must consider the cost factors to effectively integrate these strands, as up to date technology needs to be positioned into the classrooms, as well as the appropriate training for teachers. If the teachers are not properly trained for such a task, then it will all be in vain.

While there are baby steps being taken toward integration of online education within our schools, I must concur with Minister Minnis that we have not integrated the basic computer technology as yet. Of course there are many Bahamians who are technology savvy, many have computers in their homes, many use smart phones, et cetera. However, there are still numerous Bahamians who cannot afford a computer or Internet service.

What is the position of the Bahamas regarding online education? I can say that I see my country as a sprinter, at the starting line, getting in position to start the race. Sadly the staring pistol has already been fired. Perhaps one day we will begin the race in spite of others lapping us.

REFERENCES

Berge, Z., & Muilenburg, L. (2000). Barriers to distance education as perceived by managers and administrators: Result of survey. In M. Clay (Ed.), *Distance learning administration annual 2000.* Baltimore, MD: University of Maryland-Baltimore.

Massey, J. (2009). The learning crisis: A Bahamian public policy essay. Retrieved from http://www.thebahamaschamber.com/UserFiles/HTMLEditor/Bah_Edu_Book.pdf

Minnis, H. (2013, November 4). The new Bahamas: Technological proficiency. The quest toward effective management of our nation. *The Nassau Guardian.* Retrieved from http://www.thenassauguardian.com/index.php?option=com_content&view=article&id=42924:the-new-bahamas-technological-proficiency&catid=49:op-ed&Itemid=86

Simonson, M., Smaldino, S., Albright, M., & Zvacek. S. (2012). *Teaching and learning at a distance: Foundations of distance education* (5th ed.). Boston, MA: Pearson.

Stancil, S. (2011). Wired for success: Alabama's ACCESS to distance learning. *Distance Learning, 8*(4), 19-26.

The Evolution of ODL System in Nigeria
The Place of Nigerian Students of Conventional University Age Bracket

Janet O. Odeyemi

INTRODUCTION

Nigeria's guiding principle on education is the equipping of every citizen with knowledge, skills, attitudes, and values that will enable the individual to derive maximum benefit from being a member of the society and to lead a fulfilling life as well as contribute to both the development and welfare of the society. Educational objectives in Nigeria include the inculcation of national con-

Janet O. Odeyemi,
Centre for Lifelong Learning,
National Open University of Nigeria,
14/16, Ahmadu Bello Way,
Victoria Island Lagos, Nigeria.

sciousness and national unity, inculcation of true values and attitudes needed for the survival of an individual and the society, and training for understanding the world as a whole. These objectives are viable; however, educational development has faced many constraints. Globally, education is seen as the enabler for all, and the continent of Africa particularly needs education for its continued development—the type that can cushion the effect of war, famine, and other man-made/natural catastrophes.

A closer look at the educational scene in Nigeria reveals many disparities, including disparities observed between rural and urban schools and federal-owned and privately owned schools. Gaps are also observed in the enrolment of the genders; admission figures and the available teaching resources.

Figure 1 shows the Nigeria education system and the expected age range toward attaining the educational objectives. It shows the primary school and its expected age bracket, as well as secondary and the tertiary institutions. The higher education is shown as including the colleges of education, polytechnics, colleges of technology and the universities. This paper has as its purview, the Nigerian youths of university age bracket. It will therefore, look into higher education alone.

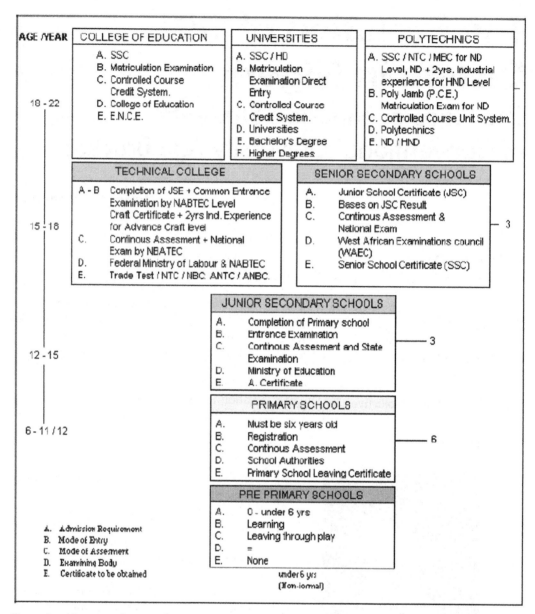

Figure 1. Nigerian educational system—age range.

OVERVIEW OF HIGHER EDUCATION IN NIGERIA

Higher education holds a strategic place in national development; it is the platform for the production of quality graduates to drive the various sectors of the economy. Higher education is also seen as the bedrock of the human capital development in economic, agriculture, infrastructure, energy, oil and gas, and other sectors. The importance of higher education in Nigeria and Africa as a whole in catalyzing national development cannot be overemphasized (Adei, 2001).

The polytechnics, colleges of education, and universities are the subsectors that produce higher education in Nigeria. Within its 774 local governments in 6 geo-political zones there are 104 universities. The breakdown includes 40 federal, 39 state, and 50 private universities ("Nigerian Universities," 2013). All these universities are to produce highly skilled manpower for the nation and as a segment of the public service; their management is being guided by various policies. A survey of higher education faces an increasingly hostile and complex issues pertaining to enrolment in conventional education in Africa. This remains a great challenge all over Africa, including Nigeria where closer survey of university education shows serious constraints in the issues of enrollment. In Africa alone, it is said that 10.1 million people are out of school. In Nigeria, 16% of the population accounts for school children, of which 26% are not able to complete the cycle of education. There are an astounding 40 million illiterates (EFA: Profile, 2007). All these have put a peg in the current efforts of developing the educational sector to meet the goals of both the Millennium Development Goals and the Education for All (EFA) targets by 2015. Dodds (2002) observed that globally, 125 million are out-of-school; Africa has more than 50 million out of this total. What, then, are the challenges inhibiting the educational development in Africa, especially in Nigeria?

CHALLENGES OF HIGHER EDUCATION

The demand for university education is growing in leaps and bounds. This is as a result of high birthrate in some parts of Africa. Nigeria alone is witnessing exponential population growth. According to the EFA profile on Nigeria on Global status (2007), the high rate of population growth has put immense pressure on the country's resources and overstretched public services and the available infrastructure. An after-effect of population growth is the increased enrollment rate, which has cre-

ated a challenge in ensuring quality education and satisfactory learning outcomes as available educational resources are more thinly spread.

The EFA profile still exposes the fact that despite the heavy investment on infra-structure over the recent years, the number of educational facilities available remains inadequate for the eligible number of education seekers; the teaching curricular are also tilted toward academics and less on skills; and there remains a huge apathy for technical and vocational education. The table below illustrates enrollment rate and its percentages in Nigeria tertiary institutions.

According to Okojie (Table 1), Nigerian universities had a total enrollment of 1,096,312 during the 2006-2007 school year. This is a low rate compared to the number of Nigerian youths who are denied access to university enrollment each year as shown on the table below:

Table 2 shows a huge gap in the enrollment rate of tertiary institutions in Nigeria. Only 20% of applicants out of the percentage are admitted to universities, polytechnics, and colleges of education; others are not given access. For years, in Africa as a whole the educational systems have been saddled with the problem of accessibility, equity, and relevance. Nigeria faces more challenge due to its ever-increasing population rate. The table also shows that the formal education system in the country cannot cope with the admission request of young school-leavers. Kanwar (2008) observed that the conventional universities have problems with the enrollment of new entrants because they lack the capacity—space, facilities, and resources—to admit and cater for the huge number of the populace seeking admission. She also observed that their capacities can never be raised to meet the ever-increasing demand for educational pursuit by the masses. More than a decade after so many forums and conferences—Jomtien, March 1990; Delhi declaration, December 1993; Dakar

Table 1. Enrollment in Nigerian Universities (2006/2007)

Proprietorship	Subdegree	Undergraduate	Postgraduate	Total	Percentage
Federal	4,999	503,154	57,300	610,453	55.7
State	8,734	419,901	19,459	448,094	40.9
Private	357	36,641	767	37,765	3.4
Total	59,090	959,696	77,526	1,096,312	
Percentage	5.4	87.5	7.1		100
Grand total	1,096,312.4				

Source: Okojie (2008).

Table 2. Enrollment of Nigerian Students, By Level

Level	Number	Learners	No Access
Primary	44,000	24,000,000	20,000,000
Secondary and Voc Tech	10,000	8,000,000	
	63	280,000	27,000,000
College of Education and Polytechnics	64	550,000	
	80	350,000	2,000,000
Universities	95 + 4IUC	1,196,312	6,000,000

Source: Jegede (2010).

framework for Action, 2000; Millennium Development Goals—the objectives for all of these are still far from being achieved; most, according to Rumajogee (1999), have been churned into another distant dream for the next 10 or more years. The enrollment in universities in Nigeria compares unfavorably with that of many developing countries. Low female participation and achievement remains a salient feature; lack of access to rural and dispersed youths, lack of appropriately trained teachers, non-inclusive practices in conventional universities, long-term disrupted educational provision, lack of access to habitation prone to destruction and insurgency, and poverty are all factors limiting access to conventional education.

Rumajogee (1999) further observes that the traditional face-to-face teaching is a historical heritage that is a disappointment to the masses and has failed to ensure the human capital formation required for Africa's economic edge. Increasingly, alternative or complementary approaches to education delivery are needed to create access, equity and socioeconomic development. What, then, do we need to create access?

OPEN LEARNING: THE WAY FORWARD

The demand for higher education is on the increase all over the world. Consequently, there must be a proactive orchestration of efforts to satisfy the yearnings of the admission seekers and create access for people thirsty for education at all levels. Open learning is a philosophy of learning that promotes the concepts of flexibility in order to promote access and equity. Open learning has as its major advantage the "seven league boots" which made it, unlike the conventional system of education, able to operate over a distance; cater for widely scattered bodies; with its evolving technology, can be used as an effective tool for addressing the needs of geographically isolated populations; broaden access to multi-level and multi-sector education; academic and professional training; and lifelong learning for personal and social development of an individual. Other accompanying advantages of open learning include flexibility and cost effectiveness. Stretching the intake of conventional universities will not only imply considerable up-front investment but also training and retraining of teachers. However, in the context of competing priorities, such investment is not possible due to tight budgetary constraints placed on education in Nigeria. Furthermore, the conventional system forbids learning while earning, mostly where the enrollment ratio has been almost stagnant for some years. Open learning does not have the constraint of time and space; its flexible teaching approach promotes lifelong learning. Open learning is a subset of open and distance learning (ODL). ODL is an emerging paradigm in teaching and learning method that is facilitated by information communication technologies. In most countries of the world, ODL has become a dominant force in educational management, especially in higher education. Its main advantage is that it helps to reduce the stress on physical infrastructure and reduces pressure on the limited financial resources in universities while giving access to the unreached and those denied access by conventional universities.

According to Association for the Development of Education in Africa (2002), not one of the African countries in Sub-Saharan Africa has fulfilled the promise of providing education to the entire population through the educational system, Nigeria inclusive. It is in view of all the aforementioned challenges in the Nigerian education system that the government set up the National Open University of Nigeria (NOUN), an ODL institution set up to cater for and give access to all in need of education irrespective of age, status and gender.

NOUN: VISION, QUALITY, AND THE NIGERIAN YOUTHS OF UNIVERSITY-AGE BRACKET

The problem of inaccessibility in conventional universities in Nigeria with the resultant effect of low human capital index prompted the federal government to join her other counterparts to set up NOUN. This is not only to give access, but to change attitude toward the knowledge economy and see higher education as a critical partner in development. The concept of ODL in Nigeria has come to stay. It was introduced to Nigeria in 1983 (established and dismantled in 1984) but was resuscitated and became functional in the year 2002 with the establishment of NOUN. The vision is to provide highly accessible and enhanced quality education anchored by social justice, equity, and national cohesion through a comprehensive reach that transcends all barriers (Alaezi, 2006).

NOUN, at 11 years since resuscitation, has 49 study centres located across the 36 states of the federation. It is the only single mode open and distance learning institution in West Africa.

Instructional delivery is predominantly through print, multimedia, and face-to-face tutorials, seminars, workshops and practicum. The print materials often referred to as course materials are either developed in-house by NOUN or adapted from materials obtained from outside sources—other open universities. They are put together in a manner that activates the dormant critical and analytical abilities of the learner; hence, the course materials are written in an interactive manner

In many cases distance learning is the only way to achieve the scale, the scope, and the impact required to tackle the challenges of education and training faced in Africa (Daniel, 2005). It is not enough to

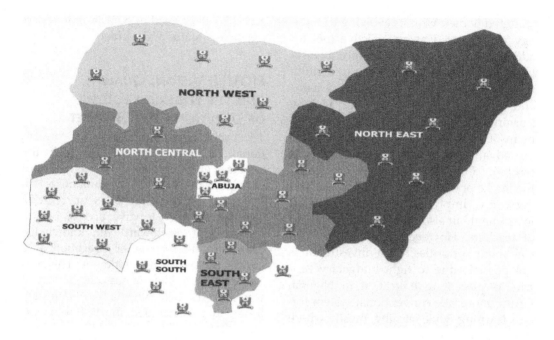

Figure 2. NOUN study centers in Nigeria.

licence a higher education institution to operate; there must be a constant evaluation to ensure that set standards and operational guides are not violated. A system that grows is such that sets standards and disciplines itself to attain them. Accreditation is a way of examining the state of an institution in relation to where it ought to be (Okojie, 2008). This is a quality assurance process. NOUN has gone through the accreditation process and has been given a merit mark by the National Universities Commission. Thirty-three programs presented by the institution, including MBA and MPA, were accredited by National Universities Commission. The courses have been publicly measured with the rate of enrollment that the university has witnessed—with over 50,000 students. The institution, as single-mode distance learning, follows an established process and standards as expected of open and distance learning institutions all over the world.

NOUN caters to professionals, skilled and nonskilled workers, the qualified, and the underqualified at work level. The mode is to work and learn, with an entry requirement that has no age barrier, and maturity, which is also a key prerequisite in admission. Also the use of feeder approaches creates a niche for admission to NOUN, in that there is room for an individual to partake in foundational programmes in a bid to transit from a deficiency in any entry requirement to the course such individual will like to pursue.

Nigerian youths of conventional age bracket have a lot to gain in NOUN, bearing in mind all the roles the institution plays. NOUN has successfully blurred the normally rather rigid distinctions between formal and nonformal approaches to learning. For youths in geographically isolated, disaster-ridden areas, and habitations prone to destruction, NOUN has overcome all these by filling the isolated areas and bringing education to all at their door steps with the study centres at all nooks and crannies of Nigeria. For youths who have dropped out of the school system due to financial constraints or other factors, NOUN provides reintegration or a second chance. With the use of ready-made, self-study educational resources, and courses tailored to learner's needs, youths can benefit more in the institution. The institution is adaptable and flexible, learners can accumulate credits that are transferable, and the examination system gives room for youths to retake examinations because it is learning at one's own pace and space. The educational resources are also structured toward learners' needs; that is, it is learner-centered. There is provision of e-library at the centres as well as visual materials for the hearing and visually impaired learners. Access is given to all, irrespective of age, geographical location, and to the handicapped.

There is a quick deployment of education to where there are no infrastructures in place through the NOUN mode of delivery; with the institution's heterogeneous nature, there is an equitable access to publicly—funded educational services.

CONCLUSION

With the advent of NOUN in Nigeria, the nation has been able to close the seemingly irreparable and widening gap between the reached and the unreached. The institution has to a large extent mitigated the effect of inaccessibility of those seeking admission in conventional universities by not only giving access but by increasing enrolment for those deprived of such while maintaining sufficient quality to meet the demands of global competition.

The Nigerian youths of conventional university age bracket have a place of pride in the delivery mode of NOUN and according to its vision it has heralded a major breakthrough in opening access to higher education for such and other unreached populations. Therefore, the NOUN vision has removed the constraint of time and space with its mode of delivery.

REFERENCES

Adei, S. (2001, November). *Reform in higher education and the use of information technology.* Paper presented at the Ad Hoc Expert Group Meeting of UNECA, Nairobi.

Aleazi, O. (2006). Open university as a model of excellence. Retrieved from http://people .usi.edu/schri/onlinelearning/2013/10/ nationalopenuniversityof Nigeria

Association for the Development of Education in Africa. (2002). Retrieved from http://www .adeanet.org/publications/docs/ open%20learning%201.pdf

Daniel, J. (2005). Open and distance learning in Africa. *15 CCEM mid-term review for Africa and Europe.* Retrieved from http://www.col.org/ colweb/site/pid/3585

Dodds, A.(2002, Winter). GATS: Higher education and public libraries. *Information for Social change,* 21-25.

Kanwar, A. (2008, January). *Signs of the times: Change or be changed?* Presentation at the Third Convocation of the Tamil Nadu Open University, Chennai, India. Retrieved from http://www.col.org/colweb/site/pid/5072

Jegede, O. J (2010, July). Teacher education and ODL. Keynote address delivered at the National Workshop on New Trends in Teacher Education and Professional Development, NOUN Abuja.

Nigerian Universities. (2013, August). *NUC News Bulletin.*

Okojie, A. J. (2008, June). Licensing, accreditation and quality assurance in Nigerian universities: Achievements and challenges. Paper presented at the CHEA Summer Workshop, Abuja.

Rumajogee, A. R. (1999). *Distance education and open learning in Sub-Saharan Africa: Survey on policy and practice.* Paris, France: ADEA working Group on Distance Education and Open Learning. Retrieved from http://www .adea-net.org

UNESCO. (2007). EFA profile 2007. Retrieved from www.unesco.org/new/en/eduation/ themes/leading-the-international-agenda/ efareport/reports/2007-early-childhood/

Delivering an Online MBA Program for Future Business Leaders in Ukraine

A Success Story

Carol A. Gravel and Lilia Dubko

INTRODUCTION

A driving force for economic growth in the European Union (EU) has been the movement of goods, services, and people throughout the union countries. With this change comes the need for citizens of EU countries to enhance their knowledge and skills in order to be more marketable in the expanding open market. An advanced business degree is a foundation for professional growth for many citizens in the EU and beyond. It could be a challenge for many of EU professionals to obtain an advanced degree from a university, especially an advanced degree from an Ameri-

Carol A. Gravel,
Associate Professor, Franklin Pierce University.
Telephone: (603) 490-9374.
E-mail: gravelc@franklinpierce.edu

Lilia Dubko,
Online MBA Ukraine Student.
Telephone: 011-28-050-927-99-57.
E-mail: lilia.dubko@gmail.com

can university. This article provides a review of an online master of business administration (MBA) program, developed as a partnership between Luhansk National University (Ukraine) and Franklin Pierce University (New Hampshire, United States), that was designed for working professions who were citizens of Ukraine. The purpose was to address the country's need for advanced knowledge in business that would in turn enhance the ability for citizens of Ukraine to participate in the economic growth within the European Union.

Franklin Pierce University is a liberal arts university whose mission is to prepare students to become active, engaged citizens and leaders of conscience. Its academic programs are grounded in a liberal arts tradition and are unified by the theme of individual and community—the individual's responsibility to community. The university has been nationally recognized for its commitment to its mission upon receiving the Templeton Award for Character-Building Colleges as well as being one of Forbes' America's Top Colleges for several years.

PROGRAM RESULTS

Franklin Pierce University joined with Luhansk National University in a partnership to offer an online MBA program in December 2005. The relationship between the two institutions has yielded a number of positive results:

- A 13-course online MBA that included customization of the curriculum to address European business practices and principles.
- Faculty training for teaching in an online environment. Luhansk National University faculty received training on the online environment.
- Faculty collaboration among Luhansk faculty and Franklin Pierce University to provide support to online Ukraine MBA students and courses when needed.

- Development and delivery of an Accelerated English Language Institute developed in order to promote English literacy for students who might consider entering the online Ukraine MBA program. The institute was conducted on location in Luhansk, Ukraine and has certified over 130 graduates.
- Two entrepreneurial summer seminars in the United States. The seminar provided a select number of online Ukraine MBA students with the opportunity to apply their emerging understanding of entrepreneurship and meet chief executive officers of United States companies where they could learn firsthand what it takes to be an entrepreneur.

INSTRUCTIONAL DESIGN ELEMENTS

In order to cultivate the desire to manage or lead a business, an educational approach that incorporated the following elements of instructional design was developed:

1. *Project-Based Approach*: Several the classes took the form of a project. While working on a project, students develop a variety of skills. The project approach provides a meaning and a context to the learning process. Projects explore topics that enhance business knowledge while at the same time contributing to the students' current work setting. The finished project for a class could be such things as proposal for a new organizational design, improvements to the current accounting process, or a detailed marketing plan.

2. *Flexibility:* Because this program was for working adults, the program provided opportunity to for a flexible but effective classroom schedule, while at the same time ensuring that the key elements of the standard curriculum. There are learning objectives and lessons plans for all classes, but also there

was the opportunity to explore issues that come up in the course of a class that directly related to the students' current work environment, when it is appropriate.

3. *Technology as a Tool*: While technology is one of the key elements of the curriculum, technology was also a powerful enabling tool, which supported critical thinking and other developmental skills. The use of an online learning environment created the opportunity for all students to participate in discussions, to share a broader array of knowledge and information, and collaborate with individuals and organizations around the world.

A STUDENT'S PERCEPTION

An online MBA, like any university degree, is challenging and time-consuming. However, for many professionals throughout the EU an online MBA degree is an ideal way to obtain an advanced degree from well respected universities. The following is a review of the online Ukraine MBA experience from a student's perspective.

Studying to obtain an online degree has certain peculiarities. As with a traditional graduate degree it is necessary to be ready to devote many hours to reading, writing papers, discussing topics with the teacher and classmates. To be successful in an online degree program, however, requires strong skills in self-organization and time management. On the one hand, an online program does not mean that all the work is done online: there are regular textbooks to read, and some sessions with offline instructors to visit. On the other hand, the online program gives more freedom in terms of time planning: a student can start his or her studying session early in the morning or late at night, during a workday or during the weekend. Being flexible means a lot since the majority of the online MBA program students are full-time employees, and many have families to take care of. Normally, a person who must leave on a business trip would miss classes; this is not an issue with the online program. Fortunately, Internet technologies do not have borders, so leaving the country would equally not interfere with the learning process.

Internet technologies are vital for the online program and not only in that they provide access to the Web, which is required. They are a precondition for any online educational program because the learning process employs a system like eCollege, WebCT, or Blackboard, which is in reality the classroom. Indeed, this system offers everything that the learning environment needs: discussion areas for discussing a variety of questions on a weekly basis; easy-to-use tools for communication with the teacher or classmates through the integrated e-mail system, or synchronous tools like chat and ClassLive, a document sharing option by which a professor or any of the students can upload a document to share with the rest of the class; a gradebook, which allows professor-customized grading of each particular student; a dropbox for submitting the weekly assignments; and an online library, which gives access to hundreds of books, journals, and the most up-to-date business reports. Once students log into his online classroom, they find themselves in a well structured online campus with all the requirements for each particular course and the course area, which is divided into 12 weekly sessions (as it is at Franklin Pierce University). Twelve weeks is the time for mastering each course. Each weekly session is unique: each week the students make one step up the course ladder by making new projects, watching educational movies, presenting new milestones, participating in discussions with their classmates and their instructors, solving problems, or analyzing case studies.

Practical application of the theories learned is meaningful; discussing case studies, students analyze external and internal factors that have led to the success or failure of a given department/company; however, trying to foresee all the possible pitfalls when creating one's own business plan or an e-commerce project is times more challenging. Giving this opportunity to its students is a great advantage of the online MBA program.

Each course requires a lot of individual efforts, but students are not alone in the process. Even though professors are thousands of miles away from their students, the input they provide is no less than in a regular class environment; tricky questions during discussions, comments provided to students' threads, personalized e-mails, as well as feedback on the written assignments and projects are but a few activities they are actively involved in. A great importance in such interaction belongs to web conferences with students, when they have a chance to model a real-class environment using available Internet technologies. This experience is truly invaluable. It is an opportunity to discuss ideas related to the learning process, but also a chance to get acquainted with a professor in person. It is necessary for students to see the so-called psychological portrait of their teacher, as the personal charisma of the latter can play a big role in motivating his or her students to fully integrate into the learning process. Despite any available technologies, a human factor in education is significant; therefore the value of face-to-face interaction between students and professors, even if performed through technical means, is difficult to overestimate.

All these technologies and methodologies, when combined into one common process, create a unique learning environment for the students: a computer with Internet access, a well-thought-out time schedule multiplied by the desire and motivation to learn and apply the learning in practice, under condition of absolute mobility.

PROGRAM OUTCOMES AND SUCCESS

The primary objective of the online Ukraine MBA program was to foster economic opportunity for citizens of Ukraine. This was accomplished via the following:

1. Education through a variety of applied graduate-level assignments and projects.

   - Twenty-six citizens (women and men) of Ukraine received a customized and innovative MBA.
   - Nine were awarded the highest honor for a graduate business student; Sigma Beta Delta Honor Society membership.
   - Fifteen students traveled to the United States and attended the Entrepreneurial Summer Seminar that was specifically designed and developed for these students, allowing them to meet and collaborate with U.S. business leaders.
   - One hundred thirty-five citizens (woman and men) of Ukraine graduated from the Luhansk Summer English Language Program.
   - A computer lab that can support distance education coursework and an MBA library is available to future students who attend Luhansk University.

2. Enhanced business skills for both current and future business professionals.

   - Fifty percent received a promotion or advancement during or after their MBA program;
   - Ten percent title of consultant;
   - Ten percent title of general manger;
   - Thirty percent title of marketing or sales manager;
   - Fifty percent junior manger; and
   - An Education and Business Working Group has been established at the American Chamber of Commerce in Kiev to help education met the needs of the businesses.

Instructional Technology and Distance Education in Nigeria
Historical Background and a Critical Appraisal

Titilola Obilade

INTRODUCTION

The purpose of this article is to examine the use of instructional technology in distance education in Nigeria and to trace the historical origins of distance education in Nigeria. Nigeria is the most populous country in Africa. It is located in West Africa and bordered by

Titilola Obilade,
Department of Learning Sciences
and Technologies (0313), 205 War Memorial
Hall, Virginia Tech, Blacksburg, VA 24061.
E-mail: obilade@vt.edu

Niger to the North, Benin to the West, Cameroon to the East and the Atlantic Ocean on the South. One-third larger than the state of Texas (Infoplease, 2011), it is the sixth largest country in the world. Nigeria had a population of 167 Million in 2011 (National Population Commission Nigeria, 2011). It has 36 states and a Federal Capital territory. The fifth largest producer of crude oil in the world, it has been a member of Organization of Petroleum Exporting Countries (OPEC) since 1971 (2010/ 2011 OPEC Statistical Annual Report). Oil is responsible for 20% of its gross product.

English is the official language. Nigeria has over 250 ethnic groups and more than 300 languages (National Commission for Mass Literacy, 2008). The literacy level among the male population is between 40.9% and 82.6% (National Commission for Mass Literacy, 2008). In the female population, the literacy level is between 14.6% and 74.7%. In the adult population, for those aged 15 years and above, the percentage range of females that are literate is between 14.6% and 62.8% while for males, it is between 40.9% and 81.3% (National Commission for Mass Literacy, 2008).

There have been various definitions of distance learning and e-learning (Oguzor, 2011; Olusola & Alaba, 2011). In this article, e-learning is defined as delivery of instruction through electronic media. Distance education is defined as a form of learning that involves less physical contact than the traditional classrooms and communication through electronic means or print. These electronic means include mobile telephones, e-mail, CD-ROM Packages, videophone system, computer, digital library, and radio and television broadcasts.

In Nigeria, students involved in distance learning are sometimes referred to as sandwich students or part-time students (Adesoye & Amusa, 2011). They are usually workers or students who were not able to gain admission into a university, as the entrance examinations into the various universities are highly competitive and spaces are limited (Adesoye & Amusa, 2011). They usually take a correspondence course during the year. During this time, the instructional materials may be sent through mail or the student drives to designated centers to pick up the study materials and use the library resources. At Olabisi Onabanjo University and Tai Solarin University of Education, in addition to the distance education, the students get face-to-face instruction for a period of a few weeks while the full-time students are on the semester break (Adesoye & Amusa, 2011).

The first education ordinance took place in 1882 while Nigeria was still a protectorate under the British government. These ordinances were revised and several educational policies were established because the Nigerian government wanted to close the gaps in educational disparities among the over 300 ethnic groups in Nigeria (Fabunmi, 2006). Nigeria has 36 federal universities, 37 state universities and 45 private universities (NUC, 2011).

The earliest offering of distance education in Nigeria was in the 1930s, when some Nigerians had to take courses through correspondence from British universities (Enukwu & Ojogwu, 2006). Distance education between Nigeria and Britain progressed until the establishment of the first Nigerian university, the University of Ibadan in 1948. By 1950, the University of Ibadan began a part time course for workers in the faculty of education.

The establishment of distance education took off in various universities under different names. At the University of Lagos, in 1973, a distance education unit was established under the name "Correspondence and Open Studies Unit." As distance education developed this name was later changed to "Correspondence and Open Studies Institute" in 1983. In 1997, for the first time at the University of Lagos, the name of the Correspondence and Open Studies Institute was changed to "Distance Learning Institute."

In 2002, Nigeria's first open university, National Open University became fully functional. The National Teacher Institute is the second national establishment that caters to distance education in Nigeria (Adesoye & Amusa, 2011). Other institutions that provide distance education include University of Lagos, Olabisi Onabanjo University, and Tai Solarin University of Education (Adesoye & Amusa, 2011; Enukwu & Ojogwu, 2006).

The mode of delivery of instructional materials at the National Open University is through television and radio broadcasts, through physical transportation of the printed materials, and through "electronic transmission of materials in multimedia (voice, data, graphics, video) over fixed line (telephone or leased lines) terrestrial and VSAT [very small aperture terminal] wireless communications" (Enukwu & Ojogwu, 2006, p. 190).

CHALLENGES

Distance learners are unable to access the Internet on a 24-hour basis because of the bottlenecks in the development of infrastructure by the Nigerian government (Ofulue, 2011). Several Nigerian researchers have concluded that the main challenges facing information communication technology in distance education is the high cost of Internet connections, the inconsistent electric power supply, and the long hours that distance learners (in the Open University) have to commute to the study centers to get the print materials and use the library resources (Ofulue, 2011).

In Nigeria, distance education is not just for students at tertiary institutions. Distance education can be effectively used to reach elementary school children in rural areas (Isiaka, 2007). According to a report cited in Aderinoye, Ojokheta, & Olojede (2007), a 2000 report by the Federal Ministry of Education stated that there were 9.3 million nomads and 3.1 million of these were children who were of school- and preschool age. The literacy rate of the pastoral nomads is 0.28%. The nomads have a mobile school that is easy to assemble and dissemble. Radio and television broadcasts are being used to teach the nomadic children. Mobile telephones are now being proposed to supplement the radio and television broadcast.

In a survey of 215 distance learners from three open and distance learning institutions in 2008, print media was the most common form of instruction (60.5%) (Ofulue, 2011). This was followed by radio (13%), e-mail (10.2%), text messaging (8.4%), television (6.5%), online learning (4.7%), and teleconferencing (3.7%). When the respondents were asked to identify the challenges faced in distance education, 35.8% identified lack of access to information communication and technology equipment, and 31.6% identified financial constraints as a major factor. Lack of electricity was identified as a major constraint by 26% of the respondents, while 20% identified lack of Internet as the major challenge. Some of the ways the respondents coped with these challenges included reading all the course materials and attending tutorials, participating in peer group discussions, and using Internet at cybercafés and at work. The author concluded that 60.9% of the distance learners had to print hard copies of learning materials or make photocopies of learning materials.

Adeoye and Wentling (2007) examined the relationship of culture and the use of e-learning. The 24 study participants were international students attending a university in the United States and came from 11 different countries. Two of the participants were from Nigeria. The study concluded that there was no relationship between the national culture and the use of e-learning. However, there was a relationship between uncertainty avoidance and the use of the e-learning system. Those who were not familiar with the e-learning system spent more time on the system.

In a study involving 301 lecturers from federal universities, Okore (2011) concluded that among lecturers, the use of information technology for communication was the same for both females and males, irrespective of their rank. In addition, she concluded that the gender of the lecturer was not a barrier to the development of information technology in the Nigerian academic field.

Agbonlahor (2008) conducted a study in 2003 to find out the attitudes of older professors to information technology. She surveyed 718 lecturers from ten of the federal and state universities in Nigeria. The results showed that there was no difference in the attitudes of the lecturers with respect to their academic ranks. The results also showed that the female lecturers were more anxious on the use of information technology. Lecturers from the medical sciences and veterinary group scored highest on the enjoyment scale of information technology use, while lecturers in the education and agricultural departments were the least anxious about the introduction of information technology. The implication of studies on attitudes to information technology is that the results can be used in the planning and designing of systems that would be acceptable to the user (Davis, 1993).

Similarly, in a study on web-based learning among pathologists, the results showed that 83.7% of the study participants used the Internet for their literature reviews, 67.6% used it for tutorial, and 19% used it for chats (Ekanem, Olasode, & Jombo, 2009). There were 37 study participants. These study participants had practiced for more than 10 years and they all lived in urban and semiurban areas in Nigeria. Ninety-two percent of the participants agreed that web-based learning had improved the quality of their practice. The implication of this study is that the results can help in the planning and in the development of the use of instructional technology in learning and teaching (Davis, 1993).

Some private universities in Nigeria are advocating for e-learning as part of the system and not just for administrative purposes. In some universities the electronic portal is made available for payment of fees and registration of students. It is not made available for teaching. Some of these universities are now advocating for a personal learning system (Awodele, Idowu, Anjorin, Adedire, & Akpore, 2009).

The University of Lagos, a federal university, has a student population of 30,000 and 3000 academic and administrative staff (Okiki, 2011). The students are able to register for their courses online. The university has subscribed to Moodle, Blackboard, and Makau e-learning systems. It is possible to access the portal through the university system.

However, the University of Lagos faces a lot of challenges in the area of e-learning. These challenges range from the prohibitive cost of hardware to the "maintenance culture" (Okiki, 2011, Para.18).

This article has set out to examine the historical background of distance education in Nigeria. It has described the state of distance education in Nigeria today and has also highlighted the challenges peculiar to the Nigerian situation.

CONCLUSION

Although Nigeria started distance education in the 1930s, distance education in Nigeria has not reached its full potential. Distance education began as a result of correspondence courses between students from the university of Ibadan and universities in Britain. Distance education is the only way to effectively reach nomadic children and children in rural areas (Aderinoye, Ojokheta & Olojede 2007; Isiaka, 2007).

Various articles cited in this article have identified the political situation and poor infrastructure as contributory factors to the poor development of distance education in Nigeria (Enukwu & Ojogwu, 2006; Oguzor, 2011; Okiki, 2011).

The recommendations from this article are to strengthen the existing infrastructure and to lower the costs of Internet access.

REFERENCES

Aderinoye, R. A., Ojokheta, K. O., & Olojede, A. A. (2007). Integrating mobile learning into nomadic education programs in Nigeria: Issues and perspectives. *The International Review of Open and Distance Learning, 8*(2).

Adeoye, B., & Wentling, R. (2007). The relationship between national culture and the usability of an e-learning system. *International Journal on E-learning, 6*(1), 119-146.

Adesoye, A. E., & Amusa, O. I. (2011). Investigating the information needs of sandwich and part-time students of two public universities in Ogun State, Nigeria. *Library Philosophy and Practice.* Retrieved from http://www.webpages.uidaho.edu/~mbolin/adesoye-amusa.htm

Agbonlahor, R.O., (2008). Individual characteristics as correlates of attitudes to information technology among Nigerian university lecturers. *African Journal of Library, Archives and Information Science, 18*(2), 131-146.

Awodele, O., Idowu, S., Anjorin, O., Adedire, A., & Akpore, V. (2009). University enhancement system using a social networking approach: extending e-learning. *Issues in Informing Science and Information Technology 6*, 270-283.

Davis, F. D., (1993). User acceptance of information technology: System characteristics, user perceptions and behavioral impacts. *International Journal of Man-Machine Studies, 38*(3) 475-487. doi:10.1006/imms.1993.1022

Ekanem, B. I., Olasode, B. J., & Jumbo, G. (2009). Web-based used learning as an important bridge in information divide in contemporary practice of pathology in the developing world: Findings from Nigeria. *Internet Journal of Third World Medicine, 8*(2), 10.

Enuku, U. E., & Ojogwu, C. N., (2006). Information and communication technology (ICT) in the service of the National Open University in Nigeria. *Education, 127*(2) 187-195.

Fabunmi, M., (2005). Historical analysis of educational policy formulation in Nigeria: Implications for educational planning and policy. *International Journal of African and African American Studies, 4*(2) 1-7.

Infoplease. (2011). Nigeria: Geography. Retrieved from http://www.infoplease.com/ ipa /A0107847.html

National Population Commission Nigeria. (2011). Nigeria's over 167 million population: Implications and challenges. Retrieved from http://www.population.gov.ng/

National Universities Commission. (2011). Universities in Nigeria. Retrieved from http://www.nuc.edu.ng/pages/universities .asp?ty=3&order=inst_name

Ofulue, C. I., (2011). Survey of barriers affecting the use of information communication technologies (ICTS) among distance learners: A case study of Nigeria. *Turkish Online Journal of Distance Education, 12*(3), 142-154.

Oguzor, N. S., (2011) E-learning technologies and adult education in Nigeria. *Educational Research and Reviews, 6*(4) 347-349.

Okiki, C. O., (2011) Information communication technology support for an e-learning environment at the University of Lagos, Nigeria. *Library Philosophy and Practice.* Retrieved from http://www.webpages.uidaho.edu/ ~mbolin/okiki3.pdf

Okore, A. M., (2011) Demographic and socio economic attributes as determinants of information and communication technology use for scholarly communication in Nigerian universities. *Library Philosophy and Practice.* Retrieved from http://www.webpages .uidaho.edu /~mbolin/okore.pdf

Olusola, A. J., & Alaba S. O. (2011). Globalization, information and communication technologies (icts) and open/distance learning in Nigeria: Trends, issues and solution. *The Turkish Online Journal of Distance Education, 12*(3), 66-77.

OPEC. (2011) Countries producing oil. Annual statistical bulletin 2010/2011 edition. Retrieved from http://www.opec.org/ opec_web/static_files_project/media/ downloads/ publications/ASB2010_2011.pdf

UNESCO. (2008). The development and state-of-the-art of adult learning and education national report on Nigeria. National Commission for Mass Literacy, Adult and Non-Formal Education. Retrieved from http:// www.unesco.org/fileadmin/MULTIMEDIA / INSTITUTES/UIL/confintea/pdf/National_Reports/Africa/Africa/Nigeria.pdf

Distance Learning in Belize
A Benefit for Youths and Adults

Yvonne Palma

In today's changing world with its economic challenges, addressing the needs of underprivileged youths and adults becomes a growing challenge for any small nation such as Belize. Belize, a Caribbean country in Central America, is the only English-speaking country in the region. With a diversity of people, sites, and a democratically elected government, Belize has a population of 310,000 (Statistical Institute of Belize, 2007).

DEMOGRAPHICS OF BELIZE

As a developing nation, Belize suffers from many societal ailments, such as youths leaving school early with limited opportu-

Yvonne Palma,
2917 Albert Hoy Street, P O Box 2419,
Belize City, Belize.
Telephone: (501) 620-9256

nity for meaningful employment, and adults who are unskilled and unable to occupy job positions that are available to sustain their families. The problem of crime starts with youths dropping out of school; poor adults received little education, have big families, and are unable to meet their expenses (Crawford, 2010). A survey of the *Police Notebook* (Belize Police Department, 2010) shows crime and violence on the rise, and the age of criminals being youths 13 and 17 years and early 20s.

In 2007, the unemployment rate among youths was 24%. While female unemployment rate was 32.8% of 41.8% participation rate; males were 18.7% of a participation rate of 77.5% (Statistical Institute of Belize, 2007). The concentration of unemployment, according to the Statistical Institute of Belize (2007), has been in the rural area of the country, with high rates of unemployment recorded in the northern and southern districts. The highest unemployment rate for females was in the southern district. In 2009, the highest unemployment was concentrated in the northern district. This was credited to the decline in the sugar industry located in the northern districts and the economic downturn (Statistical Institute of Belize, January 2010)

PROFILE OF THE BELIZEAN STUDENT

Belize, aware of the global environment, is focused on guaranteeing quality education as a basic human right to all through "allocating public funding to schools equitably by funding schools on a per student basis" and "free tuition policy. We know that many of the students who do not attend secondary school because of poverty and limited access (United Democratic Party, 2008). Through the establishment of these policies, more students will have access to a quality education.

According to the Ministry of Education (2008), of 42,000 students who begin elementary school, 38,000 transition to secondary school, and 20% drop out of secondary school. According to Ingels, Chen, and Owings (2005) students perceive positive school experiences based upon the attitude and skills of their teachers, the degree of safety they feel within their school, their perception of victimization at a school, their perception of school rules, the importance they place on good grades and their reason for being in school. The secondary schools in the country with the highest student enrollment are the urban areas (Ministry of Education, 2008).

The Belizean student lives with mother and father, father, mother, stepfathers or stepmothers, relatives, on their own, boarding with boarders, grandparents or grandparent. The parents of these students have varying levels of education ranging from primary level education to postgraduate degrees. Based on the availability of distance education within the country, more and more parents are returning to school to pursue higher education (E. J. Lopez, personal communication, April 20, 2010).

DISTANCE EDUCATION: A POSSIBLE SOLUTION?

In attempting to address the needs of youths' and adults' unemployment or underemployment, Belize has over the years recognized that the traditional system of education no longer meets the needs of these learners. According to United Nations Educational Scientific and Cultural Organization (n.d.-a), conventional education systems are poorly prepared to deal with the challenges and opportunities that are present in the emerging information and communication technologies and little has been done to address the growing problem of social fragmentation, human frustration and disempowerment, cultural dislocation, and technological alienation (p. 2). According to Adaji, Salawu, and Adeoye (2008), distance education provides avenues for higher education for vast under-privileged population.

According to Simonson, Smaldino, Albright, and Zvacek (2009) distance education is institution-based formal education where the learning group is separated, and where interactive telecommunications systems are used to connect learners, resources and instruction. Furthermore, research has found no significant difference between distance education and traditional education in terms of student achievement.

According to E. Raymond (personal communication, April 21, 2010) learners in Belize have been participating in distance learning since 1964. This was in the form of examinations for teachers, where teachers attending the teachers' training school in Belize take qualifying examinations through correspondence. Two-way communication was between student and examination authority through postal services. Students from Belize also completed qualifying subject specific examinations from London's Royal Society of Arts and General Certificate of Education in ordinary and advance levels. Teachers were also able to obtain professional teachers' certification, advancing to the doctorate level through correspondence. Today, these examinations can be taken at a distance online, or via postal and courier services.

Telesecundaria. In 1999, the Ministry of Education through technical assistance from the Mexican government as part of the EDUSAT project embarked on a distance learning initiative. According to Ministry of Education (2009) the EDUSAT project was to establish secondary education through satellite and television throughout remote parts of the country of the country, to provide secondary education opportunities to students who otherwise would not receive the opportunity. Technical assistance from Mexico included the training of facilitators in the methodology and use of course materials, technicians to provide equipment support, donation of satellite dishes and televisions, as well as course materials for students. The telesecundaria was implemented in the northern district of Corozal at Escuela Secundaria Mexico because the language of the materials was in Spanish, and people in the northern districts were considered more competent in speaking Spanish and hence would immediately benefit from the training (D. Eck, personal communication, 2009).

Telesecundaria, which was launched in Mexico in 1968, provided lower secondary school learning with television support to remote and small communities; lessons corresponding to Grades 7 to 9 were transmitted live, through open public channels to television sets placed in distant classrooms where students listened and took notes in the presence of a teacher (United Nations Educational, Scientific and Cultural Organization, n.d.-b, p. 2). This program was operational from 2005 to June 2008. After being informed of the program being discontinued, the Ministry of Education conducting an investigation to determine the circumstances that led to the program being discontinued; upon completion of the investigation the explanation received from the principal was the need for additional classroom space (A. Castillo, personal communication, April 20, 2010). Although this program was accessed by many youths and adult learners, training time for the program was Monday to Friday between the hours of 8 A.M. to 2:30 P.M. The time factor also allowed for fewer individuals to access the program and restricted the benefit of utilizing existing

space and available teachers. Although the signal could be accessed in any part of the country, the program was never expanded to other areas within the country. An additional factor may have been language, as the language of course materials and instruction was in Spanish.

TECHNICAL AND VOCATIONAL EDUCATION AND TRAINING

Technical and vocational education and training has been recognized as an important element in a nation's development. According to Caribbean Secretariat (1990) TVET is looked upon by developing countries as "a vehicle for the development of marketable skills as an engine for development" (p. 1). As a measure of preparing countries within the region to become more competitive in the global economy, TVET is called upon to help unemployed young people, upgrade existing workers' competencies, reduce the burden of higher education, provide qualified labors to attract foreign investment, and any investment in human development draws return on the individual as well as the society as a whole (CARICOM, 2001). Individuals will benefit from a better career, increased earnings, and a better quality of life. What benefits the society is a skilled-workforce that enables global competitiveness and economic growth.

In an effort to expand and improve TVET in the country of Belize, and provide opportunities for its people, the government of Belize invested $4.4 million into the establishment and development of Institutes for Technical and Vocational Education and Training (ITVETs) (Caribbean Development Bank, 2001). The Institutes for Technical and Vocational Education and Training (ITVET) are government of Belize skills training institutions that provide training for employment. These institutions are located in each of the seven districts of Belize and provide training based on employment training needs in each district.

Stann Creek ITVET is located in the southern district of Stann Creek. The institution provides training in the area of tourism and hospitality, automotive, masonry, carpentry, and electricity. The main industries in the district are tourism, hospitality, and citrus. New resorts are being built in the district, requiring persons skilled in masonry, carpentry, and electrical installation. Once the resorts have been built, skilled persons will be required to provide services in tourism and hospitality. Automotive training was provided to address the needs of the citrus industry. According to S. W. Bowman (personal communication, February 26, 2010) work has began to expand training to secondary school students within the Stann Creek district. He hopes to provide more employment opportunities for the students with the inclusion of a TVET program as part of their training.

Similar to Stann Creek ITVET, Belize ITVET provides similar training with the addition of customized training to specific groups based on request. The institute provides customized training for the Belize Defense Force, along with courses offered at night in the area of air conditioning and refrigeration and auto body repair. Further, request for training has been received from several different organizations, and these programs are customized programs (K. Ellis, personal communication, March 11, 2010).

Orange Walk ITVET, located in the district of Orange Walk, provides training in the area of building construction trades, computer repair, and automotive repair. Orange Walk ITVET focuses on preparing trainees to become competent and excel in the Belize National Vocational Qualification examination. Beyond the entry level program offerings, the institution has moved to offering training in level two, which prepares employees to perform tasks requiring some level of autonomy.

The other four institutions provide similar training with the inclusion of training in the agricultural area in the Toledo district.

According to Bowman (2010, January) the enrollment for Stann Creek ITVET has experienced a decline in the student population. Twelve trainees dropped, out leaving 58 participating in training. Toledo ITVET has 35 trainees enrolled in the programs, which is very small to justify the expense in operating the programs. Bowman (2010, January) attributes the decline in enrollment to financial problems experienced by the trainee in meeting the cost of the program.

DISTANCE LEARNING IN TECHNICAL AND VOCATIONAL EDUCATION

As the economic situation of individuals continue to decline, the management of the various institutions recognizes the need to expand and increase access for persons who would otherwise be unable to access training. Distance learning in technical and vocational education can allow for underprivileged youths and adults to obtain skills that will make them employable. Although presently the institutions have only computers and Internet, with regards to technological capabilities to provide distance learning using telecommunications systems, the process of trying to provide training for youths and adults in other locations is considered a priority. Belize ITVET began implementing its first distance learning initiative in San Pedro, Ambergris Caye (K. Ellis, personal communication April 20, 2010). This town is approximately 45 miles outside of the city. This initiative provides training to electricians who are unable to travel to Belize City to attend classes. Students will be able to perform the practical aspect of the training by conducting installations within the workplace. This initiative falls within the category of traditional distance learning program that used postal services, and the EDUSAT concept, though without the technology of satellite and television. For the institution, this is a start and the intention is to expand the distance education program to more individuals through the use of the Internet and other communications technology. There are many open software and available support web-based sites that can be accessed by purchasing licenses or obtaining permission to use the resources.

It is anticipated that programs will be expanded to include students attending secondary schools within the district; satellite centers located in smaller communities would be able to transmit the course using satellite dish and television, as well as videoconferencing and the Internet. (S. W. Bowman, personal communication, February 26, 2010). Distance learning programs will expand opportunities for other students as well as for students at the Orange Walk ITVET (A. Gomez, personal communication, March 11, 2010). The advantage will be that students will be able to take course in programs not offered at that specific ITVET. With distance learning programs offered through the ITVETs, the youths and adults who are ultimately the clients that the ITVET targets will benefit from such an initiative. This will facilitate quality skills training being provided with the introduction of communications technology to persons who would otherwise be unable to access training offered using technology. According to Moore and Tait (2002), many countries have developed vocational and other types of short-cycle colleges, sometimes spanning both secondary and postsecondary levels to provide training to adults and youths. In this sector there are many examples of open and distance learning programmes that may be useful to the ITVETs.

A Coordinated Effort

In order to be successful, the plans and efforts of the ITVETs in providing distance education to clients requires coordination and funding. A distance learning division within the TVET system is required. The division will offer individuals the opportunity that would otherwise be inaccessible to them within their own location through a system of telecommunications and internet technology. This initiative will not only provide programs that will be offered through the distance unit, but also allow existing customers from the traditional face to face division, local community, and other targeted groups to access training from the convenience of their own location. According to Simonson et al. (2009), the unavailability of technical support creates a major barrier that discourages many faculties from teaching online course. The need to offer the relevant support to the institutions will also be required, and that will require the Ministry of Education to invest in infrastructure development and teacher training.

Benefit to Youths and Adults

According to the Commonwealth of Learning (n.d.), benefits of distance education include overcoming problems of physical distance, solving time or scheduling issues for learners and schools, expanding limited number of places available for learners, and it makes the best use of few teachers. In 2008, the Ministry of Education began a subsidy program, in which students entering secondary schools and those entering the second year receive subsidies to assist with cost of school. In 2010, students completing elementary schools from the Stann Creek and Toledo districts were automatically entitled to subsidies to offset the cost of schooling (A. Genitty, personal communication, April 22, 2010). With the availability of this program, underprivileged students living in remote areas will have the opportunity to obtain relevant materials required for schooling face-to-face or at a distance.

With its small population and high unemployment rate, Belize can benefit tremendously from distance education. The ratification of the free labour movement among Caribbean countries, now more than ever, highlights the need for Belizean youths and adults to become skilled, certified, and competent to meaningfully participate in employment. The vast amount of capital investment made by the government of Belize into infrastructure development in technical and vocational education and training can be further expanded with additional investments to include the development of distance learning initiatives. This will allow for the participation in distance education of more underprivileged youths and adults throughout the country.

REFERENCES

Ajadi, T. O., Salawu, I. O., & Adeoye, F. A. (2008). E-learning and distance education in Nigeria. *Turkish online journal of educational technology*. Retrieved from http://0-www.eric.ed .gov.novacat.nova.edu/ERICWebPortal/ Home.portal?

Belize Police Department. (2010, April). Police notebook. *Amandala*, p. 4.

Bowman, S. W. (2010, January). Monthly report. Stann Creek ITVET.

Caribbean Development Bank. (2001). *Appraisal document: Loan to government of Belize*. Bridgetown, Barbados: Author.

Caribbean Secretariat. (1990). *Regional strategy on TVET*. Georgetown, Guyana: CARICOM.

CARICOM. (2001). *CARICOM regional TVET strategy*. Georgetown, Belize: Author.

Commonwealth of Learning. (n.d.). *Advantages of open and distance learning*. Retrieved from http://www.commonwealth of learning.org

Crawford, J. I. (2010, April 25). Treasury lane car washers: "Its tough, but it's honest work." *Amandala*, p. 19.

Ingels, S. J., Chen, X., & Owings, J. A. (2005, March). A profile of the American high school sophomore in 2002; initial results from the base year of the education longitudinal study of 2002. *Statistical Analysis Report*. Washington, DC: U.S. Department of Education, NCES.

Ministry of Education. (2008). *Statistical digest*. Projects & Planning Unit.

Ministry of Education. (2009). *Report on Telesecundaria*. Belmopan, Belize: Author.

Moore, M. M., & Tait, A. (2002). *Open and distance learning: Trends, policy and strategy consideration*. Paris, France: UNESCO. Retrieved from http://unesdoc.unesco.org/images/0012 /001284/128463e.pdf

Simonson, M., Smaldino, S., Albright, M., & Zvacek, S. (2009). *Teaching and learning at a distance: Foundations of distance education* (4th ed.). Boston, MA: Allyn & Bacon.

Statistical Institute of Belize. (2010). *Annual report 2009*. Belmopan, Belize: Author.

United Democratic Party. (2008). *United Democratic Party manifesto*. Retrieved from http:// www.udp.org.bz/UDP-Manifesto9.htm

United Nations Educational Scientific and Cultural Organization. (n.d.-a). *Learning Without Frontiers*: Constructing open learning communities for lifelong learning. Retrieved from http://www.unesco.org/education/lwf/

United Nations Educational Scientific and Cultural Organization. (n.d.-b). Telesecundaria, Mexico. (Lower secondary school learning with television support). Retrieved from http://www.unesco.org/education/educprog/ lwf/doc/portfolio/abstract8.htm

Challenges in Higher Education Distance Learning in the Democratic Republic of Congo

Banza Nsomwe-a-nfunkwa

INTRODUCTION

Open and distance learning has created opportunities for all sorts of people in all walks of life to access education (Badza & Chakuchichi 2009). However, distance learning in the Democratic Republic of Congo is still a field demanding a lot of research and practice to ensure successful implementation.

Banza Nsomwe-a-nfunkwa,
Associate Professor,
University of Kinshasa,
Democratic Republic of Congo.
E-mail: nfunkwa@hotmail.com

The use of information and communication technology (ICT) in distance learning in the higher education sector is facing a lot of problems in the Democratic Republic of Congo. This article addresses only some of the main obstacles; the complete list is very long.

The first problem is the limited technologies. The Democratic Republic of Congo depends on its ICT through imported goods; all hardware and software are made outside of Democratic Republic of Congo.

The second problem is the exorbitant costs for such technologies; because all the equipment is imported, it is subject to taxes, shipment fees, and so on.

The third problem is that many higher education institutions are located in rural areas that stable electricity—or lack electricity entirely, creating a major obstacle to the effective use of ICT for distance learning.

The fourth problem is that in some corners of my country, old technologies such as tape recorders and video are still a novelty; how can we even think to talk about new technologies in those areas?

The fifth is a lack of trained instructors. Technologies can be readily available at any place, but it will be very complicated to use it effectively because of the lack of trained people.

NEED FOR DISTANCE LEARNING

The Democratic Republic of Congo, with 49 years of independence from Belgium, has never entered such a huge problem of reconstruction and development as today. The program of reconstruction of the country is divided into five sectors: education, electricity, water, health, and infrastructure. In light of this huge program, the country is in great need of skilled people to contribute to and participate in the Congolese work market.

Because the country has a high rate of illiteracy, a new condensed and functional version of the content of learning is needed so the population can learn in their spare time. Many workers are highly interested and motivated to learn in their spare time, because they can be working and learning at convenient times, improving their skills to match the evolution of their jobs. People are working under stress created by new jobs, social need, and economic situation; self-training is needed for many people to update their skills and knowledge.

CHALLENGES TO DISTANCE LEARNING IN THE HIGHER EDUCATION SECTOR

It is easy to talk about distance learning and its needs in the Democratic Republic of Congo but is very hard to talk about the challenges because they are so numerous.

The first challenge is connected to the quality of materials. Here the big question is how much the people trying to develop these materials are qualified for this job, abiding by national requirement and policy.

The second challenge is related to a lack of financial resources. In the last few years of war, the financial area is facing many problems. It is unclear if the Democratic Republic of Congo is ready to provide adequate financial resources to distance learning.

The third challenge concerns the attitude of Congolese society to distance learning. From the colonial educational system, psychology, and the attitude of the Congolese people, they were and still are prepared to respect and accept conventional education and not really to consider distance learning. They argue that the face-to-face educational system is the best.

The fourth challenge is the lack of distance learning management skills. In the Democratic Republic of Congo, distance learning is hesitantly being accepted step-by-step by few people. However, the management of the distance learning system is still a huge challenge.

The last challenge is technophobia.

STRATEGIES

Distance learning is a very complex and complicated system. To find solutions to all challenges facing the Democratic Republic of Congo in the establishment of distance learning in the higher education sector, I put forward some suggestions:

1. Information about distance learning should be provided to the people of the Democratic Republic of Congo.
2. If distance learning in the Democratic Republic of Congo is to succeed, it is an obligation to prepare distance educators.
3. Organize conferences, seminars, discussions and reflection on the topic of distance learning and its impact on the Congolese people's well-being.
4. Organizing training on the management of distance learning by the Congolese people.
5. Organizing workshops on the design and development of distance learning courses.
6. Help new distance educators learn about methods of teaching
7. A huge campaign to encourage the people of the Democratic Republic of Congo to study at a distance.

8. Organizing training on the evaluation system before, during, and after the lesson.
9. Prepare counseling and support services for distance learners.

CONCLUSION

Effective use of distance learning in higher education in the Democratic Republic of Congo is still a long way from realization. I do believe that a huge campaign on the impact and benefit of distance learning in the Democratic Republic of Congo will contribute to development of appropriate solutions to the many challenges facing distance learning in my country. Then this developing country can enjoy the benefits of new information and communication technologies.

REFERENCE

Badza, A., & Chakuchichi, D. (2009). Women access to higher education through open and distance learning: Challenges and learner support. *International Journal of Open and Distance Learning, 2,* 45-57.

BARRIERS TO DISTANCE EDUCATION IN THE REPUBLIC OF CONGO

1. LIMITED TECHNOLOGIES
2. EXORBITANT COSTS FOR TECHNOLOGIES
3. UNSTABLE ELECTRICITY
4. NEW TECHNOLOGIES HAVE NOT REPLACED OLD TECHNOLOGIES

Distance Education and the Well-Being of the Rural Poor

Case Study of the Kabongo Region in the Democratic Republic of Congo

Banza Nsomwe-a-nfunkwa

As a result of war and the economic situation in the Democratic Republic of Congo, the people of the country are suffering extreme poverty. The population of Kabongo depends on agricultural output and the generated income, primarily from the production of cassava. At present, cassava is suffering from diseases and the consequence is a decrease in production. The decreased production leads to less food, and there-fore even higher rates of malnutrition. Also, there are fewer products to sell, resulting in less money, more children with no access to school, a higher rate of school dropout, a lack of clothing, a lack of access to medicines and a higher rate of street kids stealing or begging. As a result of the problems leading to decreased pro-duction of cassava, the rural people in the Kabongo region are seeking a solution to the problem. By solving the problem of the diseases affecting cassava there will be increased production of cassava and an increase in farmers' incomes.

To solve this problem, we suggest a functional education program for the rural people on cassava. The objective is to develop a teaching and learning curricu-lum designed specifically to meet the needs of rural people; this curriculum will be focused on adult learners who are illit-erate, as well as not able to speak the offi-cial language, French, or even the four national languages. The people of Kabongo will frequently only speak the local dialect. These people are geographi-cally scattered and isolated in the local area. To solve the problem of the scattered nature of the target audience, where there is an absence of electricity, telecommunica-tion (and in short all new technologies are lacking), we have chosen to produce a dis-tance education program using radio broadcast. To enable learners to provide

Banza Nsomwe-a-nfunkwa, Faculty of Psychology and Educational Sciences, Kinshasa University, Congo and Docto-ral Candidate in Educational Techno-logy, Nanjing Normal University, China. Telephone: +86-25-83715127.
E-mail: nfunkwa@hotmail.com
paralotodo@yahoo.fr

feedback and reduce the need for direct contact between the rural adult learners, our plan is to use "radio broadcasting reception centers." These centers will be staffed by trained people, who are qualified teachers, and at the end of training they will be posted to the reception centers. These facilitators will assist adult learners, answer their questions, explain complex aspects of information broadcasted, organize workshops and practical activities, as well as provide "counseling" services.

In the case of this rural distance education by radio, linear design will be predominantly used; in some cases in which the learner or learning activities need another rhythm of learning, the linear design will be combined with other instructional designs to achieve the objective.

This curriculum will be the first in the domain of rural, illiterate, adult learners. Also, it will be the first time a curriculum has been designed to meet the specific needs of the rural people in the Kabongo region.

INTRODUCTION

Kabongo is located in the province of Katanga in Democratic Republic of Congo. This region is characterized by various daily problems. Transportation in this region is a major issue, and reaching nearby major cities is problematic. The principal means of transportation to Kamina, a city only 200 kilometers away, are truck, train, and bicycles. During rainy season, this 200-kilometer trip can take up to two days by truck or slow train. This area also does not have electricity, running water, television, radio broadcasting, and Internet; essentially, there is a total absence of all new technologies.

In the Kabongo region, the vast majority of people are farmers, and they live off their agricultural produce. From the sale of their produce they gain money and participate in the standard economic cycle; there-

fore, they are able to buy clothes, medicines, send children to school, and try to fight against premature school dropout, along with being able to deal with the normal daily problems.

This corner of Congo is facing a very high level of poverty. The poverty was intensified by the consequences of 5 years of war, and recently diseases present in cassava plants. Cassava is the staple food source for most people in the Kabongo region. Its importance is that the root is eaten as bread and the leaves as vegetables. Cassava is central to the rural economy. Cassava is currently suffering from diseases, and these have very negative consequences on the production rate and quality; the decrease of cassava production seriously affects the well-being of rural people.

In order to see an improvement in the well-being of the rural people, it is essential to solve the problem with cassava production. The best way to solve this is to provide information and functional education about cassava production, diseases present in cassava, and related environmental issues.

Education in the rural area of Kabongo faces many obstacles: these include a high rate of adult illiteracy, language problems because these adults are often able to speak only local dialects and not the national languages, and the scattered geographical nature of the people within the area. As a result, it is essential that there is a specific curriculum designed for adult learners to counteract the issues related to cassava.

The development of a teaching and learning curriculum for isolated rural adult learners, and the delivery of such a curriculum via radio broadcasting is the most effective means to inform and educate the people facing such circumstances. This curriculum will be divided into two sections: a compulsory (in some ways) and an elective component. The compulsory section will contain information about cassava production, cassava diseases, and some content will be focused on the environment and issues related to soil. The elective section will contain lessons about Kabongo's history, general knowledge, public awareness campaigns, and community building.

Cassava Problems and Solutions

Network of Cassava Problems, Causes, and Effects

As a result of war and the economic situation in Democratic Republic of Congo, the population is suffering extreme poverty. The population of Kabongo depends on agricultural output for their income, and much of this income generated from the production of cassava. Cassava is the most important staple food and accounts for up to 70% of the population's income in the Democratic Republic of Congo (IITA, 2000). At present, cassava is suffering from diseases, and these diseases are resulting in a decrease in production. The decreased production leads to less available food, and consequently higher malnutrition. Also, there are fewer products to sell as a result of less money in the economic cycle, and therefore more children are not able to access education, there is a higher rate of premature school dropout, a lack of clothing and medicines, and an increase in the rate of stealing and begging. From the decrease of cassava production the level of poverty is increasing; and the well-being of the people of Kabongo is negatively affected.

As a result of the problems leading to decreased production of cassava, the people in the Kabongo region are seeking a solution to the problem. The result of solving the problem of the diseases affecting cassava will lead to increased cassava production and hence an increase in the incomes of the rural peoples.

From Figure 1, we can read that the central problem is the decrease in the production of cassava. Some of the causes for this reduction are diseases (mosaique du manioc, bacterie du manioc, anthracnose du manioc, structure brune du manioc, cercosporioses), magical beliefs, bad luck from ancestors, lack of knowledge of diseases, agricultural cycles, environmental issues, and problems with the soil. The consequences of the reduced production are malnutrition and under-nourishment, inability to send children to schools, higher school dropout, poor choices for lifestyle, and a lack of clothing and medicine.

Network of Methods and Solutions

The aforementioned information outlined how the decreased production of cassava is affecting the well-being of the rural poor of the Kabongo area. Hence, there will now be an analysis of how to solve such decreased production of cassava and suggestions presenting the methods and means used to solve the problems. The promise is that a functional education program designed for the rural people about cassava diseases, its origin, and how to fight against such diseases can alleviate the situation. Also, this program should include the new techniques of cassava cultivation and practices, along with information on soil and the environmental situation.

An increase in cassava production is central to overcoming decreased cassava production. To seek this solution, functional education regards the present diseases and their origins as critical. Also, the people need to be educated to overcome the acceptance of diseases, education including more modern farming methods, an awareness of environmental issues, cultivation of cassava, and replacement crops, all of which will result in improved conditions for the rural people.

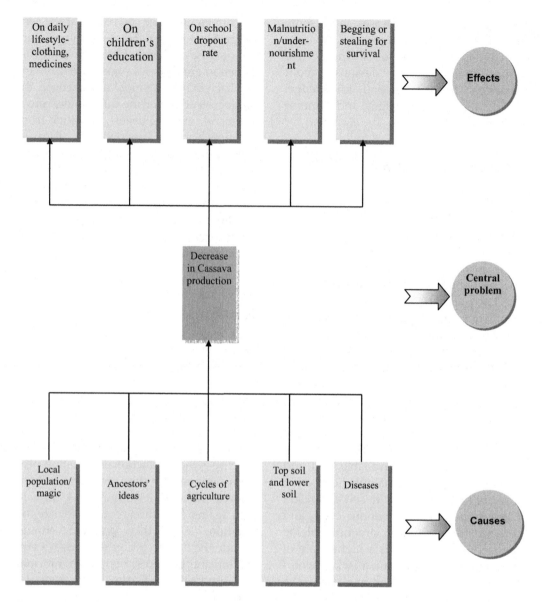

Figure 1. Network of Cassava problems, causes, and effects.

CURRICULUM FOR RURAL DISTANT LEARNERS

Our objective is to develop a teaching and learning curriculum for rural people. This program will be focused on adult learners who are illiterate, cannot read and write French or any of the four national languages but are only able to speak their local dialect. These same learners are geo-graphically very scattered in the local area; hence distance education is our chosen mode of teaching.

Furthermore, instructional objectives will assist the teacher in selecting appropriate content, teaching strategies, resources, and assessment, and can also support the teacher in educational activities (Cohen, Manion, & Morrison, 1998).

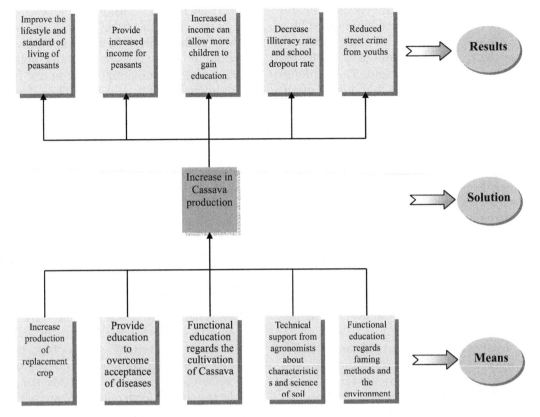

Figure 2.　Network of methods and solutions.

As stated above, this program has two parts: a compulsory and an elective. In this specific case of distance education for adult learners who are illiterate, some questions concerning planning, implementation, and evaluation will constantly present themselves when designing the curriculum.

PLAN

When planning, many questions are raised: How is the curriculum developed? How is the subject matter developed? How are curriculum objectives defined? How is curriculum content selected? How to organize the curriculum content? We start to think about the learner (target audience), teacher (and facilitator), and the instructional technology. Dunn, Beaudry, and Klavas (1989) contend that it is crucial for teachers to match their teaching styles

with students' learning styles; every person has a learning style. It is as individual as a signature. When the students' learning styles are identified, then classrooms can be organized to respond to their individual needs.

The Kabongo target audience constitutes adult learners (who are illiterate) living in scattered rural areas of the Kabongo region, and who are generally only able to speak the local dialect (Kilubakat), but not French (the official language) or the four national languages. Most of our learners are farmers, leaving the village in the morning at about 5 a.m. to go to the fields; they work all day and return home in the afternoon at about 5 p.m.

Research was conducted in the Kabongo region to ascertain the most convenient times for the local citizens to receive educational broadcasts and the reasons for this preferred time. The results showed that 79.9% responded that evening time was the most convenient and 20.1% felt that mornings were convenient. Those preferring evenings indicated that during morning time, they were busy with agricultural work and other daily activities. Their preference for evening time was because by evening time everyone is already back at home and ready to listen to the broadcast and available to meet others for discussion. As a consequence, it is important that the classroom environment provides opportunities for the adult learners to feel accepted in the classroom and have teachers/facilitators who listen to their requests and can respond to their specific questions. That is why Tomlinson (2002) contends that students seek affirmation that they are significant in the classroom.

In the planning of curriculum and delivery, a major point of consideration has been to place the learners at the center and make the program meet their needs, such as taking into account the time available for the learners, the age of the learners, and the cultural behaviors of the learners. The primary goal is the overall well-being of the learner, so we have to equip learners with skills to address and overcome daily problems. These skills will enable them to address the problem of the decreased production of cassava and help them develop the skills to solve future problems. This program will also enable these adult learners to draw on their previous experience in agricultural fields to deal with present and future problems, all of which can allow the learners to participate in the new lessons. This method will provide the adult learners, who culturally must be respected because of age and experience, to draw on their farming experience with cassava and share their methods and successes. The learning plan is to keep the adult learners motivated by involving them in all kinds of activities and practices; in this way they will cooperate and participate to the program.

Teachers need to consider the following questions when matching their learners. How is each learner's self concept being developed? How does a teaching style meet learners' individual differences of need, interest, ability, and skill? How does a teaching style develop in each learner? How does the organization of the class and school facilities foster security in each learner?

In this stage of planning, the distance educator is determining tasks to be done at the end of each module and by the end of the curriculum. They must also plan the way learners will cooperate among themselves, with the teachers, or with the facilitators. Here we think that practical activities, workshops, small seminars, and simple discussion will enable the learners to have a hands-on, interactive role in their learning. Also the teacher must plan and think about the technological tools to be used for delivering content. In the case of the Kabongo region, radio broadcasting will be the chosen form of technology, with the use of other media, such as DVD, CD-ROM, tapes, print, and booklets. Those technologies will help with the transmission, but the content should always respond to the needs of the learners and should be translated into their local language (Kilubakat). During the research survey, local citizens were asked which language they would prefer the broadcast in. The local citizens overwhelmingly requested Kilubakat (92.1%). Other languages that were offered as choices were Tshiluba (0%), Kikongo (0%), Lingala (0%), Swahili (4.9%) and French (3%) (Nsomwe-a-nfunkwa, 2005).

Geographical distance between the broadcasting center, teachers, and learners will certainly be an issue. The reality for the local citizens in the Kabongo region is that the people are scattered throughout different rural villages. To address this problem, qualified teachers will be trained in the content and they will become facilitators at the end of training sessions and will be sent to different "radio broadcasting reception centers." These facilitators will have the role of assisting adult learners by answering their questions, explaining sections of the broadcast that were not understood, and organizing workshops and practical activities. They will also provide counseling services to support students through their learning.

After introducing the situation for the learners and teachers, it is then appropriate that the instructional technology and design is discussed. The article has mentioned some of the realities of Kabongo, which can plainly be characterized by no electricity and no access to advanced technology; hence, the primary technology to be employed is radio broadcasting and other media. Considering the old machines, the target audience, and their needs and challenges, what kind of instructional design is going to be used for the Kabongo distance education adult learners?

Many authors have written about instructional design models: linear design, branched design, hyper-content design, and learner-directed design. Taking into account the differences between the learners in Kabongo, a linear design, designed by Simonson (2006), will be predominantly used.

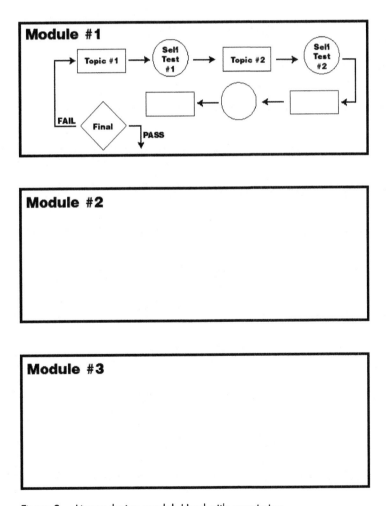

Figure 3. Linear design model. Used with permission.

In the case that a learner or learning activities need another rhythm of learning, other instructional designs will be employed. The overall goal is to meet the objective for every module and for every adult learner.

IMPLEMENT

Scott (1999) said a curriculum, however well designed, must be implemented if it is to have any impact on students. Fullan and Panfret (1977) said that implementation is a critical phase in the cycle of planning and teaching a curriculum.

After planning, it is time to implement what has been planned. This implementation is where the adult learners start to receive lessons from radio broadcasting. Before starting the broadcast, the reception center will have already received all didactic supports such as booklets, prints, pictures, DVDs, CD, tapes, and so forth.

Students will study every day, and the facilitators must ensure that the adult learners master the daily module, pass the daily test and, after success, then pass on to the following module. In some cases, the student will have to pass a practical test held out of the reception center; the facilitator can then confer with the student if he can continue on to the next module and if necessary pass the oral or practical test. Here, all distance learners will be receiving the same content at the same time, but they will be in different locations within the region.

A common problem facing distance education programs is feedback; in the case of the Kabongo's cassava education program, the solution lies in the training of facilitators who will be located in the local area. The facilitators will report to the radio broadcasting center; these reports will encompass didactics needs, difficult questions where support is required, the evolution of learners and their participation, the quality of content broadcasted, and the attitude of adult learners towards the pro-

gram. Also, the facilitators will be the connection between the radio broadcasting reception centers and the radio broadcasting center. The radio broadcasting center will try in some ways to help learners of different radio broadcasting reception centers to share their experiences by inviting some adult learners to participate in the preparation and broadcast content and engage in discussions at times. During the research survey stage local citizens were asked if they would like to participate in the preparation and broadcasting processes in a community radio on a weekly basis. There was an overwhelmingly positive response, with 86.7% asking to be involved and 10.3% who indicated they did not want to participate and only 3% who were undecided.

As this will be the first opportunity for the rural people to have a radio broadcasting center in their own area, it will be important to try to respond to the requests of the local people. If the information gained from the survey can be followed, then it is possible to meet the needs of the community. During the research survey, citizens were asked if such things as agricultural issues, health issues, educational issues and cultural issues would be good points to focus on. 89.3% of the community responded with a definite yes to the aforementioned issues and 0.1% said no with 10.6% of the responders undecided.

Following the implementation steps is the evaluation of the two precedent steps.

EVALUATION

Mager (1984) points out that if you are teaching things that cannot be evaluated, you are in the awkward position of being unable to demonstrate that you are teaching anything at all. Intangibles are often intangible because we have been lazy to think about what it is we want students to be able to do. This is another important step, from which the designer will discover if the curriculum was helpful and useful following the need of the learner.

Talking about evaluation, we think about planning and implementation. From here, it can evaluate the work of the student and discover if he has mastered what was planned for him to master. In the case of the Kabongo distance education broadcasting, the evaluation process must include an assessment to ensure the learners understand the issues related to cassava and are able to transfer this knowledge to daily life. If the result of students' evaluation is very good, this can enable the designer to understand that the plan was greatly successful; if the results are poor, this will let the designer reconsider the design, the content, the tools used to deliver the content, the environment, and the instructional design, and hence review the areas that are leading to poor performance.

Formative evaluation, and in some ways the summative evaluation, will be used to evaluate learners. The formative evaluation will allow the teacher and the learners to understand the evolution and the mastery of the present module prior to continuing on to the next module. From the formative evaluation the teacher will be able to provide some assistance and advice to learners. That is why Fehring (2005) stated that students have the right to know about their own literacy learning achievements, and that this is still the most salient reason for the assessment and reporting processes used in teaching and learning educational environments.

In terms of formative evaluation, the Kabongo distance education broadcast also faces some obstacles due to the illiteracy of the local citizen, and hence we must use oral evaluation. Questions will be asked to adult learners and, from their answers, decisions will be made concerning their mastery of the modules. Also, from practical activities, discussions, presentations and explanations, and workshops on the module, the teachers and facilitators will decide if the students can make the transition to the new module.

Concerning summative evaluation, attention should be paid to the cultural issues of local people in the Kabongo region. These cultural values include that adult answers are the correct answers. If we have to tell the adult learners, who are fathers to at least five children and considered the spirit, the chief, the decider, the person most responsible for the family, that their answers are incorrect; this will manifest itself as a frustration for those adult learners. Possible consequences could be that, step-by-step, the learners will lose motivation towards the program and, potentially, adult learners could drop out.

Summative evaluation is important in the sense of motivating learners. The Kabongo distance education broadcasting case is the first experience of teaching adults and often illiterate learners in that corner of Congo, and hence the plan is to provide a "certificate of participation" to all adults who participate in the program. This can motivate others to come and join the program in the future, for either agriculturally based curriculum or for other social/educational based curriculum.

RADIO BROADCASTING

When assessing the technology, each resource should be examined for its unique qualities and its potential benefits for rural teachers and adult learners. In the case of the Kabongo region, we should not use a tool because it is new and available. Each innovation should be suited to the needs and the realities of the environment. It has been said by many that there is a tendency to dispose of old machines. This is a good idea for some parts of the world, but a very bad decision for those who have never seen nor touched such "outdated machines." This is the case in the Kabongo region in the Democratic Republic of Congo. In Congo, 60% of people are affected by a high rate of poverty and live in rural areas, where they have never seen electricity, television, radio broadcasting or computers. The area has roads in very poor condition, slow trains, and the people are scattered throughout the region. In such a situation, if we have to deliver distance education to isolated learners, the first choice would be radio broadcast. Such a method is practical; people are able to buy a radio receiver and batteries, and not rely on electricity. They can all receive the lessons simultaneously. Given the local realities: the scattered population, the high rate of illiteracy and language diversity, we believe that radio remains the most popular, accessible, and cost-effective means of communication for rural people of the Kabongo area. Radio can overcome all of the aforementioned obstacles.

In order to achieve success, radio broadcasting combined with booklets, DVD, CD, and tapes can ensure the delivery of information. All content to be broadcasted must be contained on DVD, CD, tapes, and printed booklets. These will be used as didactic support. The content will be the same in the DVD, CD, tapes, and booklets. This means that the DVD will use local language and will contain voice, images, and content. The CD will contain voice, images, and texts; and tapes will contain voices, and the booklets will have written text and pictures. (Booklets will be useful for literate people.)

In comparison to other distance education based on radio broadcasting, our innovation is that the rural people will first be trained to become facilitators in different villages that are chosen as centers of reception for the broadcasting. Second, before the broadcasting of lessons, all materials such as booklets, DVD, CD, and tapes will be sent to the areas. Third, when broadcasting the content, the facilitators must be with the rural adult learners, organize a short explanation on location, collect and answer any questions from the learners, discuss the content with the learners, and

plan some activities as practice for the learners. Fourth, the trained group originating from different villages (centers of broadcast reception) will travel to the central broadcast place for curriculum evaluation and from this evaluation consider alterations to the curriculum.

TIME OF DELIVERY

The radio will broadcast every day from morning to evening, but the educational content will only be in the evening, following the wishes of the target audience. There will be lessons three times per week focused on agriculture, three times for lessons on values and community building, and two times for general knowledge. Sunday morning is culturally the time of religion, and at noon as for all days, the national news will be broadcast.

MANAGEMENT AND BROADCAST

The radio broadcasting will be managed by the nongovernment organization called Community and Social Development Organization (www.odcs-rdc.org) located in Kabongo. Experts who make up the broadcasting management team will be native speakers of the local language, Kilubakat. This team will include expertise in areas such as: information and communication technologies, distance education, adult education, adult psychology, journalism, agriculture, and climatology.

In terms of the broadcasting regulations, the first regulation will be that everyone hoping to become a broadcaster for this educational radio must be an educator. They must understand the principles of education; teaching and learning and the psychological principles of rural adults. The radio will be used as a tool to reach the remote target audience, so it is very important in this step to follow the qualification criterion to become a qualified teacher of distance education. The second condition is also very important, and that is mastery of the local language (Kilubakat). The target audience, as stated previously, constitutes rural adult learners who are illiterate, and often cannot speak French or other national languages, only their own local language.

It is hoped that gradually they can train the local people to become presenters to share local farming knowledge. The local people expressed in the survey that 88% would like to listen to broadcasts made by the local community and only 1.3% answered no. There was 10.7% undecided on the topic.

TIMETABLE

As noted above, every week there will be three lessons focused on agriculture, three lessons focused on values and community building, and two lessons devoted to general knowledge. Each lesson we take one hour; there will be two information delivery sessions, the first segment will be 20 minutes and then a 5-minute break (containing some music, perhaps), the second segment is 20 minutes, and 15 minutes at the end of the lesson for review and discussion.

SUGGESTION

Distance education should be regarded in the case of the Kabongo region as a vital option in continuous rural problem solving, youth empowerment, and a means to fight premature school dropout. The Democratic Republic of Congo, and in particular the region of Kabongo, has a majority of the population living in rural areas, and they are poor, illiterate, physically isolated and scattered, and facing all kinds of daily problems. The schools are characterized by late primary entrance, high grade repetition and a high rate of dropout. Distance education can be a good way to empower the rural people, youth, and women. These groups can be offered all kinds of skills and then they will be able to solve the daily problems encountered in the agricultural sector, along with other sectors such as education and training, family planning, environment and pollution, communication and transportation, and electricity and water.

CONCLUSION

This curriculum is innovative as it is the first one in the domain for rural, illiterate, adult learners. Also, it is the first time a curriculum has been designed to take into account the needs of rural people in the Kabongo region.

This distance education curriculum will be delivered by radio broadcast and it will use an experimental curriculum. After its effective implementation, evaluation will

Table 1
Broadcast Timetable

	MON	TUES	WED	THURS	FRI	SAT	SUN
AM	LI	LI	LI	LI	LI	LI	LI
	ADV	ADV	ADV	ADV	ADV	ADV	RELIG
NOON	NI	NI	NI	NI	NI	NI	NI
PM	M	M	M	M	M	M	M
	RA	RA	RA	RA	RA	RA	KB
EVENING	KH	KB	KH	K	KH	KB	K

Key: LI = local information; ADV = advertisement; NI = national information; M = messages; RA = recreation activities; KH = know how; KB = knowledge being; K = knowledge; REL = religion.

allow for development and enhancement as well as develop into other subjects.

It is believed that distance education is an appropriate means to educate rural people in different ways on all kinds of challenges they are facing in their daily life. Also in the case of the Kabongo region, where they are facing numerous social and economic issues such as a high rate of illiteracy and permanent school dropout, family-related problems, issues of environment and pollution, agricultural problems, bad roads and transportation, and a lack of telecommunication, we are sure that through distance education we will succeed to educate the population of Kabongo. This education will empower them with specific transferable skills and these skills will allow them to be able to solve the different kinds of problems they are facing and those that may be encountered in the future.

REFERENCES

Cohen, L., Manion, L, & Morrison, K. (1998). *A guide to teaching practice* (4th ed.). London: Routledge.

Dunn, R., Beaudry, J. S., & Klavas, A. (1989). Survey of research on learning styles. *Educational Leadership, 46*(6), 50-58.

Fullan, M. G., & Pomfret, A. (1977). Research on curriculum and instruction implementation. *Review of Education Research, 47*(2), 335-339.

Fehring, H. (2005). Critical analytical and reflective literacy assessment: Reconstructing practice. *Australian Journal of Language and Literacy, 28*, 335-339.

IITA. (2000). *Mission Report: In the context of war and the resulting distrurbance of trading activities, the phytosanitary situation of cassava.* Retrieved February 20, 2006, from http://www.rdfs.net/linked-docs/booklet/bookl_-congo_en.pdf

Mager, R. F. (1984). *Preparing instructional objectives* (3rd ed.). Belmont, CA: Lake.

Nsomwe-a-nfunkwa, B. (2005). Survey concerning the implementation of a community radio in Kabongo's region. *PSE review, 1*(2).

Scott, G. (1999). *Change matters*. Sydney, Australia: Allen & Unwin.

Simonson, M. (2006). *Seven key concepts: Integrating instructional technology in the classroom.* Retrieved January 17, 2006, from http://www.Fgse.nova.edu/itde/faculty/Simonson/it/intro_it.ppt

Tomlinson, C. A. (2002). *The third wave*. New York: Bantam Books.

Distance Learning and Bilingual Educational CD-ROMs in Rural Areas of the Democratic Republic of Congo

Banza Nsomwe-a-nfunkwa

Nowadays, many countries, especially those that are developed, are concerned by the use of new technologies in teaching and learning in different areas of the daily life of their citizens in different societies. But this is not the case in developing countries, such as

Banza Nsomwe-a-nfunkwa,
Nanjing Normal University, China.
E-mail: nfunkwa@hotmail.com

the Democratic Republic of Congo, where even the old technologies are still a huge obstacle. In a country such as the Democratic Republic of Congo where, in the case of rural areas, everything is lacking in terms of the information and communication technology (ICT) infrastructure, add to this the lack of electricity and not even a generator nor solar power in some corners of rural areas. Addressing this situation, and our need to participate in, and improve, the well being of the scattered population in the rural areas, is the concept of development of a distance learning system. *What should be the content of this distance learning program? What kind of technology should we use in order to meet the needs of all distance learners? Which language should be used for the teaching and learning?*

In rural areas of the Democratic Republic of Congo, people are facing different kinds of problems connected to the lack of education and training on a daily level. These are adults characterized by a high level of illiteracy. In the case of the research done in the Kabongo region, the province of Katanga, in the Democratic Republic of Congo, people are facing huge problems related to Cassava diseases and its effect. The effects include a loss in their daily income and consequently a lack of food and hunger, higher child school-dropout rates because there is not enough money for schooling fees, a lack of clothing, and a lack of money to buy medicine in the case they are sick.

The rural people hope to solve the problem of cassava diseases. The best way to help them is to educate and train them about cassava diseases and the possible ways to fight against those diseases. In this case, the teaching and learning must be done in the local language of the illiterate distant learners.

In this article, the author explains the process of the design and development of the content contained in an educational CD-ROM. In this age of high technology, everyone is trying to focus on new technologies and in some way trying to bypass the old technologies. This is the case of many developed countries, but not in developing countries, such as the Democratic Republic of Congo, where the situation is catastrophic in term of the use of technologies in teaching and learning activities. In rural areas for example, there are still some people who have never seen or used a television, never seen or touched a computer, never used the old and new technologies and, in addition to this, the rural areas lack electricity and all kinds of ICT infrastructure. In these rural areas, there is a high rate of illiteracy and extremely high child school-dropout rates. At the same time, the people in the rural areas of Congo are facing all kind of problems and need to be educated or trained in the way to be able to solve their daily problems. The majority of rural dwellers are farmers living scattered across huge areas in villages. In this case, the use of distance learning is the best way to reach the people. At this point, the question is to know what technology can be used correctly, reliably, and appropriately.

Distance learning via CD-ROM is an opportunity for rural people of the Kabongo region to study wherever, and at whatever time, they choose. All content— audio, evaluation, and photographs—is provided on CD-ROM, and additional prints and tapes will also be provided to help facilitate the successful use of the CD-ROM. To help give students feedback, facilitators will be available for consultation via mail, or face to face.

Distance education uses various media to deliver learning information and to link students and teachers. Some media can be used for both purposes, but they generally fall into two categories: those that can be used to convey subject content, such as print materials, video tapes, audio tapes, television, computer-based courseware, and CD-ROM, and those that permit communication between teachers and students, such as fax, radio, teleconferencing, videoconferencing, and the Internet (The Commonwealth of Learning, 2006). With the CD-ROM, distance learners have a huge opportunity to learn or to train in their own time at their own place (Distance Learning Zone, 2006).

CD-ROM PRESENTATION

The program contained in this CD-ROM is designed to address the basic needs of the rural people in order to solve their daily problems connected to cassava disease and its impact on their daily life, on kids' education, on clothing, etc. This CD-ROM "Le Manioc et ses Maladies" is an educational CD-ROM containing several elements: Images of Cassava, summary, introduction and conclusion; including seven chapters. Chapter 1: History of Cassava, Chapter 2: Importance of Cassava, Chapter 3: Cassava Diseases and Insects, Chapter 4: Importance of Cassava Diseases, Chapter 5: Moment of Decreased Production, Chapter 6: Fight Against Cassava Diseases, Chapter 7: Cassava Dangers and Solutions.

LEARNING DESIGN

This CD-Rom is adheres to all steps of instructional design. Another advantage with this CD-ROM is that the self-directed learner has flexibility to opt for linear, branched, hypercontent, or learner directed design. The chapters are connected in terms of numbers, but in terms of the content, the learners are free to decide from which chapter to start. But to complete the program, the learner must learn all modules and pass the test for each chapter. For the self-directed learner, the CD-ROM also contains questions for evaluation. But for adult learners who are illiterate, the evaluation will be oral and practical.

In terms of learning design, the specificity of this CD-ROM is that the learners have multiple choices of daily content; they can start from any chapter and head to the evaluation of the chapter (see Figures 1 and 2).

CHOICE OF LANGUAGE

Here we have to say that this CD-ROM allows the learner to make a language preference following his skills in one language or another. As noted above, our target audience constitutes a huge percentage of illiterates learners; to help them to have a chance to study something on the cassava matter, we decided to design the same content in two languages. This has the advantage of giving each learner the choice of language in which he prefers to learn.

To make a choice between languages is very easy for everyone even for the illiterate learners. It only requires you to move the mouse on the top of the name of the language and click once, and the result is that you have the content in that language (Figures 3, 4, and 5).

FLEXIBILITY OF USING VOICE

An advantage of this educational CD-ROM is that it has voice in both French and Kilubakat language. The voice can be used following the pattern of the learner. It can be stopped in order to make a comment or assess if the learner understood the teacher, or just for a small pause. Also it

Figure 1.   Learning design giving multiple choice of study (French version of CD-ROM).

Figure 2.   Learning Design giving multiple choice of study (Kilubakat version of CD-ROM).

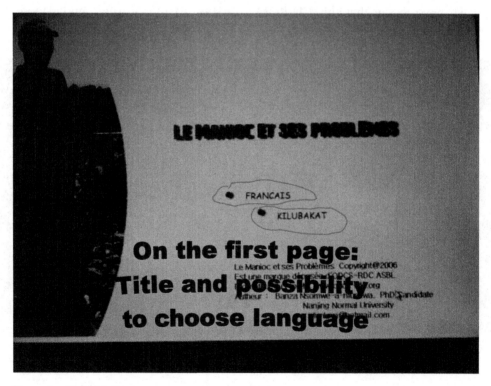

Figure 3.   French language.

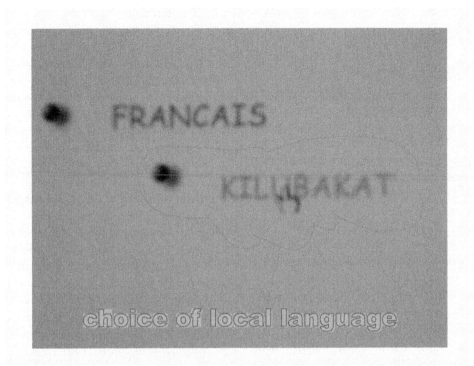

Figure 4. Kilubakat language.

Figure 5. Choice of language.

gives the possibility to preview or to forward through the content.

DIFFICULTIES AND OBSTACLES

When designing this CD-ROM, we faced many kinds of difficulties and obstacles connected to time and financial matters. This CD-ROM was designed to meet the needs of the rural people living in the rural areas of Kabongo, in province of Katanga in the Democratic Republic of Congo. The economic situation of this country has a negative impact on all sectors of the people's lives. From the major city (Lubumbashi) to the rural area where I collected data, the distance is approximately 800 kilometers. It took me 3 to 4 days to reach this area because of bad roads and the lack of good transportation.

The survey I conducted with the local people in order to identify their problems was in French, it took me time to translate it into the local language so as to be understood by the local illiterate people (the people who have not had an education and do not speak French).

From their answers to the survey, I discovered that their problems were connected to the agricultural sector, the economic foundation of their well-being. After discussions with them, I discovered that the main issue of focus was cassava diseases and its impact on their life, their children's education, their clothing problem and so on.

Not being an expert in the agricultural sector, I contacted experts and they informed me that there are many kinds of research completed on cassava disease, and the research results were available in the library. After visiting different libraries, I discovered that all research was completed and published in the French language (the official language of the Democratic Republic of Congo), but French is used by few rural illiterate peo-

ple. The language problem was the first obstacle for the rural people in accessing this information. The second obstacle was the lack of trust in the diseases, the third obstacle was also the resistance to the new agricultural practice, and the lack of appropriate educational strategies for educating rural adult people, and another obstacle was the scattered nature of the population.

From this situation, I developed a program suitable for adult learners living in the rural areas of Kabongo, Katanga Province, in the Democratic Republic of Congo. This program would make efforts to find a resolution to the aforementioned obstacles.

Because of the poor technological infrastructure present in Congo, the choice was made for the use of radio broadcasting to reach the scattered adult learners. The radio will be used in combination with print, audio and video. From this I decided to also design an educational CD-ROM to be used both by teachers, facilitators and self-directed distant learners.

SUGGESTIONS

In the case of developing countries such as the Democratic Republic of Congo, the use of educational CD-ROM plays a huge importance in urban and rural areas. Attention should be paid to all obstacles enumerated such as language problem, location of target audience, the nature of the audience, needs of learners, etc.

I do believe that given the lack of new technologies, radio broadcasting, print, CD-ROM, audio, video are all still needed in developing countries, and especially in local regions, where almost all forms of technologies are currently lacking. The realities of the absence of technologies in these areas mean that the use of new technologies is not viable. But in some cases the use of older technologies can meet some of the needs of the population in the terms of education and training.

CONCLUSION

From this experience from the rural area of Kabongo, Katanga Province, Democratic Republic of Congo, I do believe that the use of radio, CD-ROM, audio, video, print, etc can facilitate distance learning (distance education) for the rural people, and they can benefit from this.

The main goal of distance education should be firstly, and most importantly, focussed on the educational objectives, and not firstly on the technological equipment. This is not to say that new technologies are not welcome in the rural areas of developing countries, such as Congo.

The meaning is that at this level where the economical situation of developing countries, such as Congo, is still delayed, the countries cannot afford all new technologies for rural areas; therefore it is better at present to think of new technologies, but in the meantime use the old technologies.

REFERENCES

The Commonwealth of Learning. (2006). *The use of multimedia in distance education.* Retrieved June 15, 2006, from http://www.col.org/knowldges/ks_multimedia.htm

Distance Learning Zone. (2006). *QM&T'S distance learning products.* Retrieved June 2, 2006, from http://www.qmt.co.uk/distl.htm

---

IN RURAL AREAS OF THE DEMOCRATIC REPUBLIC OF CONGO, PEOPLE ARE FACING DIFFERENT KINDS OF PROBLEMS CONNECTED TO THE LACK OF EDUCATION AND TRAINING ON A DAILY LEVEL.

Education Leaders Perspectives
Pros and Cons of Distance Education in a Small Caribbean Island

Noverene Taylor

INTRODUCTION

Due to the rapid advance in computer technology and Internet access, the landscape of education has changed drastically over the years. Because of this dramatic change, many educational institutions today have realized that teaching, and learning are no longer confined to delivery models such as face-to face instruction, and are in the process or restructuring what goes on inside

Noverene Taylor, Grand Turk, Turks and Caicos Islands, B.W.I.
Telephone: (649) 946-1471.
E-mail: noverene@nova.edu

their school walls. As part of their restructuring effort, distance education plays an important role. Owing to the myriad of benefits for K-12 education offered by distance learning technologies, schools are using these technologies to reach all students, especially those in remote locations, and provide them with challenging and appropriate educational experiences.

This article examines education leaders' perspectives regarding the advantages and disadvantages of distance education in the Turks and Caicos Islands. In order to understand these, it is important that readers have a basic understanding of the islands' geography, people, and education.

THE TURKS AND CAICOS ISLANDS

The Turks and Caicos Islands consist of eight inhabited islands and about 40 cays. The islands are located at the southeastern end of the Bahamas chain, 575 miles southeast of Miami, and 90 miles north of the island of Hispaniola. The islands are accessible by aeroplanes and boats. The native people are of African descent. The expatriate community of British, American, French, Canadian, Haitians, Dominicans, and Jamaicans gives the islands some international influences.

Education is an important feature of the Turks and Caicos Islands and, as such, is provided for students up to the secondary level on most of the islands. With a student population of approximately 6,000 students, enrollment data shows that close to 3,000 students are from culturally diverse backgrounds for the 2006-2007 school year. Similar trends in enrollment were also observed for the 2005-2006 school year. Students completing their primary school education sit for the Grade Six Achievement Test (GSAT), while those after five years of secondary school sit for the Caribbean Secondary Education Certificate (CSEC) examinations.

Students who have completed elementary education and do not have immediate access to traditional high school would normally relocate to one of the other islands where the necessary facilities for education are provided. With only two community colleges on these islands, the same can be said for students who have finished high school and want to access college-level education. With the hassle of relocation, costly airline tickets, and the islands being multicultural in nature, distance education technologies can offer a great deal of flexibility, and convenience as to when, where, and how education is distributed to students at the elementary school, high school, and community college in the Turks and Caicos Islands.

DEFINING DISTANCE EDUCATION

It is important that definitions that are associated with this approach to instruction be examined so that readers will have a better understanding of the pros and cons of distance education in the Turks and Caicos Islands. Distance education can be defined as: "institution based formal education where the learning group is separated, and where interactive telecommunications systems are used to connect learners, resources, and instructors" (Simonson, 2003, as cited in, Simonson, Smaldino, Albright, & Zvacek, 2006, p. 32). Traditionally, this includes a variety of activities from correspondence program using postal services; courses

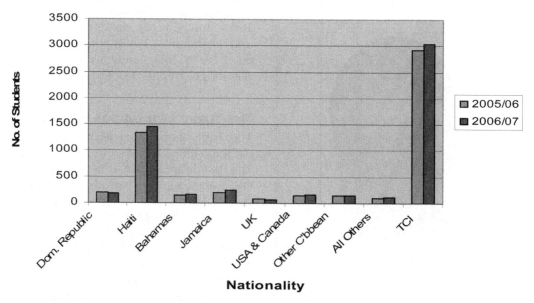

Source: Ministry of Education, Youth, Sports, and Gender Affairs (2007).

Figure 1. Enrollment by nationality in both government and private schools for the school years 2005/2006 and 2006/2007.

broadcasted using the radio, distributed video lectures, or other materials to enhance instruction. Today, with the rapid increase in technology, more attention is given to online distance education.

ONLINE DISTANCE EDUCATION

Distance education has been in existence for at least 160 years (Simonson et al., 2006), and the medium has changed from paper-and-pencil correspondence study to real-time online education. The development of this "subfield" of distance education has become a central focus of the field of education due to its flexibility, affordability, convenience, and attractiveness. It is distinguished from other previous paradigms of distance education by its ability to create critical communities of inquiry (Garrison, Anderson, & Archer, 2003). Many may still use distance education and online education interchangeably, but it is believed that the distinction is useful in helping us to see the development of this "subfield" of distance education in which technologies have played a major role.

Online education is delivered over the Internet. It may be synchronous, in which the teacher and the student interact with each other in "real time." For example, with two-way videoconferences, students interact with "live" video of an instructor. Telephone conversations are also considered synchronous. Asynchronous delivery, on the other hand, does not take place simultaneously. In this case, the teacher may deliver the instruction using video, discussion board postings, Web sites, or other means, and the students respond at a later time. While adult students are benefiting from online distance education programs, the young and traditional students have increasingly begun to realize the new opportunities that are available to increase their academic achievement.

DISTANCE EDUCATION VERSUS TRADITIONAL INSTRUCTION

Distance education's quality is often compared with that of traditional instruction. Most recent reports have shown that there are no significant difference between online learning and traditional instruction in terms of student grades, test scores, and other measures of student achievement (Worley, 2000). Phipps and Merisotis (1999) completed a review of distance education's effectiveness and concluded that no matter what technology is used, distance education courses are as favourable as traditional face-to-face learning.

ADVANTAGES OF DISTANCE EDUCATION IN THE TURKS AND CAICOS ISLANDS

In the Turks and Caicos Islands (TCI), education leaders consider some of the key strengths of distance education to rest in its capacity to provide "anytime" and "anywhere" education to students. According to the views expressed by some of the education leaders, distance education affords many adults on these islands the opportunity to access education that would not otherwise be possible.

The director of education, Beatrice Fulford, who is presently pursuing her doctoral degree, indicated that distance education is a great learning opportunity for individuals who have jobs and families, and do not want to interrupt their job to go back to school but really want to pursue higher education. While distance education is different from the face-to face traditional setting, she noted that it is very convenient, flexible, and affordable. Convenience suggests that students do not have to spend time commuting to classes during the week or at a particular time of the day. As a distant learning student, she has great freedom to study at times that suit her, be it early morning or middle of the night, and completes her assignments when the time is convenient, whether during lunch hours or after work in the convenience of her home.

Thomas Joyner (personal communication, March 20, 2007), the education psychologist, stated that, in these islands, distance education is of tremendous benefit to adult learners who have difficult schedules because they can learn at their own pace and time. In other words, distance learners control their learning environment; school is brought to the student, and not the student to school. Joyner also noted that certain learners, for example those who are shy, will find distance education suitable to meeting their educational needs. Distance learning, he said, eliminates the need for some students to feel judged or embarrassed by their classmates.

Distance education can be a worthwhile experience for learners. It can provide convenient locations for both students and instructors because many of the technologies, such as the Internet, videotape, and telephone, can be easily accessed at home, noted the education officer for the literacy program, Kaydeen Miles. She also pointed out that when you look at the benefits of learning new technological skills in order to adequately prepare yourself for the virtual environment, distance learners are at an advantage above the traditional student. She noted that distance education offers great potential for alleviating educational inequity in these islands because the islands are multicultural in nature. Distance education she believes, can also be less costly than that of traditional education. Books, course content provided by the instructor, and other resources are only a click away.

In order for students to move on to high school, they have to achieve an average of 50% or more on the Grade Six Achievement Test. When results for the June 2006 examination were analyzed, it was found that of the 292 students who sat the exam, approximately 188 students received a score of 50% or more. This clearly indicates that these students could have benefited from distance education, which could be used as a legitimate teaching method to provide appropriate instruction for students to enhance their academic performance. Students who did not achieve a score of up to 50% might not necessarily be weak students. They could be students with different learning styles, needs, and abilities. Placed in a different learning environment, such as a distance learning setting, where they can work at their own pace, they could show marked improvement.

Pass marks for the Caribbean Secondary Education Certificate (CSEC) examinations range from grade one to three, with one being the highest and three the lowest. On the May/June 2006 examinations, 88 students received a grade one, 226 students received a grade two, and 338 students received a grade three. Therefore, if these students were provided with a distance learning environment, where they can collaborate and work together, and be more actively involved in their own learning, the possibility exists that the number of students who receive a grade one could increase, thereby decreasing the number of students who receive a grade three.

Several teachers who were interviewed agreed that, while adult learners are using distance education programs to achieve higher education, in the Turks and Caicos Islands, elementary school students, high school students, and the traditional college students should have access to the new opportunities presented by distance education. Indeed, distance learning represents a network of technologies that can connect the public school systems, and provide greater motivation, reduced learning time, and higher achievements, among others.

The community college offers associate degrees to students who have completed high school education. Distance education could allow students studying at this level

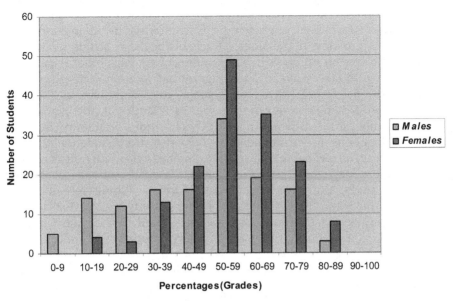

Source: Ministry of Education, Youth, Sports, and Gender Affairs (2007).

Figure 2.   Grade Six Achievement Test Results for June 2006 (males = 135, females = 157).

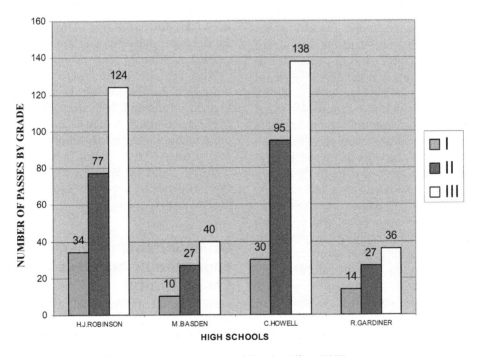

Source: Ministry of Education, Youth, Sports, and Gender Affairs (2007).

Figure 3.   Caribbean Secondary Education Certification passes by grade and school for May/June 2006.

to pursue courses that are not available on these islands. This educational approach could also address growing populations, limited space, and permit students who have failed a course to take it again. This could eliminate the hassle of getting student visas, and transportation to and from campuses. In addition, students would not have to worry about housing accommodation or the expense of airline tickets to return home because they would not have to go overseas to study. And even if they do, traveling to the institutions campus would not be for any extended period. Distance education is not normally tailored around the schedules of traditional semester schedules. Therefore, students would be more flexible with their time in completing courses.

In a multicultural society where students may have language challenges, the distance education environment would be quite appropriate to make them feel more comfortable and relaxed using the English language without the fear of being embarrassed or judged by their peers. Additionally, distance education can afford traditional teachers the opportunity to move away from a mechanistic style of teaching where knowledge is imparted by the teacher to students, to a more active and creative process, one in which teachers design and facilitate activities that are geared towards students using technology to generate, discover, and build their own framework of knowledge collaboratively. Montgomery (1998) argues that not all students learn the same way, and so using multimedia allows students to take an active role in learning in ways that the traditional classroom cannot afford. This implies that distance education environments can be designed in ways that meet each student's needs.

Students' interisland interaction is limited to inter-island school events, where only the competitors from each school get to interact with each other. Having established a platform for distance education, this would open up the gateway for complete interislands interaction. All of the schools in these islands would be able to interact with each other regardless of geographical location. The adoption of distance education here in the Turks and Caicos Islands, at the elementary, high school, and community college levels could also afford students the opportunity to interact with other students across the globe. Imagine students collaborating with each other, sharing research ideas, and forming study groups for the Grade Six Achievement Test or the Caribbean Secondary Education Certificate. This could be a great motivator and a wonderful learning experience!

Teachers believe that they could work collaboratively in developing online courses for students at the different grade levels and share resources for the benefit of the students. This could be seen as an advantage wherein, the teachers would not have to develop courses on their own. The design of distance education courses does take time, and much effort, and must be done properly for students to be successful.

Through the technologies of distance education, students would be at an advantage in interacting with first world countries classrooms that may be using cutting-edge technologies. Furthermore, the Turks and Caicos Islands, being a third world country, could be brought to modernization, in order to become more productive and inventive.

DISADVANTAGES OF DISTANCE EDUCATION IN THE TURKS AND CAICOS ISLANDS

Lack of vision and financial resources may be considered two of the major factors that can disadvantage elementary school, secondary school, and community college students from distance education opportunities on these islands. Other drawbacks include, but are not limited to, lack of face to face interaction, academic dishonesty, no campus atmosphere, stigma attached, and the requirement of new skills for both the instructor and student.

The director pointed out that, with her experience in a distance education environment, she believes that the "distance" aspect of distance education seems to have taken away much of the social interaction that is present in traditional instruction. She noted that distance learning may not be for everyone. Those who do not have a strong desire to learn on their own can become easily distracted, playing online games such as pool or simply chatting with friends. In addition, when a student needs assistance with a particular assignment, it can be very difficult for the instructor to assist without being physically present. A student working alone at times can also feel isolated and depressed. Therefore, it is important that distance learners feel connected one way or another to the learning environment.

The director stated that some students are at a disadvantage when participating in certain activities for their distance education program. For example, for her program of study, the university offers weekly and monthly on-campus workshops and seminars that are beneficial to her professional development. But as a student in the distance education environment she does not have these opportunities readily available at her "fingertips." She mentioned that even though students are able to interact with people across the globe, the interaction is not necessarily the same as when you are in a traditional setting. Mediated communication takes away a lot of cues and personalized attention. Fulford also stated that some employers might not value certification through distance education. They tend to believe that the reputation of distance education is questionable. Therefore, students pursuing distance education courses must ensure that the course or program is accredited by a valid educational agency.

According to Joyner (personal communication, March 20, 2007), when students pursue online courses, it can be very hard to detect cheating. In the privacy of one's home students can easily receive an A grade by submitting another student's work. Hence, this is a matter that must be dealt with by teachers who are considering teaching at a distance. Joyner added that teachers must ensure that instruction is designed so that each student submits authentic work.

Miles, the literacy officer, noted that if you are afraid of change or learning new technology skills, then online distance education might not be suitable for you. She further claimed that if the instructor is not adequately prepared to deal with the virtual classroom, learners can become frustrated and drop the course. Therefore, in order for distance education to be successful in these islands, technical barriers would have to be a nonissue.

Some teachers believe that the lack of exposure to distance education settings would put some students at a disadvantage. When asked the reason for drawing such conclusion, the teachers simply stated that some students are already accustomed to the traditional classroom, and so exposing them to a faceless classroom environment could prove difficult. They believe that the transition from a face-to-face classroom to a faceless classroom might not be an easy task for some students.

The teachers further indicated that students in the current school system who are not yet exposed to the technological skills needed to succeed in a virtual environment would have to be properly trained. Teachers would have to be equipped technically and be trained to develop online courses and implement them accordingly. Institutions would have to acquire and install the needed equipment, course management systems, and other resources required. This could be very costly for the institutions, especially those operating on a tight budget. The success of any distance education program is dependent on the efficiency and effectiveness of a distance instructor and how prepared students are for the virtual environment. Therefore, if adequate training and support are not provided, in the initial stage of participating in distance education programs the attrition rate could be very high.

It is also unrealistic to expect young children to attend distance education courses at their own time and convenience. Someone must be able to supervise them. Elementary school students would not have recess time to socialize and play, and of course, social development is vital to the development of the whole child, especially when preparing students to survive in a highly socialized work environment. Not being able to attend important workshops, seminars, and special functions on campus would disadvantage some distance learners, especially those students who are just leaving high school.

Students who are weaker academically may be at a disadvantage in the distance learning environment. Distance learners have to be self-directed and intrinsically motivated. They also have to have good reading and comprehension skills. The weaker students may not be disciplined enough to use their own initiative to be successful. These are usually the students who require face-to-face interaction in the traditional classroom setting. Therefore, online education may not be for all types of learners.

Being in a third world environment, access to computers may be difficult on the part of some students. This would certainly put some of these students at a disadvantage where distance education is concerned. The monthly cost of Internet access might not be affordable to some students.

Tradition affects a wide cross-section of society. Most recent research demonstrates that there is no significant difference in terms of students' course grades, rating of course content and the instructor, and other outcomes. Therefore, it is incumbent of educators to make it clear to parents, and the wider community that distance education has been proven to be just as effective as traditional face-to-face instruction. One point is of paramount importance; if distance education is successfully implemented at all levels of the education system in these islands, it will have a promising future!

SUMMARY AND CONCLUSION

Distance education can be just as effective as any other category of instruction here in the Turks and Caicos Islands because when used effectively, learning occurs and knowledge is gained, which is the objective of teaching. Distance education is also cost effective, flexible, and convenient for many adult learners on these islands. Even though distance learning courses originally catered to nontraditional students as its target group, students at the elementary, high school, and community college levels can benefit from the new opportunities provided by distance education. The teacher's ability to create an interactive environment is vital for quality online education. Not all students may benefit from distance learning opportunities. Students who are intrinsically motivated and self-directed are most likely to succeed. Distance education may create feelings of isolation, and depression for some students. However, the advantages of distance learning seem to far outweigh the disadvantages. Therefore, by carefully identifying, and dealing with drawbacks that are within their influence, institutions on these islands may very well find that such actions are sufficient to provide students with distance education opportunities so that they can become contributing citizens in a global, diverse, and technologically advanced society.

REFERENCES

Garrison, R., Anderson, T., & Archer, W. (2003). In M. G. Moore & W. G. Anderson (Eds.), *Handbook of distance education*. Mahwah, NJ: Erlbaum.

Ministry of Education, Youth, Sports, and Gender Affairs. (2007). Turks and Caicos Islands Education Statistical Digest.

Montgomery, S. M. (1998). *Addressing diverse learning styles through the use of multimedia* [online]. Retrieved March 25, 2007, http://www.vpaa.uillinois.edu/tid/resources/montgomery.html

Phipps, R., & Merisotis, J. (1999). *What's the difference? A review of contemporary research on the effectiveness of distance learning in higher education*, Washington, DC: The Institute for Higher Education Policy. Retrieved April 11, 2007, from http://eric.ed.gov/ERICDocs/data/ericdocs2/content_storage_01/0000000b/80/11/6f/e4.pdf

Simonson, M., Smaldino, S., Albright, M., & Zvacek, S. (2006). *Teaching and learning at a distance: Foundations of distance education* (3rd ed.). Upper Saddle River, NJ: Prentice Hall.

Worley, R. B. (2000). The medium is not the message. *Business Communication Quarterly, 63*(2), 93-103.

Educational Colonialism

Michael Simonson

Colonialism is the policy or practice of acquiring full or partial political control over another country, occupying it with settlers, and exploiting it economically. Education is the process of receiving or giving systematic, formal instruction, usually at a school or university—also, an enlightening experience involving teaching and learning.

So, is there such a thing as educational colonialism, which could be defined as the policy of acquiring full or partial control over another country's educational sys-

Michael Simonson, Editor, *Distance Learning,* and Program Professor, Programs in Instructional Technology and Distance Education, Fischler School of Education, Nova Southeastern University, 1750 NE 167 St., North Miami Beach, FL 33162. Telephone: (954) 262-8563. E-mail: simsmich@nsu.nova.edu

tem, occupying it with nonlocal teachers, and exploiting it educationally?

Distance education may be an example of educational colonialism, as the practice of teaching and learning at a distance seems to be the antithesis of local education. Yet, most readers of this journal probably think it may be possible to combine the advantages of distance education with local control of schools, colleges and universities.

The massive open online course is a notable application of distance education. MOOCs utilize the expertise of eminent scholars and teachers, often from the most prestigious universities, to offer world-class education to anyone in the world, sometimes for free.

Is it possible for the field of distance education to be tailored to meet local needs? Can distance education, defined as "institutionally based formal education with interactive telecommunications systems used to connect learners, instructors, and resources" (Schlosser & Simonson, 2009, p. 1) be community, region, or state based? Or, must distance education ultimately be a massive system?

Possibly we should be advocating a new approach to distance education—the localization of distance education. For that, another definition—of localization or local control—is needed. Here is what the Great Schools Partnership (2013) says about local control in education:

In education, local control refers to (1) the governing and management of public schools by elected or appointed representatives serving on governing bodies, such as school boards or school committees, that are located in the communities served by the schools, and (2) the degree to which local leaders, institutions, and governing bodies can make independent or autonomous decisions about the governance and operation of public schools. (para. 1)

The concept of local control is grounded in a philosophy of government premised on the belief that the individuals and institutions closest to the students and most knowledgeable about a school—and most invested in the welfare and success of its educators, students, and communities—are best suited to making important decisions related to its operation, leadership, staffing, academics, teaching, and improvement.

Wow, an interesting situation. Distance education provides the promise of teaching and learning from the best people and places to nearly anyone, anywhere. Yet, there is considerable and important relevance to the local control of education, especially in the United States. Is localized distance education possible? Perhaps it is a topic worthy of study.

And finally, as Thomas Jefferson is purported to have said, perhaps written, "an educated citizenry is a vital requisite for our survival as a free people."

REFERENCES

Great Schools Partnership. (2013). Local control. Retrieved from the glossary of education reform website: http://edglossary.org/local-control/

Schlosser, L. A., & Simonson. (2009). *Distance education: Definition and glossary of terms* (3rd ed.). Charlotte, NC: Information Age.

CPSIA information can be obtained
at www.ICGtesting.com
Printed in the USA
LVOW03*0549240916

506038LV00007B/32/P

9 781681 236421